St. John de Crèvecoeur

After the portrait by Vallière, 1786,
in the possession of
M. le Comte Louis de Crèvecoeur

SKETCHES OF
EIGHTEENTH CENTURY
AMERICA

More "Letters from an American Farmer"

BY

Crèvecoeur, Michel Guillaume St. Jean de, called

ST. JOHN DE CRÈVECŒUR

EDITED BY

HENRI L. BOURDIN, RALPH H. GABRIEL
AND STANLEY T. WILLIAMS

NEW HAVEN · YALE UNIVERSITY PRESS
London, Humphrey Milford, Oxford University Press
M DCCCC XXV

THE

PHILIP HAMILTON McMILLAN MEMORIAL
PUBLICATION FUND

The present volume is the third work published by the Yale University Press on the Philip Hamilton McMillan Memorial Publication Fund. This Foundation was established December 12, 1922, by a gift to Yale University in pursuance of a pledge announced on Alumni University Day in February, 1922, of a fund of $100,000 bequeathed to James Thayer McMillan and Alexis Caswell Angell, as Trustees, by Mrs. Elizabeth Anderson McMillan, of Detroit, to be devoted by them to the establishment of a memorial in honor of her husband.

He was born in Detroit, Michigan, December 28, 1872, prepared for college at Phillips Academy, Andover, and was graduated from Yale in the Class of 1894. As an undergraduate he was a leader in many of the college activities of his day, and within a brief period of his graduation was called upon to assume heavy responsibilities in the management and direction of numerous business enterprises in Detroit; where he was also a Trustee of the Young Men's Christian Association and of Grace Hospital. His untimely death, from heart disease, on October 4, 1919, deprived his city of one of its leading citizens and his University of one of its most loyal sons.

ACKNOWLEDGMENT

THIS volume of letters of St. John de Crèvecœur has been made possible through the kindness of M. le Comte Louis de Crèvecœur, who loaned me the manuscripts for publication and who cordially aided me in my investigations. My thanks are also due to Mr. Carl Van Doren of the Century Magazine *and Professor Frank Senour of the University of Indiana.*

H. L. B.

TABLE OF CONTENTS

CRÈVECŒUR AND HIS TIMES

ABOUT the year 1759 or 1760, a young Frenchman came into the northern English colonies from Canada. At different times he seems to have been a surveyor in the region of Albany, a resident of Pennsylvania and of Ulster county in the province of New York. In Orange county he ultimately acquired a farm, "Pine Hill." About two months before the purchase of this, in 1769, he was married to Mehetable Tippet of Yonkers. So, for the time being at least, the wanderings of Hector St. John de Crèvecœur came to an end.

Behind this enthusiastic young farmer was an interesting story. He had been born near Caen, France, in 1735, the son of a well-bred country gentleman and of a mother who belonged to a family of distinction and who herself was educated beyond the usual woman of her time. When a young man, Crèvecœur, always in pursuit of new experiences, came out to New France. Here he joined the army and became a lieutenant under Montcalm in his battle for the preservation of the French Empire in America in the last great French and Indian war. His military duties seem to have sent him on a map-making expedition into the wilderness beyond the Great Lakes. He went to Detroit and turned southward through the forests to the Ohio River. He learned much of the valleys of the Scioto and the Muskingum and something of the habits and character of the powerful Indian tribes who lived south of Lake

I

Erie. In 1758 he made an extensive map of the French
claims. After the fall of Quebec, in 1759, he turned his
back on Canada.

During the next few years Crèvecœur seems to have
travelled widely. His first book, *Letters from an American
Farmer*, published in England in 1782, shows that
he was familiar with Nova Scotia, the country about
the Kennebec, Massachusetts, Connecticut, Nantucket,
Martha's Vineyard, New York, and Pennsylvania. He
also made a journey into some of the southern colonies
and perhaps to Bermuda and Jamaica. When he finally
married and made his home at Pine Hill, there were
few men who knew French and English America as
well as he.

He knew the forest and, like the borderer, he could
find his way about in it. He knew the life of the Indians
and, according to his own statement, was once adopted
into a tribe. He had the Frenchman's sympathetic attitude toward the culture of the redskins which made the
Canadian *couriers-de-bois* better traders than the English. But Crèvecœur was a man of few illusions and he
was never guilty of the fanciful idealization of Indian
life that was characteristic of some of the French fol-
lowers of Rousseau. Such was the background of the
man who for ten years after his marriage lived among
the farmers some few miles northwest of the steadily
growing little seaport of New York. "Few writers
about America," he observed in 1782, "have resided
here, and those who have, have not pervaded every part
of the country, nor carefully examined the nature and
principles of our association." Certainly Crèvecœur was
qualified by experience to describe life in the new
world.

The papers which appear in this volume have, with

Crèvecœur and His Times.

four exceptions, lain unpublished for nearly a century and a half in the cabinets of the family of Crèvecœur in France. They give an insight into eighteenth century American life, both intimate and authoritative. By nature Crèvecœur was an observer, and he set his observations against a background of wide contact with men and communities and a broad philosophy of life which made for sane and unprejudiced judgment. He has been called a sentimentalist whose tears flowed easily when something aroused his sympathy. One certainly cannot read the following pages without becoming vividly conscious of the emotional side of his nature. Yet sympathy in the presence of distress is not of necessity a hindrance to clear thinking. There is something distinctively French in the clearness of thought and cogency of reasoning that is found in even the most moving passages. This blend of the emotions and the intellect gives a completeness to his pictures of American life that is rarely found in writing of such character. And America, when he wrote these papers, was passing through one of the most significant periods of its history.

Four years before St. John de Crèvecœur and Mehetable Tippet were married, one George Grenville, a chancellor of the British exchequer, had attempted to raise new taxes in America by means of the Stamp Act. Then followed the details of a now familiar story. The Stamp Act was repealed in 1766, and the next year Charles Townshend levied new taxes in a different form. Americans, liking little the taxes ordered by their own assemblies, were strongly antagonistic to those imposed upon them from London. Crèvecœur, in the four papers on farm life in the following chapters, reflects the American farmer's point of view with

3

regard to taxation. They were probably written some time between 1770 and 1774, for the most part years of widespread political quiet when all the unpopular Townshend taxes had been repealed save the tax on tea.

Crèvecœur, the American farmer, advancing arguments against English taxation of his fellow countrymen, was led into a statement of the difficulties that surrounded the husbandman in the new world. He described the problem of acquiring, from rascally land agents, a bona fide title to a tract on the frontier. He pictured the work of clearing away the trees and difficulties of living alone in the forest. He did not forget the heavy burden of mortgage that pressed on practically every frontier holding. Then, when the forest was cleared and the farm established, he told of the early settler's fight with an astonishing variety of natural enemies. In this description he was aided by his great interest in nature and by his acute observation of the world of birds, animals and insects. Frequently, as in "Ant-Hill Town," Crèvecœur describes wild life for the pure love of nature. In honest disgust he wrote: "Strange that you should have in England so many learned and wise men, and that none should ever have come over here to describe some part of this great field which nature presents." But he took pains to record that this same nature caused the farmer no end of difficulty.

The chapters dealing with the farmer's troubles are a complete refutation of the old charge against Crèvecœur that he idealized agricultural conditions in the new world. But Crèvecœur knew also and sketched the pleasant side of country life. One is led to believe that the years after his marriage and before the outbreak of war were the happiest of his life. There can be no doubt that he liked farming and was fond of his neighbours.

Crèvecœur and His Times.

He lived in a typical American community of the day. Descendants of the Dutch worked their farms side by side with the English, and there were a few scattered Frenchmen like himself. About him were the poor who had no land, and the rich who owned vast estates. European feudalism had taken firm root in the valley of the Hudson. The Dutch had established the patroon system, and their English successors had in many places granted vast tracts of land to favoured persons. Such landowners, like the Livingstons or the Van Rensselaers, were country gentlemen, colonial aristocrats. They had an aristocrat's influence in the communities in which they lived, and had a very large share in the political life of its people.

Such a farming community as that in which Crèvecœur lived was, in a very real sense, America. Probably ninety or more percent of Americans in his time lived on the soil, and a very great proportion of these were small farmers like himself. There were only four seaports of any consequence, Boston, New York, Philadelphia and Charleston. These, at best, were struggling little cities whose aggregate population did not bulk large when compared with the million and a half people living in the thirteen English colonies in 1760. When Crèvecœur describes the snow-storm in the Mohawk valley or the manners and customs of the people about him, he is describing conditions typical of America north of the Potomac. Other writers have left a record of the mode of life of the grand folk of the great estates. With a wealth of detail Crèvecœur pictures the everyday experiences of the humbler people. Looking back at his work from the vantage point of the twentieth century, Crèvecœur's writings take an interesting place in a significant development.

5

Eighteenth Century America.

By the end of the eighteenth century land along the
Atlantic seaboard which had been cropped for a century
or more was beginning to give out. This was apparently
not so true of Crèvecœur's own community. But here,
as elsewhere, the methods of husbandry were bad.
They had been born of frontier conditions and were ill
adjusted to soil that was beginning to show the impov-
erishment which inevitably came from exploitative
cropping. The farms still remained largely self-sufficient, the farmer producing on his acres most of the
things that life required. To Crèvecœur's mind the
store was chiefly a place where country families were
tempted to buy things they did not need and could ill
afford. The independent family on a self-sufficient
farm came close to his ideal of perfect social conditions.
With a vividness and an intimacy unequalled by any
other writers of the time, he described the life of this
group where the husband and wife laboured together in
partnership to provide the food, clothing, and fuel that
the family needed. He was not aware that the methods
of husbandry were bad, for apparently the fields of
Orange county were still but little impaired. But other
Americans were conscious of the need for better farming. Just a few years before Crèvecœur wrote these
"letters," Jared Eliot, a Connecticut clergyman, published the first treatise on American husbandry that had
for its purpose the betterment of conditions. The movement thus inaugurated was checked by the war, but after
the Revolution was revived by a group of prominent
Americans scattered along the coast. It was led by large
landholders, country gentlemen, from Charleston to
Boston. Robert Livingston, Crèvecœur's neighbour in
the Hudson valley, was one of the chief of these. He
with others made an earnest effort to introduce better

methods into American agriculture. Out of this movement, which had its inception in the last third of the
eighteenth century, has come that science of agriculture
that has revolutionized American farming. The sig-
nificance of these hitherto unpublished letters of Crèvecœur lies in the fact that they picture fairly completely
the round of life of the ordinary country family whose
methods of husbandry the reformers were trying to
change. No important phase is omitted. Side by side
with the account of the labours of the field and the
household is the description of the frolics that played so
important a part in the community social life. The political interests of the countryman and his religious
problems seemed as important to Crèvecœur as the
manner in which he cared for his cattle and his sheep.
Crèvecœur understood the farm people of his day, and
had the ability to put his knowledge into permanent
form. Though not primarily a literary man, he was the
forerunner of other writers who have portrayed American farm life, Riley and Hamlin Garland.

But Crèvecœur had probably scarcely completed the
writing of his descriptions of American rural folk when
he beheld the people of his adopted country swept into
war. In the spring of 1775, word spread rapidly
through the colonies that Massachusetts Minute Men
had clashed with British Regulars at Lexington and
Concord, and that Massachusetts was rising in revolt.
Apparently, at first, the war puzzled Crèvecœur. At
one time he despaired of ever judging truly which side
had the right. Later he wrote: "No European can possibly conceive the secret ways, the great combination of
poisons and subtle sophisms which have from one end
of the continent to the other, allured the minds [of
Americans], removed ancient prejudice, and, in short,

prepared the way for the exhibition of this astonishing revolution." Crèvecœur chose the Loyalist rather than the Patriot cause.

The war brought an end to the happiness of the "American Farmer." A friend wrote concerning him: "During the Rebellion it is well known he has suffered much for his steady attachment to His Majesty's Government and friends." Finally the Patriots drove him and one son from his farm. He turned his face towards New York where the British army, under General Clinton, offered a refuge. The measure of the misfortunes which the conflict had brought him is suggested in a letter which he wrote in New York to the inspector of the claims of refugees. "Myself and son are now become refugees in this town, and find myself obliged to apply to you for the indulgence of rations for us both from this date, the only reward of four years of contumely received, of fines imposed, imprisonments, and the inclosed letters from persons better known to you than myself will, I hope, convince you that my request is founded on necessity, and will enable you to judge how far I am justifiable in making this application." He spent some months in New York, and on Long Island, working at such tasks as he could find. Then the British authorities threw him into a military prison as a result of a charge contained in an anonymous letter, that he was in secret correspondence with General Washington. After his release he, along with other refugees, was reduced to abject want. At last, in September, 1780, he sailed for England, and from there he went to France.

One can only guess why Crèvecœur became a Loyalist. The support which France early gave to the American cause seems to have amazed him, if we understand the sentiments which he expressed in "The English and the French before the Revolution." Certainly when Lafayette was a general on Washington's staff, and when France was shipping large quantities of munitions and supplies to the American forces, it is strange that Crèvecœur should support the cause of England, against whose armies he had campaigned twenty years before under the command of the great Montcalm. While Crèvecœur was a refugee in New York, came the news that France had openly allied herself with the revolting colonies. "The American Belisarius" and "American Landscapes" seem to hold the clue to the reasons behind Crèvecœur's party affiliation. After all, he was a gentleman born. With all his friendship for his humble neighbours, he could never quite shake off his aristocratic point of view. The greater part of the more prominent people in New York instinctively became Loyalists at the outbreak of the war. One suspects that the Patriots from the poorer folk were as much interested in the overthrow of the power of the American country squires as in combating the legislation of a British parliament. Crèvecœur, apparently, was convinced of this, and considered the talk about "liberty" and "democracy" as the jargon of hypocrisy. He spoke contemptuously of "the citizens of Boston, perpetually brawling about liberty without knowing what it was." Crèvecœur, like the Patriots, was opposed to the British legislation, but he was more opposed to groundlings making it the excuse for the overthrow of the established order. Whole-heartedly he cast his lot with the gentry, and the professional people who formed the larger part of the New York Loyalist group. When he could no longer stay in America, he returned to the country of his ancestors. After the war was over, more than thirty thousand of his fellow partizans were

Eighteenth Century America.

driven into exile in Canada, the islands of the Bahamas, Bermuda, and England.

One would expect Crèvecœur's writings during the war period to be charged with prejudice. Civil war, such as the Revolution in reality was, inevitably warps the judgment and inflames the passions. Crèvecœur was no exception. Remembering that some of the country folk about whom he had written so intimately had come to the new world under a cloud, he once rather venomously referred to his fellow Americans as sprung from "felons and banditti." Yet in the seven war pieces that follow, two, "The American Belisarius" and "American Landscapes," deal with the persecution of the Loyalists by the Patriots; two, "The Wyoming Massacre" and "The Frontier Woman," describe with the utmost vividness the sufferings of the frontier people at the hands of the bands of Indians and Loyalist whites; and two, "The History of Mrs. B." and "The Man of Sorrows," narrate events in the lives of Loyalists without the least show of animosity toward the Patriots. Crèvecœur's sympathy with the unfortunate rose above his political principles. To him the war was one vast tragedy for all concerned. The thing which, apparently, his mind most dwelt on was the sufferings of humble people who had no part in and little understanding of this battle between the nations. The larger phases of the Revolution do not appear in his pages. His story is of the moral and material desolation that the conflict brought to the common folk.

Crèvecœur was not a historian; he was a chronicler of unrelated episodes. He was an observer whose main interest was not in ideas or causes but in people. His writings before the Revolution contain a picture of the life of the average American community in the middle colonies; his sketches during the conflict picture such communities convulsed by war. In reading him one has to be on guard against certain peculiarities of the author. His remarks about the past beyond a few years are apt to be quite inaccurate. Some of his references to his father, and probably some of those to his wife, in his letters on farming should not be taken as autobiographical. Crèvecœur gathered many anecdotes which he embellished and incorporated in his writing, frequently associating himself in a minor way with the episode. His purpose in these slight twistings of fact seems to have been to enhance the vividness of his account, to cover up his French identity, and to give his statements a more authentic ring. Keeping these things in mind, the reader can get an interesting view of the years before and during the Revolution, and an intimate insight into the extraordinary personality of Crèvecœur himself.

A few details of his career after the writing of these papers may add interest to certain passages. Immediately after the war, France sent Crèvecœur to America as consul. Upon his arrival he anxiously enquired for his wife and children, only to learn that his home had been burned, that his wife was dead, and that his children had vanished. "I should have fallen to the ground," he wrote afterward, "but for the support, at this instant, of my friend Mr. Seton, who had come to conduct me from the French vessel to his house." His anxiety was deepened when he learned that an Indian raid in the region of his old home had been the cause of much of the calamity that had befallen his family. For days he searched without avail for news of the boy and girl he had left with their mother. Then quite by accident, the first details of a strange story became clear.

Shortly after he had gone to France, he had befriended five American naval officers, refugees from an English prison, who had escaped and crossed the channel in an open boat. He had taken them to his father's house, and had put them in touch with Benjamin Franklin, the American representative at Paris. When they had set out for America, he had pressed upon them a packet of letters with the urgent request that they be delivered to his wife. One of the group had informed him that, being under the command of Congress, they could not themselves comply with his wishes, but that they would put them in the hands of a friend in Boston. So it came about that Captain Gustavus Fellows, a Boston merchant, received the letters and out of gratitude to Crèvecœur for his kindness to the Americans made a long, hard winter journey to Orange county. He located the children in the house of a neighbour who had been left in pitiable destitution by the Indian raid. He bundled them into his sleigh, and took them back to Boston, where he made them a part of his family. Here Crèvecœur found them in the spring after his arrival in New York.

As French consul to New York, New Jersey, and Connecticut, Crèvecœur laboured hard to improve relations between his country and the new republic. In this his old interests were of value. To his great surprise and pleasure he was made a member of the French Academy of Science, to which he contributed much information about the natural history of the new world. He became deeply interested in the American movement for better agriculture, and played a part in furthering it by writing for the American press a series of articles over the signature of "Agricola." He wrote to a friend in France that he had introduced into America,

Crèvecœur and His Times.

sain foin, lucerne (alfalfa), the vetches, vignon, and racine de disette. On agricultural matters he corresponded with Jefferson and Washington, about whom he had once written with much animosity in "The English and the French before the Revolution." He materially assisted in establishing the botanical gardens at New Haven.

In the spring of 1790, as the first year of Washington's presidency was closing, Crèvecœur received permission to return to France on a leave of absence. Before he left he witnessed the marriage of his daughter, America-Francés, to M. Louis-Guillaume Otto, the French chargé d'affaires at the American capital. The Secretary of State, Thomas Jefferson, was present at the ceremony. A few weeks later, from the deck of a fast-sailing packet standing out to sea from the port of New York, the "American Farmer" saw for the last time the shores of the country wherein he had known so much joy and sorrow. He had seen his adopted country pass through the throes of war, and had returned as a foreign official to aid in the founding of a nation. While his ship was hurrying eastward across the Atlantic, the conflagration of the French Revolution was sweeping over his native land. France claimed the years that remained to him. In his later life, his thoughts turned again to America, and he wrote *Voyage dans la haute Pensylvanie et dans l'état de New York*. One wonders what he thought of the shelf of folios that contained the unpublished letters of an American Farmer and the manuscripts that had been composed in the heat of the American Revolution.

RALPH H. GABRIEL

13

THE CRÈVECŒUR
MANUSCRIPTS

IT is probable that Michel Guillaume de Crèvecœur landed in the little harbour of New York on the sixteenth of December, 1759.* Though the few years he had spent in Canada had not been very successful,† yet they had not daunted his adventurous spirit. He appears to us as a carefree youth of twenty-four, still unwilling to bow to the conventions and restrictions of his former European surroundings and determined to enjoy more of the free existence of the new continent.

For ten years he led a more or less roving life in this half-settled country which so delighted him that he

---

* This is the date set in the *Dictionary of National Biography* for the arrival in New York of Lieutenant General Monckton. It is highly probable from the extract of the letter quoted below that Crèvecœur had taken passage on the same boat.

. . . En conséquence il [Monckton] a ordonné pour demain l'embarquement de MM. Tourville, Deschambault, de Léry, la Chevrotière et MM. de St. Félix et de Crèvecœur. . . . C'est un mystère où ces officiers qui seront embarqués doivent être transportés. J'ai ouï dire que tous les vaisseaux destinés pour l'Europe étaient partis. Comme ce général [Monckton] part dans deux ou trois jours pour New York, je croirais volontiers que ces officiers iront au même endroit. M. de St. Félix accepte toute route qui les conduira en Europe, et Crèvecœur n'aspire qu'à aller chercher fortune ailleurs. (Lettre de M. Bernier à M. de Bougainville. 21 Octobre 1759.) *Extraits de lettres de divers particuliers au Chevalier de Lévis;* publiées sous la direction de l'abbé H. R. Casgrain D.ès.L, Professeur à l'Université Laval, etc. (Québec, 1895.)

† J'ai donné à Crèvecœur deux cent quarante livres, je ne pouvais moins faire pour nous en débarasser. D'ailleurs, il ne serait et ne pouvait partir sans ce secours. Il m'a laissé un état de ses dettes actives et pas-

The Crèvecœur Manuscripts.

chose it for his own in 1764. Then in 1769, having married and settled on his estate of Pine Hill, he decided, in his enthusiasm, to sketch for the sake of his former countrymen a picture of the land of his adoption. So it was that he wrote a number of essays, most of which breathe a genuine admiration for the rough but independent life of the American freeholders.

Another decade passes and in 1779 we again find Crèvecœur in New York, more destitute than on the day when he landed there, twenty years before. But he carries with him—and of all the harvests the American Farmer had reaped on American soil, it was the only thing he had succeeded in preserving—his collection of writings.* Though probably driven away from his

sives. (Lettre de M. Bernier à M. de Bougainville. 21 Octobre 1759. *Ibid.*, p. 37.)

In spite of the statements of Miss Julia Post Mitchell both in the preface and chapter 2 of her monograph, *St. Jean de Crèvecœur, New York* (Columbia University Press, 1916), there cannot exist the slightest doubt that the personage referred to in the previous letters is no other than the American Farmer. It is impossible to discuss this point at any length here. I shall only quote an extract of the letter of the Marquis de Lotbinière which Miss Mitchell was not able to procure and on which, in her opinion, "the whole case hangs." I may add that there are, besides this most convincing document, many other indications which confirm the identity of the two personages.

De New York, le 7 Juin 1790.—M. Otto chargé des affaires du Roi auprès de ces Etats-Unis est depuis huit à dix jours à Elisabethtown à 18 milles d'ici avec sa nouvelle femme, fille du fameux St. Jean de Crèvecœur, dont vous avez pu entendre parler dans la campagne de Québec, en 1759, qui a été pour lui la dernière à la vive demande des lieutenans et sous lieutenans de la Sarre ce qui l'obligea de forcément se réfugier de suite dans le haut de la rivière d'Albanie où végétant il faisait le métier d'arpenteur. . . . Le Mis. Chartier de Lotbinière a M. des Méloizes rue Royale No. 1 à Paris.

* These papers were inventoried in New York by Major General Pattison, who reported to his chief, Sir Henry Clinton: . . . "they likewise found a small Trunk which he [Crèvecœur] had put in the care of Mr. Brown, which they brought to me, it was opened and examined

15

home by "the new rage" of the American Patriots, he clings to these narratives of his former happy days, and his first move, once he has managed to cross the Atlantic, is to offer them to a London publisher.

What passed then between Crèvecœur and the publishers in May, 1781,† will always remain a matter of conjecture. There is not the slightest doubt that Crèvecœur intended, at least at the time he wrote his papers, to publish all of them. The little sketches which he had drawn at the end of the essay "Ant-Hill Town," and the directions given for four plates at the end of "Landscapes" are excellent evidence that such pieces were designed for publication. The insertion in his first French edition of such essays as "A Snow Storm as It Affects the American Farmer," "The Man of Sorrows," "The History of Mrs. B.," and his sketch "On the Manners of Americans," show also that such portions of his writings were highly regarded by the author. Why, then, did so small a part of the entire work (about one-third) go into print?

In the second edition of the *Letters from an American Farmer*, published by Thomas Davies and Lockyer Davis less than one year after the first, the publishers inserted this note which seems to throw the responsibility on Crèvecœur himself, because of his desire to re-

in my presence, and contained a great Number of Manuscripts, the general Purport of which appears to be a sort of irregular Journal of America, and a State of the Times of some Years back, interspersed with occasional Remarks, Philosophical and Political; the tendency of the latter is to favor the side of Government and to throw odium on the proceedings of the Opposite Party, and upon the Tyranny of their Popular Government." (Letter reprinted in the *Mag. of Amer. Hist.*, Dec., 1889, pp. 511-512.)

† The Crèvecœur's manuscripts which were published by Thomas Davies and Lockyer Davis in 1872 under the title *Letters from an American Farmer* were sold to the publishers on May 20, 1781.

vise his hasty writing. "Since the publication of this volume, we hear that Mr. St. John has accepted a public employment at New York. It is therefore, perhaps, doubtful whether he will soon be at leisure to revise his papers, and give the world a second collection of the American Farmer Letters." Yet the manuscripts which went to press bear testimony that they were pitilessly corrected and apparently not by Crèvecœur himself, but by a strange hand which was probably employed by the publishers for this purpose. The whole set of papers could easily have been submitted to the revision in the same way. So we must try to find another solution for this puzzling problem, and I feel inclined to throw the guilt on an overprudent publisher, who wanted to sound his public before undertaking the publication of a second volume. The following sentence, which ended the advertisement of the first edition, warrants, it seems, such an explanation: "Should our Farmer's letters be found to afford matter of useful entertainment to an intelligent and candid public, a second volume, equally interesting with those now published, may soon be expected."

Anyone at all familiar with the life of Crèvecœur after his return to France, knows that another English edition of his papers was out of the question. Lionized by his friend, the Comtesse d'Houtetot, who was only too glad to produce a living illustration of the theories of her beloved Jean Jacques Rousseau, received and feasted by the literary men of the day as well as by the liberal group of the aristocracy, the only ambition of the American Farmer was to adapt such pieces of his writings as he could to the sentimental taste of the period, and thus achieve a reputation as a French writer.

But since the selection of the papers seems to have

been the work of the English publisher, why is it that such strongly loyalist pieces as "The American Belisarius" and "Landscapes" were not published? It may appear to us now that the English public would have been only too glad to find a justification for the policy of its government in trying to overcome the "lawless American revolutionists," but we must not forget that, especially during the last period of the American Revolution, there was in England a strong current of opinion against the war waged by King George III. So it is not at all surprising to find a cautious publisher selecting from the Crèvecœur papers exactly those which appealed to this popular thought, even though they threw a favourable light on the enemies of his country. It is also possible, however, that the treatment Crèvecœur had received at the hands of the English authorities in New York had shaken his Tory sympathies, and that he himself opposed the publication of his loyalist papers.

At any rate, whatever may have been the motives for such a scanty selection, out of material of such obvious interest, the fact remains that the author had to be satisfied with the publication of one-third of his work and the thirty guineas allowed him by his publisher.

He then crossed the English Channel, laid aside the coarse homespun clothes which were the pride of his farming days, and assumed an attire more in keeping with his rank and with the social circles he was to frequent; and along with his colonial clothes he also laid aside his colonial writings. True enough, he did, some time afterwards, translate or rather adapt a number of these letters into his native language. But, like their author, the *Lettres d'un Cultivateur Américain* have discarded the homespun garb of their American originals. They lack precisely the qualities that make the

The Crèvecœur Manuscripts.

American Crèvecœur so captivating,—charming simplicity and naïve sentiment. They are defaced and adulterated by the artificial sentimentality and redundant rhetoric of eighteenth century French literature.* So, with the exception of those which the London publishers chose to run through their press, we may say that Crèvecœur's real American letters lay buried in the family closets, enshrouded in the coarse blue covers befitting their colonial origin.

There it was that I found them two summers ago. And along with them there was a small volume containing a collection of letters addressed by prominent Americans to our author during the years of his consulship.† On the title-page of the latter Crèvecœur had written in his fine pointed hand: "This collection, like old cheese, will I hope, few years hence, prove acceptable to these two dear boys for whom it is intended, as well as a much larger one of Gleanings and other Materials which I am preparing. Caen, 18 8bre, 1790."

Before I attempt a description of the manuscripts, I feel that I must answer a question which I have repeatedly been asked as to how I happened to find these papers. While engaged in the study of the Marquis de Chastellux, I stumbled on Crèvecœur. In comparing the English and the French editions of his letters, it became evident that Crèvecœur was making an especial

* The French version of the second letter "On the situation, feelings and pleasure of an American Farmer" is a striking example of it. I may also refer my readers to the difference of treatment which exists between the episodes of "The Sassafras and Vine" and "The Indian Dog," as they will be found in this volume and in their French adaptations.

† Most of these letters, especially those of Washington, Jefferson and Franklin, were communicated by M. le Comte de Crèvecœur to the American Embassy in Paris and have been published in different collections.

effort in his French letters to speak favourably of the Quakers. This marked insistence suggested that perhaps Crèvecœur had waged a sort of veiled polemic with the Marquis de Chastellux, who in his *Voyages dans l'Amérique Septentrionale** had dealt somewhat roughly with the Society of Friends. Yet these passages on the Quakers, which do not exist in the English edition, might have been suppressed for some unknown reason by the English publisher. It was primarily to satisfy myself on this point that I decided to examine the manuscripts. I must also confess that I was not without hopes of finding some material of interest in spite of the fact that Miss Mitchell, who journeyed to France in order to investigate the Crèvecœur papers, had remained silent concerning the existence of such material.

I was welcomed with the utmost cordiality by M. le Comte de Crèvecœur in his country house near Saumur, and was given free access to all the family papers. Long shall I remember my first night in the quiet little room of the château, when by the dim light of an oil lamp I perused those faded yellow folios on which, a hundred and fifty years before, the benevolent farmer had set down his thoughts. Perhaps he too had sat up late into the night hours to ponder over the same sheets, while the moon shone on the crystal ripples of Crommeline Creek much the same as it shone that night on the pla-

---

* *Voyages de M. le Marquis de Chastellux dans l'Amérique Septentrionale dans les années 1780, 1781 et 1782.* 2 volumes, Paris, Prault, 1786. Previous to this complete edition of his travels, Chastellux had had the first volume printed on board the flagship of the Rhode Island squadron. Out of this limited edition (twenty-four copies) only ten or twelve reached France. Just before Crèvecœur's arrival in France, they were distributed among the friends of the Marquis, most of whom were to be the friends of Crèvecœur.

The Crèvecœur Manuscripts.

cid waters of the lazy Loire. Deep as his emotions must sometimes have been, I wonder whether they equalled the thrill I felt while turning over those leaves. Not only had I under my eyes the original version of some of the French essays, and those "Landscapes" whose existence and interest Robert de Crèvecœur had mentioned in his ancestor's biography* but also an unsuspected wealth of forgotten material which might revolutionize the accepted ideas of Crèvecœur as an observer of American life and a man of letters.

M. de Crèvecœur loaned me his heirlooms for the period of one year. Then I spent the few days which I had left in France in making a thorough inventory of the loose bundles which were also kept in the same coffer. They were mostly copies of the numerous reports Crèvecœur sent to the French foreign office during his consulship; they were hurried notes half in French, half in English, scribbled during his consular days and while he was an emigré at Hamburg. I was satisfied that the two volumes of unpublished essays I was to take back to the United States and which for the most part are here printed were the complete literary work of the American Farmer.†

The American Farmer manuscripts are bound in three volumes. They comprise altogether three hun-

---

* Robert de Crèvecœur, *Saint John de Crèvecœur, sa vie et ses ouvrages*. Paris. Librarie des Bibliophiles, 1883. p. 197.

† M. Louis de Crèvecœur has told me that a manuscript containing short stories had been lent by his father to M. Pierre Margry and had not been recovered after the latter's death. I have tried to trace it. M. Chadenat, the bookseller who bought M. Margry's library, has never seen it, and there is nothing of the kind at the Bibliothèque Nationale, in the Margry collection. M. Henri Cluzant, near Bordeaux, also possesses another manuscript of Crèvecœur. It refers to his stay at Altona near Hamburg, 1795-1796.

dred and thirty-three folios of different sizes, which, deducting the blank folios, yield six hundred and seventeen pages of text. The largest folios measure thirteen and a quarter by eight and a quarter inches, and the smallest are nine and three quarters by seven and three quarters inches. With the exception of two or three pages they are in an excellent state of preservation.

The first volume, composed of two hundred pages of text, contains the letters published in 1782, with the exception of the "Introductory Letter." An essay entitled "An Happy Family disunited by the Spirit of Civil War," which was not included in that publication, begins at folio 65 and numbers 23 pages of text. It is not in the hand of Crèvecœur, being a second copy. The original essay in the hand of the author exists in a loose quire. The copy has been extensively corrected and considerably shortened. The corrections seem to be in the same strange hand as those which were made at the instance of the publishers.

The second and third volumes are composed respectively of two hundred and fifty-two and one hundred and sixty-five pages of text which were never published in the original English text. Besides the material included in this present publication, they contain the following essays:

In the second volume:
Rock of Lisbon. (24 pages)
Sketches of Jamaica and Bermudas. (13 pages)
Hospitals. (8 pages)
Susquehanna. (48 pages—including the Wyoming Massacre published herein)

In the third volume:
The Grotto. (14 pages)

The Crèvecœur Manuscripts.

The Commissioners. (24 pages)
Ingratitude rewarded. (14 pages)

All of the essays contained in the second and third volumes are in the hand of Crèvecœur with the exception of: in Volume II, "The Frontier Woman" (folio 101 to 106) corrected by Crèvecœur; in Volume III, "The American Belisarius" (folio 3 to 14) corrected by a strange hand, and "Ingratitude rewarded" (folio 78 to 95) no corrections.

All the folios of the manuscript were probably stamped with the arms of the de Crèvecœur family surmounted by a count's coronet at the time they were collected and bound. Only four essays are dated, but the dates they bear seem to have been inscribed when Crèvecœur wrote his French adaptations. In spite of the well-known inaccuracy of the American Farmer in the matter of dates it might be interesting to note that the earliest is 1769,* which is also the earliest found in the two French editions of the letters.† Comparisons of the watermarks, sizes of paper, differences in handwriting (Crèvecœur uses alternately a vertical and a slant hand), have failed to procure any definite indications of the exact dates of the different essays. But, roughly speaking, we may say that Crèvecœur's American writings cover a period of about ten years, from 1769 to 1779.

An interesting point which was revealed by the manuscripts is that the author often wrote an account of a journey a long time after he made it. His narrative of the excursions he made in the Susquehanna valley was not written until July, 1778, though evidence points

---

* Ant-Hill Town, Virginia 1769. (Not translated.)
† Lettre écrite par Ivan, etc. . . . Philadelphie le 12 Octobre 1769.

out that they had taken place some time before 1774. It is concluded by the account of the Wyoming Massacre which begins thus: "Soon after my return from this last excursion began the great contest between the mother-country and this." I am strongly inclined to believe that he wrote it from notes taken while on his journeys. The large amount of scribbled notes made during his consular period would indicate a long-formed habit, while the accuracy of some of the details does not seem to admit the possibility that he wrote from memory. The fact that no trace of such notes exists in the family papers is not a serious argument against this theory. It is likely that Crèvecœur either destroyed or left behind him at his farm such material, and it was subsequently scattered and lost.

HENRI L. BOURDIN

CRÈVECŒUR AS A MAN
OF LETTERS

CRÈVECŒUR longs sometimes for an artist to
limn his American scene: somone to paint the
anguished farewell in "The Man of Sorrows,"
or the retreat through the wilderness after the Wyoming Massacre. I should prefer rather a sketch of Crèvecœur himself at work on his manuscript, for he could
have given us a "Selbst bildnis." His drawings with his
own hand are charming. Crèvecœur composing would be
a characteristic pose. The American farmer is never done
with his writing, though, of course, he protests that he
lacks literary ability; and he begs his correspondent to
tear up these letters. When his wife declares that his
pen is never idle, and laughs at him, he blushes. He is
aware that writing is a dubious practice for a distinguished farmer. "There is something," he says, "truly
ridiculous in a farmer quitting his plough or his axe, and
then flying to his pen." Yet we finish reading the letters
feeling that this farmer, politician, and naturalist loves
to write. He does it not merely, as he avers, to record
events, but for the joy of composing. This may, of
course, mean nothing. Such has been the attitude toward writing of many distinguished bores. Yet Crèvecœur's zeal makes one curious. We recall the sentimental
estimates of him in histories of American literature.
Has he the characteristics of a man of letters?

Our first impulse is to accept Crèvecœur's own judgment on this question; he says he cannot write. In his
remarks to the Abbé Raynal, in the first volume of the

letters, he calls the letters "trifling lucubrations." He deplores the "method" of the thing, and he is full of apologies. So he was, we think, a wise observer, a philosopher, perhaps a dreamer,—but a man of letters? He is rather a settler, full of good farmer's talk of horses and ploughs and barns. He knows the woods and the sea, and can discourse on maple trees, mountains, courses of rivers, whaling, bees, snakes, owls, crows, wolves, mosquitoes, skunks, and what-not. He understands America's distresses, and he meditates with emotion on the deeper meaning of the Revolution. What can be the true nature of Justice? Has Providence indeed designed a future life? Such subjects,—immortality, or the corn-weevil,—subjects fit for a pioneer and a man, he dignifies with his solid, sensible, facile writing. As we read we think more and more easily of him as a chronicler of America, and less easily of him as a literary man,—so striking become his faults as a writer of English prose.

He has little book-lore. His quotations from the classics are trite, and his writing as a whole is allusive only in elementary fashion. He can refer to Lycurgus, Solon, Seneca, Zeno, and the god Arimanes, but we suspect that he has little information in reserve about these worthies. Then, too, he is not concerned, like your true devotee of literature, with characters and ideas for their own sake, but rather for their bearing on practical affairs of the world. His approach to a subject is commonly not that of the lover of books but that of the man of deeds. Above all, his royal indifference to spelling and grammar, his clumsy perorations, his flights of sentimentalism,—all proclaim a mind unenriched by careful education; unpolished by the subtle mastery of

Crèvecœur as a Man of Letters.

a style or a language; a mind unconscious, in a word, of the aims of pure literature.

No, Crèvecœur does not regard, with the eye of the literary man, the life about him as artistic material. It is rather that the spectacle itself interests him; he cannot help but set it down. He has been called an eighteenth century Thoreau, but Thoreau, a man of culture, was an experimenter in language and style, really in art. In his passionate interest in American frontier life, Crèvecœur reminds us of Parkman, but Parkman had a literary technique for obtaining effects; he was a finished master of prose. Thus it would seem that Crèvecœur belongs to a line of writers, of whom, I sometimes think, America has produced her full share: those who are first men of action, and afterwards writers. From John Smith to Theodore Roosevelt (scores of other names come to mind) we have begotten men who could explore a river, scalp an Indian or found a nation—and then write about it. With these men of action who wrote with their left hands Crèvecœur seems allied. He philosophized in no quiet English library. He knew what it was to toil and to sweat and to suffer. These new realistic letters on pioneer life should finally dispose of the myth that Crèvecœur was a Utopian romancer. When he stole an hour to write we may easily imagine what his activities were just before and after his self-indulgence. At his wife's entrance he blushed. He seemed to agree with her that writing was a strange occupation for a pioneer farmer. Crèvecœur was only incidentally, so he thought, a writer.

For all this in Crèvecœur we may be thankful. From this comes, when he drops the plough and picks up the pen, the vigour and freshness of his style. As he writes, his ardours are unrestrained by withering self-criticism.

Eighteenth Century America.

His apostrophes to the ocean, his satisfaction in his farm and his rage at Puritan hypocrisy may be naïve, but they are robust. After he has returned from caring for the cattle in the snow-storm, and has made his house and family secure, he drinks before the fire with his wife his mug of gingered cider. He is supremely happy in his lot, and he writes down his contentment. Such high spirits are contagious. Crèvecœur's emotions are strong and true, and simply expressed. In reading his pages we are spared excessive analysis; his feelings are not supersensitive like those of some artists, but sound and sweet, such as become a man. Thus as he shudders at the misery of the American Belisarius, or at the negro in the cage, we shudder too. So fervently does he feel these things that they overflow his crude sentences and reach our hearts.

This, imperfectly suggested, is one of Crèvecœur's charms as a writer. A man of far subtler mind might fail to carry us with him as does the straightforward farmer. His simplicity is convincing. He makes us, without conscious effort, feel the ferocity of the battle between the snakes; the beauty of the farmer's fireside life; the pathos of the frontier woman's struggle; the strange and dreadful joy with which the survivors of the massacre passed through the wilderness. How impressive is his acute observation without comment on that fact of human nature that some have thought so disgraceful: our tenacious clinging to life when all that makes it dear is lost. "Hundreds," he says, after describing the horrors of a massacre, and the escape of the few, "were seen in this deplorable condition, yet thinking themselves happy that they had safely passed through the great wilderness." I have read many of his descriptive passages aloud, and I have yet to find the person who forgets the tortured negro; the scene of the travellers in Crèvecœur's house; the children coming home from school in the snow-storm; or the woman's cry, as the raider enters her home. All of us have sometimes observed with wonder the power of the strong mind, undulled by learning, expressing itself for the first time in literature. This is Crèvecœur. He is untouched by halting self-criticism, by introspection, by all the fees which Nature exacts for a knowledge of books.

There is reason to suppose, however, that the farmer, had circumstances been different, might have paid this price, and have become as sophisticated as his readers. For he was not a mere frontiersman, jotting down whatever came to mind. He enjoys a certain directness of approach; he maintains grasp upon his subject; and he is free from that fumbling uncertainty which is so characteristic of untrained writers. Besides these qualities, he sometimes manifests those of the more skilled composer: free as he is from the mood of libraries, he occasionally startles by his literary insight. For example, he is describing the retreat after the Wyoming Massacre. Here is an opportunity for an enthusiastic amateur; here is a chance for a catalogue or a rhapsody. Instead he offers us that silhouette of the beast of burden with the bedding on its back as a saddle. "On it sat a wretched mother with a child at her breast, another on her lap, and two more placed behind her, . . ." Or if he wished to harrow us there is the scene after the battle, when the mourners search for their dead: "I can easily imagine," he says quietly, "or conceive the feelings of a soldier burying the bodies of his companions, but neither my imagination nor my heart permit me to think of the peculiar anguish and keen feelings which must have seized that of a father, that of a mother avidly seeking among the crowd of slain for the disfigured corpse of a beloved son, the throbbing anguish of a wife—I cannot proceed."

He is capable of restraint, and discrimination. After the beautiful pictures of the animals in the snow-storm, of the farmer's winter evening, of the family asleep in the darkened farmhouse, he concludes with a certain grace: "A long ramble like this," he says, "through a cold Canadian storm requires rest, silence, and sleep. After so long an excursion we may with propriety wish each other good-night." Again and again in Crèvecœur may be found the natural instinct of the literary man for finish. One of the most interesting experiences, indeed, in reading Crèvecœur is to study side by side his crudeness and—it is no less—his literary taste.

Thus my title is explained. Man of letters, armed and accredited for the world, he was not. Yet in some ways, potentially, he was a man of letters. Without the self-discipline of his idol, Franklin; without, during those years, the contact of cities; without literary models; he nevertheless developed unique powers as a writer. Of these the most marked is his mastery of short, vivid narratives or descriptions. These are, after all, the best parts of the *Letters*. It is unlikely that Crèvecœur could have written a novel; his writing is too uneven,—brilliant sketches, amid considerable rhetoric. Let us also be thankful that, like Franklin, he escaped being "a wretched poet," if the lyrics included in this collection are characteristic. But the episode, the thumb-nail sketch, the scene,—who in America of the eighteenth century in depicting these is superior, in spite of his faults, to Crèvecœur?

He loves to take a single event or scene; to let the

mind dwell on it till it is reflected as sharply as in an etching. There were many of these scenes in the earlier volume: Crèvecœur at the plough, as his wife sat near him in the shade, knitting; the bees; the wrens; the whales; and the battle of the snakes. Such pictures are also the essence of certain of these selections: the snow-storm, the ant-hill town, the persecution of the man of sorrows. We learn also to watch for these pictures in the longer sections. Thus in the midst of the detail of the first four letters in this collection we reach suddenly the picture of Crèvecœur and his wife looking out from their room at night at the travellers. A little later the Indian and his dog find the lost boy. Or we smile at the description of the pioneer. He is at a land-agent's look-ing at lots, laid out, Crèvecœur remarks, like linen in a draper's shop. Once the pioneer is in America, Crève-cœur, talking in the present tense, puts him through his paces as a settler. Such instances might be multiplied from the more eventful letters. We do not forget the woman who bares her breast before the murderer; the farmer peering out into the darkness of the storm; the old people in the stockade as the conquering Indians enter.

The literary powers responsible for these pictures were observation and the selection of the right detail. Verbose as he is sometimes, and repetitious, Crèvecœur in his best work sees and makes us see what we should to comprehend his story. This quality in him was later to impress the keen-eyed Hazlitt. One may find picto-rial bits in Crèvecœur worthy of Carlyle. He seems to recreate in his prose the incidents as if arrested in paint-ing or sculpture. As the patriots struggle with the man of sorrows, this episode does not appear to be a history or tale, but rather a bas-relief or frieze. "What a subject," Crèvecœur cries out, "for a painter . . .! A man leaning against a tree, hardly recovered from the agonies of death, still visible in the livid hue and altered lineaments of his face, still weak and trembling, his mind agitated with the most tumultuous thoughts, wracked by the most anxious suspense, hearing his third and final doom. At a little distance his wife, sitting on a log, almost deprived of her reason. At a more considerable distance, his house, with all his children crowded at the door, restrained by amazement and fear from following their mother, each exhibiting strong expressions of curiosity and terror, agreeable to their different ages." It is less a narrative than a tableau.

This is to insinuate that Crèvecœur had a taste for the dramatic. I should not deny this. In general it has been enough to say that Crèvecœur was a naturalist and a sentimentalist. But his literary tastes are not so easily classified. The last selection in this volume, and in some ways the most interesting, is an experiment in the drama. Crèvecœur is now for the first time introduced to the world as an American dramatist. It was a natural consummation, for Crèvecœur's love of the pictorial is perhaps merely another name for his dramatic instinct. Without being in reality a dramatist or playwright, it is clear that his fondness for vivid portraiture and his intense interest in American life found an expression in this homespun play. Looking back at the other letters, his interest in the dramatic becomes apparent. His stories seem to have suspense and his individuals personality. The farmer's wife, the enthusiast in "Liberty of Worship," the new Belisarius, Mrs. B., the foolish leaders in the stockade,—all are distinct actors in this American drama. Thus the "Landscapes" or "Country Scenes" have interest not only as a rather touching example of early, crude American drama, but also as proof of a basic tendency in Crèvecœur towards the dramatic. He admits he is not a writer of plays but he submits these people as "genuine copies." He has succeeded. We tire of the partizan and obvious irony as the Deacon reads the Bible, while his wife fleeces the Tory home; or as she longs to see the woman "with all her little Tory bastards about her." We weary of the moralizing on the Revolution in the eternal tone of "Can such things be?" The scenes are long drawn out and full of repetitions. Yet we do see Eltha as she rifles her enemies' home; we see the Quakers in the tavern; and we hear the darky's dialect. The scenes are alive.

Nor are there wanting more delicate expressions of this gift. It will not seem surprising that this sense of the pictorial should appear also in the finer flowers of metaphor and analogy. It is so that Crèvecœur often intensifies his vivid scenes, and numerous instances might be given of his felicity of phrase. Thus looking down into the labyrinthine paths of the ant-hill town, he tells us that these are like the streets of old Quebec. As he notices the ants with wings he muses: "This gaudy attire did not appear to add any celerity to their flight; they never expanded them. Like the preposterous dresses of some ladies it served only to render them more conspicuous than the rest. Upon a closer inspection they appeared more inactive and wholly deprived of that quickness of motion for which the unwinged sort are so remarkable. Perhaps they were the matrons of the republic, never departing from that formal gravity appointed to the rank by Nature; perhaps," he adds, "they were young damsels embarrassed by the rule of modesty and decorum."

There is much indeed to indicate Crèvecœur's quickness of feeling. Humour, at least from the American point of view, is not his strong point. There is some dreary fooling in the "Country Scenes," and he is solemn, I am afraid, when he asserts that the Canadian women were the handsomest on the continent, and adds: "as is proved by upwards of twenty English officers getting wives at Montreal soon after the conquest." I wish, too, that he had smiled a little as he tells us earnestly how he read on summer evenings by holding fire-flies close to his book. His remark that Colonel Washington "very civilly kills Captain Jumonville" is delightful, but, I fear, unconsciously so. His pity is easily aroused, and is sometimes overeloquent. But his tenderness for children, for dumb animals, for suffering, is beautiful, hardly less so because he lacks a certain reticence. He has been ridiculed for a tendency to tears, and a rather futile effort has been made to link him in this regard with a tendency of his age. In the earlier volume, and in this, he weeps freely. But the mood is not unpleasant, and is sincere. When he saw the labour of the beavers overturned, he beheld them weep, and he wept too. "Nor am I," he said, "ashamed to confess it." When, as at times, this sentiment runs away with him in a vehicle drawn by dozens of superlatives, apostrophes, and hanging participles, the result is overwhelming. But at his best, when he describes the sufferings of the refugees, his is the sentiment of manhood. This compassion, we learn, is a strong part of his nature, and it envelops his narrative in a gentleness which we come to love.

So it is hoped that this collection of letters will restimulate interest in Crèvecœur not merely as a literary curiosity—such has really been his status—but as a writer. All his essays taken together compare not unfavourably with other prose written in this perturbed

Crèvecœur as a Man of Letters.

era. The cloud upon Crèvecœur's writing, as upon that of Freneau, Trumbull, Barlow, or any other American writer of the century, was the Revolution. It darkened his life, and though it furnished him with materials, it may have hindered his literary development. Let no one, however, pretend that without it Crèvecœur would have become a remarkable man of letters. His talent was not primarily for literature. Yet, as in other students of the frontier, there were in him literary excellencies of taste and feeling. He is not to be dismissed as Rousseauistic or sentimental or a pseudo-naturalist or a freak. He felt moved to put the frontier into writing, and he had certain powers of expression. I believe that various Americans who have written about the frontier, with fame, might be considered in emotional response, in dramatic sense, or in persuasive power, inferior to this American farmer. Without extravagant claims, he nevertheless deserves study not as an anomalous product of this new country, but as an early man of letters in America. He has her qualities stamped upon him: her crudeness and naïveté; her strength, her sincerity.

STANLEY T. WILLIAMS

NOTE ON THE TEXT

IN preparing this text for publication the editors
have not attempted to reproduce exactly the manuscript of Crèvecœur. Such a procedure would have
meant a book of some historical and philological interest, but one encumbered with endless annotations and
explanations. Crèvecœur was a man of action; he wrote
in the intervals of a busy life. He was an acute thinker,
but no scholar. A poor speller, he was likewise careless
of punctuation and syntax. He yielded without consistency to French idioms and English phrases—echoes of
his early life—as well as to dialect pronunciations
which he heard about him in America. Thus some
parts of this manuscript, if repeated *verbatim*, would
be, because of idiosyncrasies of spelling, punctuation,
and grammar, nearly unintelligible, and occasionally
absurd.

The aim of the editors has been, therefore, to make
the manuscript readable, and, at the same time, to re-
tain scrupulously Crèvecœur's meaning,—even, except
in a few instances, his own phraseology and mannerisms
of speech. For these letters, like those already published, have a distinct flavour. Crèvecœur is certainly
unlike any other eighteenth century writer; a gifted
Frenchman, educated for a time in England, living in
and writing of pioneer America. That these letters,
when printed, should express this indefinable quality, is
one object of the present book. Everything possible,
consistent with clarity, has been done to preserve this
tone; one may be confident that it will survive the
changes made in punctuation and spelling. Punctuation

Note on the Text.

indeed hardly exists in the manuscript. The changes, moreover, made by the editors are not comparable in extent or importance with those wrought in the first published letters of Crèvecœur by Thomas Davies and Lockyer Davis, his eighteenth century English revisers.

The spelling has, then, as a whole, been modernized. Often Crèvecœur's orthography is that of his age, as in such words as *compleat* and *antient*. Sometimes, however, he alters these forms. His vagaries are numerous. He can misuse *lie* and *lay;* he can repeat *bleating,* apparently phonetically, as *blaiting;* he frankly employs French words (or versions of them) instead of their English equivalents (*volupty, agricole, colon, carrière*); he can reduce Latin derivatives to, for example, *simetry* and *indgredients;* and he can talk of *gueeres;* or of *woolfs* and *sckuncks.* These are a very few; a list of his grotesque spellings would reach far into the hundreds. Such have been corrected, and have been put into modern form. (Occasionally an obsolete or archaic word has been retained, in its proper spelling, if the meaning is clear, to avoid the use of synonyms.) Any addition to the text, or change in meaning, or in the arrangement of words (other than prepositions, pronouns, articles, etc.) has been indicated by brackets. The capitalization has been normalized. The letters have been repunctuated, always with careful consideration of Crèvecœur's emphasis and arrangement of ideas. In his grammar his awkward constructions and unusual locutions have been permitted to stand, when the meaning is clear, but hopelessly bad grammar has been corrected, and many minor changes have been made to prevent obscurity and absurdity. Such have been imperative in the use of prepositions, conjunctions, adverbs, past participles, agreement of subjects and verbs, and, particularly, in

37

Eighteenth Century America.

the case of Crèvecœur's bewilderment before English pronouns. His continual confusion of the demonstratives "this" and "that," and of the relatives "who" and "which" suggest the nature of his difficulties with English grammar. After all, Crèvecœur was bred in a foreign tongue.

The editors are sensible that these manuscripts may ultimately be subjected to intensive philological study, as interest increases in the development of the English language in America. It has seemed best at this time to present these sketches for their literary rather than their philological interest.

THE EDITORS

SKETCHES OF EIGHTEENTH CENTURY AMERICA

A SNOW STORM AS IT AFFECTS THE AMERICAN FARMER*

NO man of the least degree of sensibility can journey through any number of years in whatever climate without often being compelled to make many useful observations on the different phenomena of Nature which surround him; and without involuntarily being struck either with awe or admiration in beholding some of the elementary conflicts in the midst of which he lives. A great thunderstorm; an extensive flood; a desolating hurricane; a sudden and intense frost; an overwhelming snowstorm; a sultry day,—each of these different scenes exhibits singular beauties even in spite of the damage they cause. Often whilst the heart laments the loss to the citizen, the enlightened mind, seeking for the natural causes, and astonished at the effects, awakes itself to surprise and wonder.

Of all the scenes which this climate offers, none has struck me with a greater degree of admiration than the

* Crèvecœur translated this essay into French under the title of "Description d'une Chute de Neige," *Lettres d'un Cultivateur Américain*, p. 289, 1787 edition.

39

ushering in of our winters, and the vehemence with which their first rigour seizes and covers the earth; a rigour which, when once descended, becomes one of the principal favours and blessings this climate has to boast of. I mean to view it as connected with the welfare of husbandry; as a great flood of congealed water sheltering the grass and the grains of our fields; and overwhelming men, beasts, birds living under the care of man. [He] in the midst of this sudden alteration has to provide food and shelter for so many animals, on the preservation of which the husbandman's welfare entirely depends. This single thought is really tremendous: from grass and pastures growing in our meadows and in our fields; from various other means by which the tenants of our farms lived before, they must suddenly pass to provenders, to grains, and to other resources gathered by Man when the face of the earth teemed with a luxuriant vegetation.

'Tis at this period that the functions of a great farmer become more extended and more difficult. 'Tis from his stores that all must draw their subsistence. He must know whether they will be sufficient to reach the other end of the wintry career. He must see whether all have a sufficient quantity daily delivered to them; whether each class is properly divided; whether water can be procured; what diseases and accidents may happen. These are a few sketches of that energetic circle of foresight, knowledge, and activity which fill the space of five months; to which you must add the care of a large family as to raiment, fuel, and victuals.

The tenants of his house, like the beasts of his farm, must now depend on the collected stores of the preceding season, sagaciously distributed and prepared by the industry of his wife. There lies the "aurum potabile"

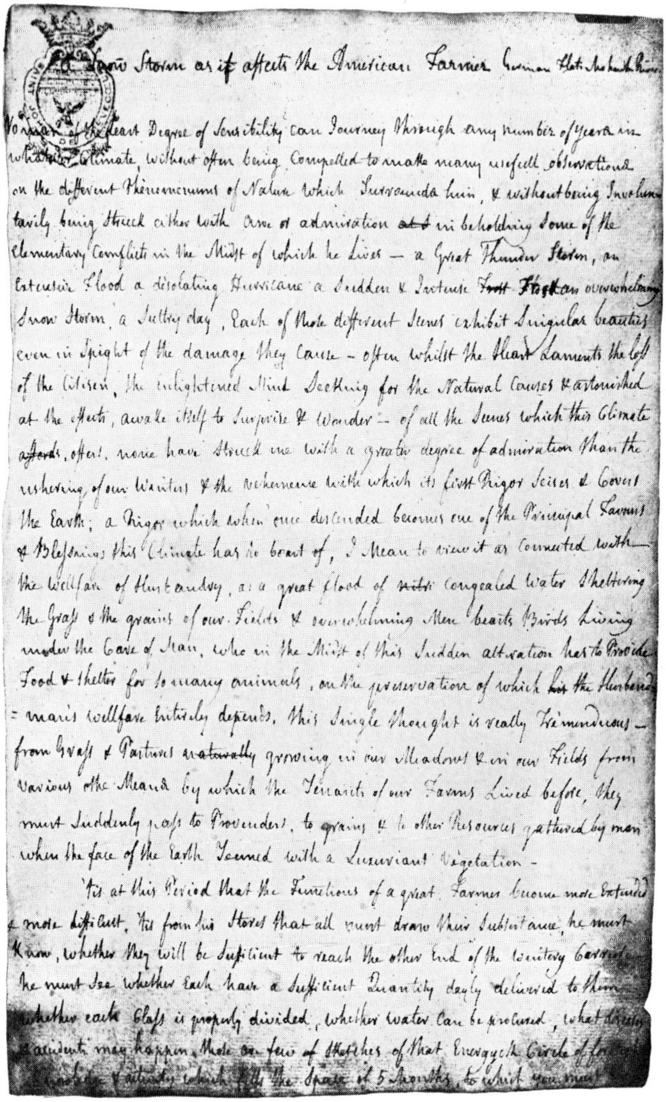

A Page of the Crèvecoeur Manuscripts

A Snow Storm.

of an American farmer. He may work and gather the choicest fruits of his farm, but if female economy fails, he loses the comfort of good victuals. He sees whole-some meats, excellent flours converted into indifferent food; whilst his neighbour, more happy, though less rich, feeds on well-cooked dishes, well-composed pud-dings. For such is our lot: if we are blessed with a good wife, we may boast of living better than any people of the same rank on the globe.

Various tokens, long since known, guide the farmer in his daily progress and various occupations from the autumnal fall of the leaves. If he is prudent and active, he makes himself ready against the worst which Nature can give. Sheds, stables, barn-yards, partitions, racks, and mangers must be carefully reviewed and repaired; the stores of corn-stalks, straw, and hay must be se-curely placed where neither rain nor snow can damage them.

Great rains at last replenish the springs, the brooks, the swamps, and impregnate the earth. Then a severe frost succeeds which prepares it to receive the volumi-nous coat of snow which is soon to follow; though it is often preceded by a short interval of smoke and mild-ness, called the Indian Summer. This is in general the invariable rule: winter is not said properly to begin until these few moderate days and the rising of the wa-ters have announced it to Man. This great mass of liq-uid once frozen spreads everywhere natural bridges; opens communications impassable before. The man of foresight neglects nothing; he has saved every object which might be damaged or lost; he is ready.

The wind, which is a great regulator of the weather, shifts to the northeast; the air becomes bleak and then intensely cold; the light of the sun becomes dimmed as if an eclipse had happened; a general night seems coming on. At last imperceptible atoms make their appearance; they are few and descend slowly, a sure prognostic of a great snow. Little or no wind is as yet felt. By degrees the number as well as the size of these white particles is increased; they descend in larger flakes; a distant wind is heard; the noise swells and seems to advance; the new element at last appears and overspreads everything. In a little time the heavy clouds seem to approach nearer the earth and discharge a winged flood, driving along towards the southwest, howling at every door, roaring in every chimney, whistling with asperous sound through the naked limbs of the trees; these are the shrill notes which mark the weight of the storm. Still the storm increases as the night approaches, and its great obscurity greatly adds to the solemnity of the scene.

Sometimes the snow is preceded by melted hail which, like a shining varnish, covers and adorns the whole surface of the earth of buildings and trees; a hurtful time for the cattle which it chills and oppresses. Mournful and solitary they retire to what shelter they can get, and, forgetting to eat, they wait with instinctive patience until the storm is over. How amazingly changed is the aspect of Nature! From the dusky hues of the autumnal shades, everything becomes refulgently white; from soft, miry roads, we pass all at once to solid icy bridges. What could an inhabitant of Africa say or think in contemplating this northern phenomenon? Would not it raise in his mind a greater degree of astonishment than his thunder-storms and his vertical suns?

A general alarm is spread through the farm. The master calls all his hands; opens the gates; lets down the bars; calls and counts all his stock as they come along. The oxen, the cows, remembering ancient experience, repair to the place where they were foddered the preceding winter; the colts wild, whilst they could unrestrained bound on the grassy fields, suddenly deprived of that liberty, become tame and docile to the hands which stroke and feed them. The sheep, more encumbered than the rest, slowly creep along, and by their incessant bleating show their instinctive apprehension; they are generally the first which attract our attention and care. The horses are led to their stables; the oxen to their stalls; the rest are confined under their proper sheds and districts. All is safe, but no fodder need be given them yet; the stings of hunger are necessary to make them eat cheerfully the dried herbage and forget the green one on which they so lately fed. Heaven be praised, no accident has happened; all is secured from the inclemency of the storm. The farmer's vigilant eye has seen every operation performed; has numbered every head; and as a good master provided for the good welfare of all.

At last he returns home loaded with hail and snow melting on his rough but warm clothes; his face is red with the repeated injury occasioned by the driving wind. His cheerful wife, not less pleased, welcomes him home with a mug of gingered cider; and whilst she helps him to dried and more comfortable clothes, she recounts to him the successful pains she has taken also in collecting all her ducks, geese, and all the rest of her numerous poultry; a province less extensive indeed but not less useful. But no sooner this simple tale is told than the cheerfulness of her mind is clouded by a sudden thought. Her children went to a distant school early in the morning whilst the sun shone, and ere any ideas were formed of this storm. They are not yet returned. What is become of them? Has the master had tenderness enough to tarry awhile and watch over his little flock until the arrival of some relief? Or has he rudely dismissed them in quest of his own safety?

These alarming thoughts are soon communicated to her husband who, starting up in all the glow of paternal anxiety, orders one of his negroes to repair to the schoolhouse with Bonny, the old faithful mare, who, like his wife, by her fecundity has replenished his farm. 'Tis done: she is mounted bare-back and hurried through the storm to the schoolhouse, at the door of which each child is impatiently waiting for this paternal assistance. At the sight of honest Tom, the negro, their joy is increased by the pleasure of going home on horseback. One is mounted before and two behind. Rachel, the poor widow's little daughter, with tears in her eyes, sees her playmates, just before her equals, as she thought, now provided with a horse and an attendant,—a sad mortification. This is the first time she ever became sensible of the difference of her situation. Her distressed mother, not less anxious to fetch her child, prays to heaven that some charitable neighbour may bring her along. She, too, has a cow to take care of; a couple of pigs hitherto tenderly fed at the door; three or four ewes, perhaps, demanding her shelter round some part of her lonely log-house. Kind heaven hears her prayers. Honest Tom lifts her [Rachel] up and, for want of room, places her on Bonny's neck; there she is upheld by the oldest boy. Thus fixed with difficulty, they turn about and boldly face the driving storm; they all scream and are afraid of falling; at last they clinch together and are hushed. With cheerfulness and instinctive patience, Bonny proceeds along, and, sensible of the valuable cargo, highly lifting her legs, she securely treads along, shaking now and then her ears as the drifted snow penetrates into them.

A joyful meeting ensues. The thoughts of avoided danger increase the pleasure of the family. The milk-biscuit, the short-cake, the newly-baked apple-pie are immediately produced, and the sudden joy these presents occasion expels every idea of cold and snow. In this country of hospitality and plenty it would be a wonder indeed if little Rachel had not partaken of the same bounty. She is fed, made to warm herself; she has forgot the little reflections she had made at the school-house door; she is happy, and to complete the goodly act, she is sent home on the same vehicle. The unfeigned thanks, the honest blessings of the poor widow, who was just going to set out, amply repays the trouble that has been taken; happy wages of this charitable attention.

The messenger returns. Everything is safe both within and without. At that instant the careful negro, Jack, who has been busily employed in carrying wood to the shed that he may not be at a loss to kindle fire in the morning, comes into his master's room carrying on his hip an enormous back-log without which a fire is supposed to be imperfectly made and to be devoid of heat. All hands rise; the fire is made to blaze; the hearth is cleaned; and all the cheerful family sit around. Rest after so many laborious operations brings along with it an involuntary silence, even among the children who grow sleepy with their victuals in their hands, as they grow warm. "Lord, hear, how it blows!" says one. "My God, what a storm!" says another. "Mammy, where does all this snow come from?" asks a third. "Last year's storm, I think, was nothing to this," observes the wife. "I hope all is fast about the house. How happy it is for us that we had daylight to prepare us for it."

The father now and then opens the door to pass judgment, and to contemplate the progress of the storm: " 'Tis dark, 'tis pitch-dark," he says; "a fence four rods off cannot be distinguished. The locust-trees hard by the door bend under the pressure of the loaded blast. Thank God, all is secured. I'll fodder my poor cattle well in the morning if it please Him I should live to see it." And this pious sentiment serves him as a reward for all his former industry, vigilance, and care. The negroes, friends to the fire, smoke and crack some coarse jokes; and, well-fed and clad, they contentedly make their brooms and ladles without any further concerns on their minds. Thus the industrious family, all gathered together under one roof, eat their wholesome supper, drink their mugs of cider, and grow imperceptibly less talkative and more thoughtless, as they grow more sleepy. Now and then, when the redoubled fury of the storm rattles in the chimney, they seem to awake. They look at the door again and again, but 'tis the work of omnipotence; it is unavoidable; their neighbours feel it as well as themselves. Finally they go to bed, not to that bed of slavery or sorrow as is the case in Europe with people of their class, but on the substantial collection of honest feathers picked and provided by the industrious wife. There, stretched between flannel sheets and covered with warm blankets made of their own sheep's wool, they enjoy the luxury of sound, undisturbed repose, earned by the fatigues of the preceding day. The Almighty has no crime to punish in this innocent family; why should He permit ominous dreams

and terrific visions to disturb the imaginations of these
good people?

As soon as day reappears, the American farmer
awakes and calls all his hands. While some are busy in
kindling the fires, the rest with anxiety repair to the
barns and sheds. What a dismal aspect presents itself to
their view! The roads, the paths are no longer visible.
The drifted snow presents obstacles which must be removed with the shovel. The fences and the trees, bend-
ing under the weight of snow which encumbers them,
bend in a thousand shapes; but by a lucky blast of wind
they are discharged, and they immediately recover their
natural situation. The cattle who had hitherto remained
immovable, their tails to the wind, appear strangely
disfigured by the long accession and adherence of the
snow to their bodies. On the sight of the master, suddenly animated, they heavily shake themselves clean,
and crowd from all parts in expectation of that fodder
which the industry of Man has provided for them.
Where their number is extensive, various and often distant are their allotments, which are generally in the
vicinity of the stacks of hay. In that case, when the
barn-yard work is done, the farmer mounts his horse,
followed by his men armed with pitch-forks. He counts
again the number of each sort, and sees that each receives a sufficient quantity. The strong are separated
from the weak, oxen with oxen, yearlings with yearlings, and so on through every class. For cattle, like
men, conscious of their superior force will abuse it when
unrestrained by any law, and often live on their neighbour's property.

What a care, what an assiduity does this life require!
Who on contemplating the great and important field of
action performed every year by a large farmer, can re-

frain from valuing and praising as they ought this useful, this dignified class of men? These are the people who, scattered on the edge of this great continent, have made it to flourish; and have without the dangerous assistance of mines, gathered, by the sweat of their honest brows and by the help of their ploughs, such a harvest of commercial emoluments for their country, uncontaminated either by spoils or rapine. These are the men who in future will replenish this huge continent even to its utmost unknown limits, and render this new found part of the world by far the happiest, the most potent as well as the most populous of any. Happy people! May the poor, the wretched of Europe, animated by our example, invited by our laws, avoid the fetters of their country, and come in shoals to partake of our toils as well as of our happiness!

The next operation is to seek for convenient watering-places. Holes must be cut through the ice; 'tis done. The veteran, experienced cattle lead the way, tread down the snow, and form a path; the rest soon follow. Two days' experience [teaches] them all the way to this place as well as the station they must occupy in their progress thither; the stoutest marching first and the weakest closing the rear. The succeeding operations with regard to the preservation of the cattle entirely depend on the judgment of the farmer. He knows, according to the weather, when it is best to give them either straw, corn-stalks, or hay. In very hard weather they are more hungry and better able to consume the coarse fodder; corn stocks are reserved for sheep and young cattle; hay is given to all in thaws.

Soon after this great fall of snow the wind shifts to the northwest and blows with great impetuosity; it gathers and drives the loose element. Everything seems

A Snow Storm.

to be involved a second time in a general whirlwind of white atoms, not so dangerous indeed as those clouds of sand raised in the deserts of Arabia. This second scourge is rather worse than the first, because it renders parts of the roads seemingly impassable. 'Tis then that with empty sleighs the neighbourhood gather, and by their united efforts open a communication along the road. If new snow falls, new endeavours must be made use of to guard against the worst of inconveniences. For, to live, it is necessary to go to market, to mill, to the woods. This is, besides, the season of merriment and mutual visiting. All the labours of the farm are now reduced to those of the barn; to the fetching of fuel and to cleaning their own flax. The fatigues of the preceding summer require now some relaxation. What can be more conducive to it than the great plenty of wholesome food we all have? Cider is to be found in every house. The convenience of travelling invites the whole country to society, pleasure, and visiting. Bees are made, by which a number of people with their sleighs resort to the inviter's house, and there in one day haul him as much wood as will serve him a whole year. Next day 'tis another man's turn; admirable contrivance which promotes good-will, kindness, and mutual assistance. By means of these associations often the widows and orphans are relieved.

After two or three falls of snow the weather becomes serene though cold. New communications are opened over lakes and rivers and through forests hitherto impassable. The ox rests from his summer labour, and the horse amply fed now does all the work. His celerity is strengthened by the steel shoes with which his hoofs are armed; he is fit to draw on the snow as well as on the ice. Immense is the value of this season: logs for future buildings are easily drawn to the saw-mills; ready-piled stones are with equal ease brought to the intended spot; grain is conveyed to the different landings on our small rivers, from whence in the spring small vessels carry it to the sea-port towns, and from which again larger ones convey it away to the different marts of the world. The constancy of this serenely cold weather is one of the greatest blessings which seldom fails us. More to the southward their winters are often interrupted by thaws and rains which are unfavourable to transportation as well as to the cattle. [This is] a happy suspension of toils and labours; happy rest without which the vegetation of our cold climates would soon be exhausted. On the other hand, 'tis an expensive season in every respect: nothing profitable can be done, and clothes of the warmest sorts must be provided for everyone. Great parts of the profits of summer are expended in carrying a family through this wintry career,—but let not that reflection diminish our happiness! We are robust, healthy, and strong; the milder climates of the South have nothing that can compensate for these advantages. It is true that the class of men who work for the farmers have less employment, but nevertheless they live with comfort and in such abundance as is proportioned to their situation; everyone has bread and meat. As for the real poor, we have none in this happy country; those who through age and infirmities are past labour, are provided for by the township to which they belong. Such are the Mohawk and Canadian winters. . . . A long ramble like this through a cold Canadian storm requires rest, silence, and sleep. After so long an excursion we may with propriety wish each other good night.

ANT-HILL TOWN*

I AM now sitting under one of the most enchanting groves of Virginia; 'tis the work of art, but executed with so much simplicity as greatly to resemble that of Nature. 'Tis an octagon frame round which vines and honeysuckles have been planted. They have grown with such luxuriancy; their limbs and foliage are so interwoven as to refuse all admittance to the rays of the sun, yet leave a free passage to the air. Round this verdant temple at an equal distance, stands a double row of the mellifluous locusts, the umbrageous catalpas, and the soft magnolias. Alternately planted, they expand their friendly limbs all round, and repel the scorching rays of the sun. 'Tis a grove of Tempé; 'tis a Druidical temple, in point of gloom, shade, and solitude.

From this predilected spot, which is my daily resort, an avenue leads to the house, a second to a private garden, and a third to a bath; while the front expands towards an extensive lawn, a very rare thing here; and opens the view to a variety of luxuriant fields of tobacco, corn, etc., reaching to the very shores of that noble river which is the boundary of this province. By extending [the view] beyond the Potomac, the country rises into a most delightful perspective, composed of plantations, buildings intermixed with copses of trees, peach orchards, etc. There is still something wanting: the pride and principal ornaments of more moist, more northern climates. Here they want the verdant lawns of

* Crèvecœur adds: Virginia 1769, from Mr. P. V.

51

Eighteenth Century America.

England, of Ireland, and Normandy; all their art cannot produce that which Nature and the soil seem to refuse. To the South you have an imperfect view of that great and capacious bay, where all the great rivers of this province disembogue themselves. The great number of small gulfs, of bays, islands, and shoals formed by the confluence of so many streams affords food and asylum to an amazing number of ducks, of geese, swans, etc. This is the place where the sport they afford presents itself to all those who care not what fatigues they undergo, provided that pleasure is annexed to it.

This rural scene where I am now, this silvan bower, appears to me so much the more enchanting on account of the cool, the calm, the placid retreat it affords; because I contrast it with the scorching fury of their sun which is now ripening with its fullest energy their extensive harvests. Here it is that I forget the toils of my late journey; the fatigues it occasioned seem now but a moderate purchase for the ease I feel. I am in that state which conveys the most harmless and indefinable happiness. The feelings of [pleasure] and ease encompass me all around. I am perfectly inactive, yet I am anxious to transmit to you some little memorial of friendship by the ——, which is to sail for England from —— in a few days. I cannot at present be very serious. Harvest and the joys it spreads are themes which ought to inspire me with the rural song. Unfortunately it is not very applicable to this country where the grain is gathered by slaves, and where their daily toils absorb the very idea of joys.

What revolutions do we experience in great as well as in small concerns! Life is but a checkered surface, every step of which is perpetually diversified. 'Tis not two months ago that in the province of Massachusetts I

Ant-Hill Town.

thought myself happy to sit by the comfortable fireside of ———, and I thought his warm room, his clean hearth afforded the greatest felicity, and amply supplied the place of their then heatless sun. 'Tis not two months since his potent Madeira, his enlivening pipe afforded me a fund of cheerfulness that now would be improper. There, reading their provincial newspapers, I beheld with pleasure a fictitious renovation of the spring in the growth of the evergreen which over-ran his mantle-piece. Now, on the contrary, I stand surrounded with these southern blasts, big with igneous particles and ready to inflame one of the most irascible of matters. We had, three days ago, a most solemn trial, one of the most awful thunderstorms ever remembered.

But however agreeable this part of America is in consequence of the hospitality of its inhabitants, the temperate zones of Europe are much superior to it. There it is that mankind enjoy a gentleness of seasons which is much more favourable to the increase of mankind and to the preservation of their health. There husbandry may be displayed in all its perfection and beauty; here one sees and feels nothing but extremes. But exclusive of those primary advantages to be enjoyed, nowhere but in the country is there a great variety of other pleasing sensations which never entered into the head of an inhabitant of cities. I don't mean those belonging to the well-pursued plan of an extensive rural economy, which govern and pursue the useful labours of a large landed estate; much less do I mean those fantastic ones often transplanted from the bosom of cities. No, those I mean are those which indeed I have often felt. They, properly speaking, afford no vulgar enjoyment; 'tis a multitude of pleasing sensations from whence one may

53

collect instruction, morality, rectitude of judgment, motives of gratitude.

Here they have no towns of any note, and I am glad of it. How I hate to dwell in these accumulated and crowded cities! They are but the confined theatre of cupidity; they exhibit nothing but the action and re-action of a variety of passions which, being confined within narrower channels, impel one another with the greatest vigour. The same passions are more rare in the country and, from their greater extent and expansion, they are but necessary gales. I always delighted to live in the country. Have you never felt at the returning of spring a glow of general pleasure, an indiscernible something that pervades our whole frame, an inward involuntary admiration of everything which surrounds us? 'Tis then the beauties of Nature, everywhere spread, seem to swell every sentiment as she swells every juice. She dissolves herself in universal love and seems to lead us to the same sentiments. Did you ever unmoved pass by a large orchard in full bloom without feeling an uncommon ravishment, not only arising from the exquisite perfumes surrounding you on all sides, but from the very splendour of the scene? Who can at this time of the year observe the ushering in of buds, the unfolding of leaves, the appearance of flowers, the whole progress of vegetation, and remain insensible? The well-known industry of bees, that excellent gov-ernment which pervades their habitations, that never-ceasing industry by which they are actuated, though sung by so many poets, and long since become the sub-ject of so many allusions, metaphors, and the theme of so many orators,—yet 'tis a subject ever new. Set your-self down under some trees in their neighbourhood, see them arriving with the spoils of the fields; observe the digested dews, the concocted ethereal particles of flowers and blossoms converted by them into honey. When these industrious citizens are all out, open one of their hives, and see the wonderful instinct which leads them by the most invariable rules to project and to execute with so much regularity that variety of cells calculated to contain their honey, their coarser food, as well as the eggs from whence new swarms are to arise.

Have not the regular arrival and departure of certain birds ever set you a-thinking whence they came? Have you never reflected on the sublimity of the knowledge they possess, in order to overcome so many difficulties, to steer so invariable a course to other more favourable regions unseen by men, either in their flight or return? When in the spring you happen to revisit some trees of your own planting, have you never felt something of the paternal affection, of that peculiar satisfaction which attends viewing the works of our hands? Have you ever enjoyed as you ought the transcendent pleasure attending that magnificent scene— unheeded, alas, by most men—because it is often repeated? Have you never worshipped the Master of Nature in the most august of all temples, in that extensive one of His own framing where He no doubt presides as the great invisible Pontiff, but where He permits His awful representative to become visible in order to bless mankind with light and life? Have you never observed the sun rising on a calm morning? What majesty pervades, then, all Nature, when the variegated aspect of the heavens, when those mixed tinges of emerging light and vanishing shades, united with that diffusive [pleasure] issuing from the fecundated earth, exhibit the most august spectacle which this transitory life affords!

Eighteenth Century America.

How often have I viewed with admiration that sublime gradation of objects reaching and filling the whole extent of my perception: from the refulgent luminary to the fainting moon, to the dimmed stars, down to the vocal choir, even to the polygonal cobweb, perpendicularly hung or horizontally suspended,—all bespangled with dew-drops refulgent as the diamond, waving to the raptured eyes! 'Tis not that I would mean to recommend to you the worship of fire in this solar appearance. I am far from believing with the disciples of Zoroaster, that the sun is the true Shekinah of the divine presence, the grand tabernacle, the Keblah where He alone resides. No, but relegated as we are at such a distance from the great Author of all, is not it a consolation to view scenes of this nature, by which we are elevated and permitted in thought to approach nearer to His throne? 'Tis in the country alone that you can follow this rotation of objects which feeds contemplation; which delights, improves, and often assuages the pains of an afflicted mind. Even the approach of a thunderstorm, though so dreaded by the generality of mankind,—how solemn, how awful, what reverence does it not inspire us with! Nature seems angry. Yes, but it is for our good, and she wisely draws from that strife of elements the salubrity of the air we breathe.

As soon as the sea breeze came, I took a walk towards the shores of the river. As I was searching for the most convenient spot to descend to the shores I perceived a large, flat stone lying on the ground. As they are very scarce in this part of the country I stopped to view it, and to consider whether it had not been left there on some peculiar account. On looking at it more attentively, I perceived the marks of ancient sea-shells incrusted on its surface. How could this stone have received these marine impressions? How could it be brought here where stones are so scarce? Hoping to find some of these shell fragments better preserved on the opposite side, I lifted it up with some difficulty, when to my great surprise and amusement I found that it served as a roof to a subterranean structure of a very singular appearance. It covered the upper walks of a town seemingly composed of arches, of vaults, of a multitude of passages intermixed throughout the whole. From these obscure mansions there were a number of apertures leading to the excavated surface which was covered by the stone. It was cut into a great number of streets; some times contiguous and parallel to each other; sometimes receding in various directions. These streets were divided from each other by little banks of earth of a different thickness, as is the case in winter-time in the streets of Quebec. The whole surface was about thirty-five inches long and about twenty-three broad. It contained seventy-one streets and had four-teen subterraneous openings. The first idea it conveyed was that of a labyrinth, but on following with attention any one of the streets, the intricacy vanished.

In order to have a fuller view of this scene of mys-terious ingenuity I removed the stone with the utmost care. On the southeast, and northwest sides I perceived two considerable breaches full three inches wide gradu-ally sloping from the surface of the ground to the subterranean avenues. These were, I suppose, the two great communications to fetch their foods and to carry off their unnecessary materials.

Here lived thousands of ants of the pismire class. But no pen can delineate the seeming confusion and affright which my bold intrusion caused among them; it was a whole republic thrown into the most imminent danger. The never-failing impulse of instinct immediately led them to provide for the preservation of their young. They appeared to be as big as small grains of wheat, and seemed to have been brought up from the lower habitations in order to receive more immediately the prolific effects of the sun's heat, and to swell their limbs into life and action. These embryos appeared to be in a different degree of animal advancement. Some seemed quite torpid and lifeless; others showed marks of feeling and pains on being suddenly seized, though by maternal claws. No sooner was the first effect of their panic over than they hurried away their young out of my sight, but as they were more numerous than the parents, more assistance immediately came from below; or else the same individuals returned to the pious office. In about five minutes not the least vestiges were left of that numerous society, and no one could have believed that it had been replenished with so many inhabitants. In this great national dismay no one quitted the mansion or attempted to make his escape, although they knew not what sort of enemy I was. The whole community, bound by the ties of the firmest confederacy, unanimously went down, trusting, perhaps, to their works of defence, or to my inability to pursue them where all appeared so dark and so intricate.

What a situation for this Virginian republic, when the refulgent sun at once pervaded every corner of their habitation, where his rays had never reached before! We may then pronounce that what the stone covered were their paths of life and health, the cradles of their rising generations. Their other and invisible recesses must have far exceeded this little insignificant surface; for, no doubt, it must have afforded them convenient rooms for their winter-stores, receptacles for

Ant-Hill Town.

their daily food, besides capacious lodgings for so many thousand inhabitants.

Should I turn up and destroy so fair a monument of industry? Should I overwhelm in death and desolation so many harmless animals? No, I could not permit myself to satisfy so impious a curiosity at the expense of so much evil and to pollute my hands by the commission of so atrocious a deed; on the contrary, I replaced the stone.

A few days afterwards I paid them a second visit, when I observed a great number of ants decorated with wings. But this gaudy attire did not appear to add any celerity to their flight; they never expanded them. Like the preposterous dress of some ladies it served only to render them more conspicuous than the rest. Upon a closer inspection they appeared more inactive and wholly deprived of that quickness of motion for which the unwinged sort are so remarkable. Perhaps they were the matrons of the republic, never departing from that formal gravity appointed to the rank by Nature; perhaps they were young damsels embarrassed by the rule of modesty and decorum; perhaps they were young ones just hatched, not having as yet ventured to traverse the air in order to harden their limbs in the aspect of the sun. How sorry [I am] that I never have read Buffon! I could have explained myself technically, whereas I am now speaking to you in the language of a school-boy who possesses as yet nothing of knowledge besides curiosity.

Within a few rods and nearer to the river were erected eleven great conical buildings three feet high and two and a half broad at the bottom. They were perforated with an immense number of holes. The whole appeared to be built of slight materials, yet by means of sticks and straws, the ends of which only were visible, they had given it a great degree of stability. The inhabitants of this second colony appeared to be of a much larger size, much stronger, and more capable of lifting heavy burthens. What surprised me was that, although so near this subterranean settlement, yet there appeared no kind of communication between them. Weak and defenseless as the first were, a perfect peace and tranquillity prevailed; a most marvellous thing considering the superiority which the one had over the other species. This harmony must have arisen from their feeding on different things. In this case there could be no room either for contention or competition; no cause that could influence their little passions and produce those sanguinary commotions so frequent among mankind. The circumjacent ground which surrounded these eleven pyramids was perfectly cleaned; neither bush, shrub, nor herbage, or any foliage whatever grew nigh that might conceal or harbour any enemy. They had made considerable paths to the waterside as well as to different fields in which they invariably travelled, but I never followed them in any of their excursions.

The same Pythagorean disposition which prevented me from turning up the bowels of the first republic, in order to satisfy a vain curiosity, made me refrain from tumbling down one of these cones which might have showed me the structure within. Whether these serve them only as summer habitations, and are but a collection of materials excavated from below, I dare not ascertain. Such as it presented itself to my view it seems to answer all their purposes, and to preserve them from the inclemency of the air, wind, and rain. What other casual accidents may happen is no doubt quickly re-

Ant-Hill Town.

paired by the mutual assistance of so many alert and vigorous insects.

When some of your friends hear of your having received a letter from North America, they will perhaps expect to hear some learned accounts of natural knowledge, botany, etc. What will they think of your correspondent when instead of useful discoveries, important dissertations, they hear you read this trifling incident not worth its passage over the Atlantic? For your sake make some sort of apology which will palliate their disappointment, without lessening your dignity. And, after all, is it not in the course of a long correspondence sometimes necessary to write as we feel? Premeditated subjects become a laborious task, and the communicating of those impulses when they arise is truly pleasurable. Indeed, had I my choice I'd much rather amuse myself with these objects of instinctive economy, knowledge, and industry than to wade over fields of battle strewn with the carcasses of friends and foes, the victims of so many phantoms. Such as this is, pray receive it, agreeable to your ancient custom for better, for worse.—Adieu.

REFLECTIONS ON THE
MANNERS OF THE AMERICANS*

IN my preceding letters I have endeavoured to show you that the prevailing modes of religion which are taught in this country, a few sects excepted, are propagated in such a manner as to preclude that particular efficacy which might be its triumph.† The situation and extent of parishes are a very great impediment. That mixture of opinions which every member of society is at liberty to follow causes in some districts a total indifference about any.

Let us follow one of these colonists in his progress towards the wilderness; he may well serve as an epitome by which we may judge of the rest. For we have all been emigrants in our turns, from the first families who planted the sea-shores, to these last ones, the labours of which I wish to describe. This man was perhaps known in the place where he was bred as a Presbyterian. It may have happened that his children have gone through a slight course of catechism, but what does it teach them that can cause a lasting impression, that can give them a permanent idea of their duties to their Creator, and of their various obligations to Man? The strongest part of their belief, the most certain idea they have of their profession arises often from this: that they remember having several times gone to meeting in company with

* Crèvecœur translated this essay into French under the title of "Histoire de S.K., colon Américain" in *Lettres d'un Cultivateur Américain*, p. 120, 1787 edition. The opening paragraphs have been omitted.

† These sentences may refer to the essay, *Liberty of Worship*. See page 152.

their parents. If, therefore, any one asks them in the new country of what profession they are, they will readily answer: "We were bred Presbyterians." This answer supplies the place of all other knowledge. If their parents are descended from progenitors among whom there prevailed some extraordinary zeal, that [causes] the contempt and jealousy of other sects. This sentiment may perhaps descend to the present generation. However, these questions are seldom asked, for the people in general, particularly in newly settled countries, care very little what the religious opinions of new-comers are. Be they what they will, they are sure to find in this new district some one or another that entertains and cherishes the same.

It may be easily supposed that in all these new establishments, often formed by chance, it must take a number of years ere a proper religious one can take place. This delay may proceed from many causes. These are always voluntary excepting in some parts of New England. For its completion, therefore, it requires the consent of a sufficient number of wills and the assistance of a certain number of purses, as well to erect the new temple as to support its minister. If the settlers happen to be greatly divided in their religious opinions, there will not be enough of any one denomination to support the establishment. None, therefore, will take place, for no family whatever is obliged to contribute unless agreeable to their will and pleasure. If in process of time any sect becomes numerous enough to attempt it, the temple will be fixed in that part of the settlement where the greatest number of this sect happens to reside. The government, unconcerned, sees and observes this great deficiency, but it cannot remedy it without departing from that system of toleration which serves as a foundation for their laws, and pervades every part of their organization. It can't put itself to the expense of building at the public charge religious edifices for every sect which inhabits the new country. The matter is, therefore, left to the people's zeal and to time.

But if among these new colonists there happens to be a considerable number who still entertain some degree of affection for those opinions they brought with them, these people will once in a while assemble themselves in the most convenient house among their own people. There the greatest scholar will undertake to read some part of the Scriptures, to say some extempore prayers and perhaps expound a text. This happy succedaneum is all they can get, and they are satisfied. This temporary priest assumes neither new airs nor new clothes in consequence of the new office. This gives him no other consequence than what he enjoyed before. The rest of the inhabitants, either more careless or lukewarm, will pass all the days of their lives in the prosecution of their labours, reading or saying prayers morning and evening to their families, industrious and peaceable, and in the most perfect religious apathy. Their children, bred still further from any religious education than their parents, must necessarily acquire a greater degree of indifference.

These people will, notwithstanding, clear these rough forests; they will enrich the soil with cattle, meadows, and buildings; they will make every vale to smile under their feet. They will fill this new country with children who perhaps never will be baptized. They will attain to a good old age, some of them with the most respectable characters. They may be raised to civil employments or to various other municipal functions. They will discharge their duty to society and to the government like the best of subjects; and, notwithstanding their having remained so many years utter strangers to the practice of any other religious duties than those I have mentioned, and perhaps to none, they will die at last in the bosoms of their families without any perturbation of mind and without any remorse of conscience. Though thus unassisted by any ministerial exhortations, prayers, or religious ceremonies, they will quit this world which they have embellished, as peaceably and with more confidence and tranquillity than a Spaniard who receives daily visits from his confessor, and whose room is filled with every vehicle of assistance his church can confer. Such is the situation of many even in more ancient, more flourishing settlements.

With regard to the real religious knowledge of these new settlers a short retrospect of what it was, ere they left their ancient habitations, will not be improper, in order to complete the picture. The parishes are in general very extensive. The minister, often occupied with the cares and solicitudes of a large family with a small stipend and a farm (for everyone tills the earth), cannot attend to every distance, to every circumstance, and to every call. He may, therefore, recommend it to all heads of families to watch over the religious principles of their children. But these have their labours to prosecute. Perhaps they are not well-instructed themselves. Perhaps they may want zeal, and that is very common. Thus these children will grow up. I don't mean that it is so in all families and in all settlements. No, but it is the prevailing method in many.

This apathy may be attributed likewise to that general happiness which proceeds from a government which does everything for us and requires little or nothing. It may be attributed to that great stream of prosperity, of which everyone here receives his full share. 'Tis only when we feel sorrow and misfortunes that we love to pray, and to take refuge in the arms of a Superior Being. Few accidents oblige us to think of God and of His judgments, except it is in consequence of a better and happier education. On the other hand, the simplicity of our worship scarcely leaves any impressions on the imagination of the vulgar. 'Tis but a mixture of theoretical divinity, ancient history, and singing. The morality of the New Testament is not taught separately but is involved in the different chapters which are read to us. The whole is intermixed with extempore prayers, dictated agreeable to the imagination of the minister. It would require more constancy and application than most of these working men can bestow to conceive and enter into the general views of this simplified system. Some part of the innovation is too spiritual for coarse understandings; some part is too controversial; some part purely anti-ceremonial; other parts abstruse and not easily brought to the standard of daily use and vulgar conceptions. 'Tis a knowledge or rather a study well enough adapted to contemplative minds, but not so well-fitted for the measure of these people who must toil, sweat, and labour the whole year. But 'tis hard to reconcile a useful, simple, rational worship, happily deprived of that mechanism which inspires but a fictitious religion, with the coarse organs of the majority of mankind. Such in general was the situation of most of these people when they left their native habitations to go to form new settlements.

Let us view now the new colonist as possessed of property. This has a great weight and a mighty influence. From earliest infancy we are accustomed to a greater exchange of things, a greater transfer of property than the people of the same class in Europe. Whether it is occasioned by that perpetual and necessary emigrating genius which constantly sends the exuberancy of full societies to replenish new tracts; whether it proceeds from our being richer; whether it is that we are fonder of trade which is but an exchange, —I cannot ascertain. This man, thus bred, from a variety of reasons is determined to improve his fortune by removing to a new district, and resolves to purchase as much land as will afford substantial farms to every one of his children,—a pious thought which causes so many even wealthy people to sell their patrimonial estates to enlarge their sphere of action and leave a sufficient inheritance to their progeny.

No sooner he is resolved than he takes all the information he can with regard to the country he proposes to go to inhabit. He finds out all travellers who have been on the spot; he views maps; attentively weighs the benefits and disadvantages of climate, seasons, situation, etc.; he compares it with his own. A world of the most ponderous reflections must needs fill his mind. He at last goes to the capital and applies to some great land-holders. He wants to make a purchase. Each party sets forth the peculiar goodness of its tracts in all the various possible circumstances of health, soil, proximity of lakes, rivers, roads, etc. Maps are presented to him; various lots are spread before him as pieces of linen in the shop of a draper. What a sagacity must this common farmer have, first, to enable him to choose the province, the country, the peculiar tract most agreeable to his fortune; then to resist, to withstand the sophistry of these learned men armed with all the pomp of their city arguments! Yet he is a match for them all. These mathematical lines and sheets of paper would represent nothing to a man of his class in Europe, yet he understands their meaning, even the various courses by which the rivers and mountains are known. He remembers them while in the woods, and is not at a loss to trace them through the impervious forest, and to reason accurately upon the errors and mistakes which may have been made by the surveyor's neglect or ignorance in the representation of them. He receives proper directions and departs for the intended place, for he wants to view and examine ere he purchases.

When near the spot, he hires a man, perhaps a hunter, of which all the frontiers are full, and instead of being lost and amazed in the middle of these gloomy retreats, he finds the place of beginning on which the whole survey is founded. This is all the difficulty he was afraid of; he follows the ancient blazed trees with a sagacity and quickness of sight which have many times astonished me, though bred in the woods. Next he judges of the soil by the size and the appearance of the trees; next he judges of the goodness of the timber by that of the soil. The humble bush which delights in the shade, the wild ginseng, the spignet,* the weeds on which he treads teach him all he wants to know. He observes the springs, the moisture of the earth, the range of the mountains, the course of the brooks. He returns at last; he has formed his judgment as to his future buildings; their situation, future roads, cultivation, etc. He has properly combined the future mixture of conveniences and inconveniences which he expects to meet with. In short the complicated arrangement of a great machine would not do greater honour to the most skilful artist than the reduction and digesting of so many thoughts and calculations by this hitherto obscure man.

* Spignet. A corruption of "spikenard" (*Aralia racemosa*).

Manners of the Americans.

He meets once more the land-proprietors; a new scene ensues. He is startled at the price. He altercates with them, for now he has something to say, having well explored the country. Now he makes them an offer; now he seems to recede; now wholly indifferent about the bargain; now willing to fulfil it if the terms are reasonable. If not, he can't but stay where he is, or perhaps accept of better offers which have been made to him by another person. He relinquishes, he pursues his object—that is his advantage—through a more complex labyrinth than a European could well imagine. He is diffident; he is mistrustful as to the title, ancientness of patent, priority of claim, etc. The idea that would occur to an Englishman of his class would be that such great and good men would not deceive such a poor farmer as he is; he would feel an inward shame to doubt their assertions. You are wrong, my friends; these are not your country parish-squires who would by so gross a deceit defame their characters and lose your vote. Besides, the price of things is better ascertained there in all possible bargains than here. This is a land-merchant who, like all other merchants, has no other rule than to get what he can. This is the general standard except where there is some competition. The native sagacity of this American colonist carries him at last through the whole bargain. He purchases fifteen hundred acres at three dollars* per acre to be paid in three equal yearly payments. He gives his bond for the same, and the whole tract is mortgaged as a security. On the other hand, he obtains bonds of indemnity to secure him against the miscarriages of the patent and other claims.

He departs with all his family, and great and many

* Three dollars is a correction of the author. Originally the text read forty shillings.

are the expenses and fatigues of this removal with cows and cattle. He at last arrives on the spot. He finds himself suddenly deprived of the assistance of friends, neighbours, tradesmen, and of all those inferior links which make a well-established society so beautiful and pleasing. He and his family are now alone. On their courage, perseverance, and skill their success depends. There is now no retreating; shame and ruin would infallibly overtake them. What is he to do in all possible cases of accidents, sickness, and other casualties which may befall his family, his cattle and horses, breaking of the implements of husbandry, etc.? A complicated scene presents itself to the contemplative mind, which does the Americans a superlative honour. Whence proceed that vigour and energy, those resources which they never fail to show on these trying occasions? From the singularity of their situation, from that locality of existence which is peculiar to themselves as a new people improving a new country?

I have purposely visited many who have spent the earliest part of their lives in this manner; now ploughmen, now mechanics, sometimes even physicians. They are and must be everything. Nay, who would believe it? This new man will commence as a hunter and learn in these woods how to pursue and overtake the game with which it abounds. He will in a short time become master of that necessary dexterity which this solitary life inspires. Husband, father, priest, principal governor,—he fills up all these stations, though in the humble vale of life. Are there any of his family taken sick, either he or his wife must recollect ancient directions received from aged people, from doctors, from a skilful grandmother, perhaps, who formerly learned of the Indians of her neighbourhood how to cure simple diseases by means of simple medicines. The swamps and woods are ransacked to find the plants, the bark, the roots prescribed. An ancient almanac, constituting perhaps all his library, with his Bible, may chance to direct him to some more learned ways.

Has he a cow or an ox sick, his anxiety is not less, for they constitute part of his riches. He applies what recipes he possesses; he bleeds, he foments; he has no farrier at hand to assist him. Does either his plough or his cart break, he runs to his tools; he repairs them as well as he can. Do they finally break down, with reluctance he undertakes to rebuild them, though he doubts of his success. This was an occupation committed before to the mechanic of his neighbourhood, but necessity gives him invention, teaches him to imitate, to recollect what he has seen. Somehow or another 'tis done, and happily there is no traveller, no inquisitive eye to grin and criticize his work. It answers the purposes for the present. Next time he arrives nearer perfection. Behold him henceforth a sort of intuitive carpenter! Happy man, thou hast nothing to demand of propitious heaven but a long life to enable thee to finish the most material part of thy labours, in order to leave each of thy children an improved inheritance. Thank God and thy fate, thy wife can weave. This happy talent constitutes the most useful part of her portion. Then all is with thee as well as it can be. The yarn which thy daughters have spun will now be converted into coarse but substantial cloth. Thus his flax and the wool clothes all the family; most women are something of tailors. Thus if they are healthy, these settlers find within themselves a resource against all probable accidents.

His ingenuity in the fields is not less remarkable in executing his rural work in the most expeditious manner. He naturally understands the use of levers, hand-spikes, etc. He studies how to catch the most favourable seasons for each task. This great field of action deters him not. But what [shall] he do for shoes? Never before did he find himself so near going barefooted. Long wintry nights come on. It ought to be a time of inactivity and repose, considering the amazing fatigues of the summer. The great fire warms the whole house; cheers all the family; it makes them think less of the severity of the season. He hugs himself with an involuntary feeling; he is conscious of present ease and security. He hears the great snow-storm driving by his door; he hears the impotent wind roaring in his chimney. If he regrets his ancient connections, the mug of cider and other conveniences he enjoyed before, he finds himself amply remunerated by the plenty of fuel he now possesses, etc. The rosy children sitting round the hearth, sweat and sleep with their basins of samp on their laps; the industrious mother is rattling at her loom, avariciously improving every minute of her time. Shall the master, the example of so happy a family, smoke and sleep and be idle? No, he has heard the children complain of sores and chilblains for want of shoes; he has leather, but no shoemaker at hand. A secret wish arises, natural enough to a father's heart: he wants to see them all happy. So noble a motive can't but have a successful end. He has, perhaps, a few lasts and some old tools; he tries to mend an old pair. Heaven be praised! The child can walk with them, and boast to the others of his new acquisition. A second pair is attempted; he succeeds as well. He ventures at last to make a new one. They are coarse, heavy, ponderous, and clumsy, but they are tight and strong, and answer all the intended purposes. What more can he want? If his gears break, he can easily repair them. Every man here understands how to spin his own yarn and to [make] his own ropes. He is a universal fabricator like Crusoe. With bark and splinters the oldest of the children amuse themselves by making little baskets. The hint being praised by the father is further improved, and in a little time they are supplied with what baskets they want.

Casks require too much labour and particular ingenuity. He in vain attempts it; he cannot succeed, but indulgent Nature offers him a sufficient compensation. In the woods which surround him hollow trees present themselves to him; he can easily distinguish them by the sound they yield when struck with the ax. They have long served as winter habitations to squirrels and other animals. Now they are cut into proper lengths, smoothed on the inside. They are placed on the floor and [are] ready to contain anything but liquids. Tight vessels are not wanted as yet, for he has no fermented liquor to preserve (save spruce beer), until his young orchard begins to bear, and by that time the natural improvement of the country will bring the necessary tradesmen into his neighbourhood.

Happy man, did'st thou but know the extent of thy good fortune! Permit me to hold for a minute the sketch of thy political felicity, that thou mayest never forget that share of gratitude which thou owest to the mild government under which thou livest. Thou hast no church-dues to pay derived from the most unaccountable donations, the pious offerings of rough ignorance or mistaken zeal; those ancient calamities are unknown to thy land. Thou mayest go to toil and exert the whole energy and circle of thy industry, and try the activity of human nature in all situations. Fear not that a clergyman whom thou never hearest, or any other, shall demand the tenth part of thy labour. Thy land, descended from its great Creator, holds not its precarious tenure either from a supercilious prince or a proud lord. Thou need'st not dread any contradictions in thy government and laws of thy country; they are simple and natural, and if they are sometimes burdensome in the execution, 'tis the fault of men. Thou need'st not fear those absurd ordinances alternately puzzling the understanding and the reason of subjects, and crushing all national industry. Thou need'st not tremble lest the most incomprehensible prohibitions shall rob thee of that sacred immunity with which the produce of thy farm may circulate from hand to hand until it reaches those of the final exporter. 'Tis all as free as the air which thou breathest. Thy land, thy canton is not claimed by any neighbouring monarch who, anxious for the new dominion, ravages, devastates, and despoils its peaceable inhabitants. Rest secure: no cruel militia-laws shall be enacted to ravish from thee thy son, and to make him serve an unknown master in his wars; to enrich a foreign land with his carcass, unrelieved in his pains and agonies, unpitied in his death. The produce of thy loins shall not feed foreign wolves and vultures.

No, undisturbed, this offspring of thine shall remain with thee to coöperate in that family partnership of which thou art the first director and manager. At a proper season thou shalt see him marry, perhaps thy neighbour's daughter. Thou then shalt have the pleasure of settling him on that land which he has helped thee to earn and to clear; henceforth he shall become also a new neighbour to thee, still remaining thy son and friend. Thy heart shall swell with inward exultation when thou shalt see him prosper and flourish, for his future prosperity will be a part of thine in the same proportion as thy family happiness is a part of that diffusive one which overspreads thy country's. In the future extensive harvests thou shalt raise; and other laborious undertakings which the seasons and the elements bid thee execute quickly. The reunited aid of the combined family by a reciprocal assistance will often throughout the year combine together to accomplish the most painful tasks.

Humanity is not obliged here, as in the old world, to pass through the slow windings of the alembic. Here 'tis an abundant spring, running and dividing itself everywhere agreeable to the nature and declivity of the ground. Neither dams nor mounds nor any other obstructions restrain it; 'tis never artificially gathered as a turbid flood to exhale in the sun, nor sunken under ground for some sinister purposes. 'Tis a regular fecundating stream left to the laws of declivity and invariably pursuing its course.

Thus this man devoid of society learns more than ever to center every idea within that of his own welfare. To him all that appears good, just, equitable, has a necessary relation to himself and family. He has been so long alone that he has almost forgot the rest of mankind except it is when he carries his crops on the snow to some distant market.

The country, however, fills with new inhabitants. His granary is resorted to from all parts by other beginners who did not come so well prepared. How will he sell his grain to these people who are strangers to him? Shall he deduct the expense of carrying it to a distant mill? This would appear just, but where is the necessity of this justice? His neighbours absolutely want his supply; they can't go to other places. He, therefore, concludes upon having the full price. He remembers his former difficulties; no one assisted him then. Why should he assist others? They are all able to work for themselves. He has a large family, and it would be giving its lawful substance away; he cannot do it. How should he be charitable? He has scarcely seen a poor man in his life. How should he be merciful, except from native instinct? He has never heard that it was a necessary qualification, and he has never seen objects that required the benefits of his sympathy. He has had to struggle alone through numbers of difficult situations and inconveniences; he, therefore, deals hardly with his new neighbours. If they are not punctual in their payment, he prosecutes them at law, for by this time its benefits have reached him. 'Tis laid out into a new county, and divided into townships. Perhaps he takes a mortgage on his neighbour's land. But it may happen that it is already encumbered by anterior and more ponderous debts. He knows instinctively the coercive power of the laws: he impeaches the cattle; he has proper writings drawn; he gets bonds in judgment. He secures himself; and all this is done from native knowledge; he has neither counsellor nor adviser. Who can be wiser than himself in this half-cultivated country? The sagacity peculiar to the American never forsakes him; it may slumber sometimes, but upon the appearance of danger it arises again as vigorous as ever.

But behold him happily passed through the course of many laborious years; his wealth and, therefore, his consequence increase with the progress of the settlement. If he is litigious, overbearing, purse-proud, which will very probably be the bent of his mind, he has a large field. Among so many beginners there need be many needy, inconsiderate, drunken, and lazy. He may bring the necessary severity of the law to flourish even in these wilds. Well may we be subjects to its lash, or else we would be too happy, for this is almost all the tribute we pay.

Now advanced in life and grown rich, he builds a good substantial stone or frame house, and the humble log one, under which he has so much prospered, becomes the kitchen. Several roads intersect and meet near this spot, which he has contrived on purpose. He becomes an innholder and a country-merchant. This introduces him into all the little mysteries of self-interest, clothed under the general name of profits and emoluments. He sells for good that which perhaps he knows to be indifferent, because he also knows that the ashes he has collected, the wheat he has taken in may not be so good or so clean as it was asserted. Fearful of fraud in all his dealings and transactions, he arms himself, therefore, with it. Strict integrity is not much wanted, as each is on his guard in his daily intercourse, and this mode of thinking and acting becomes habitual. If any one is detected in anything too glaring but without the reach of the law, where is the recollection of ancient principles, either civil or religious, that can raise the blush of conscious shame? No minister is at hand by his daily admonitions to put him in remembrance of a vindictive God punishing all frauds and bad intentions, rewarding rectitude and justice. Whatever ideas of this kind they might have imbibed when young; whatever conscience may say; these voices have been so long silent, that they are no longer heard. The law, therefore, and its plain meaning are the only forcible standards which strike and guide their senses and become their rule of action. 'Tis to them an armour serving as well for attack as for defence; 'tis all that seems useful and pervading. Its penalties and benefits are the only thing feared and remembered, and this fearful remembrance is what we might call in the closet a reverence for the law.

With such principles of conduct as these, follow him in all these situations which link men in society, in that vast variety of bargains, exchanges, barters, sales, etc.; and adduce the effects which must follow. If it is not "bellum omnium contra omnes," 'tis a general mass of keenness and sagacious acting against another mass of equal sagacity; 'tis caution against caution. Happy, when it does not degenerate into fraud against fraud! The law, which cannot pervade and direct every action, here leaves her children to themselves, and abandons those peccadilloes (which convulse not though they may [dim] some of the most beautiful colours of society) to the more invisible efficacy of religion.

But here this great resource fails in some measure, at least with a great many of them, from the weakness of their religious education, from a long inattention, from the paucity of instructions received. Is it a wonder that new rules of action should arise? It must constitute a new set of opinions, the parent of manners. You have already observed this colonist is necessarily different from what he was in the more ancient settlements he originally came from; become such by his new local situation, his new industry, that share of cunning which was absolutely necessary in consequence of his intercourse with his new neighbours.

THOUGHTS OF AN AMERICAN FARMER ON VARIOUS RURAL SUBJECTS*

I. FARM LIFE

I AM perfectly sensible of the superiority of your agriculture. England surpasses all the world for the perfection of mechanism and the peculiar excellence with which all its tools and implements are finished. We are but children and they [the English] our parents. The immense difference, therefore, ought not to make us blush. We have the same blood in our veins. In time we shall arrive likewise at perfection. All the praises we at present deserve ought to be bestowed on that strength, fortitude, and perseverance which have been requisite to clear so many fields, to drain so many swamps. Great parts of the colony of Massachusetts and Connecticut have cost more in clearing than the land was worth. The native industry of the English is nowhere more manifest than in the settlement and cultivation of those two provinces. They had every species of difficulty to struggle with: climate, stubbornness of soil, amazing trees, stones, etc. And yet now some parts of these countries, I am informed, are not inferior to the best cultivated spots in Europe, considering the short space of time in which these great works have been accomplished.

However inferior in all these rural respects we are to England, yet you seem to confess with pleasure the sur-

* This essay was divided by Crèvecœur into four letters, the titles for which have been arranged by the editors.

prise you felt in travelling from New Hampshire to this place. Everywhere you saw good houses, well-fenced fields, ample barns, large orchards. Everywhere you saw the people busy either at home or on their farms. Everywhere they seemed contented and happy. You no sooner quitted the sight of an orchard, but another presented itself to your view. Everywhere tolerable roads, pretty towns, good bridges forced you to ask yourself: When is it that these people have had time and abilities to perform so many labours? Everywhere you inform me that you met with the most cordial hospitality. Tell me in what part of Europe you could have travelled three hundred and sixty miles for four dollars? I feel proud and happy that the various accounts I gave you of this part of America did not fall short of what you have experienced. The people of New England had been represented to you in a strange light, yet I know no province which is so justly entitled to the respect of the world on many accounts. They are the true and unmixed descendants of Englishmen, and surely there is no country in America where an Englishman ought to travel with more pleasure. Here he may find the names of almost all the towns in his country and those of many families with which he is acquainted.

Some people without knowing why look with disdain on their democratic government. They do not consider that this was the very rule which prevailed in England when they left it, and that nothing more than the blessings it confers could possibly have animated these people and urged them on to undertake such labours. Slaves may cultivate the smooth and fertile plains of the South. It is the hands of freemen only that could till this asperous soil. Had they laboured under an oppressive form of government, it is very prob-

Various Rural Subjects.

able that Massachusetts and Connecticut would have been possessed yet by the Pequots, the Narragansetts, and the Wampanoags, the ancient lords of these rough countries. There is not a province in the whole continent which does not exhibit to the contemplative traveller something highly praiseworthy and highly deserving the attention of a stranger. Everywhere you find the strongest marks of industry, of activity, and of prosperous boldness. When an Englishman arrives here he should quit his insular prejudices. He should procure a small book wherein he should carefully set down the date of every establishment, and thus furnished, he might travel with more satisfaction to himself and do more justice to the inhabitants. This is the rule I always observe. For instance, who can visit some of the modern settlements in the New Hampshire grants without amazement and surprise? I know many townships that are but twelve years old which contain inhabitants worth two thousand pounds, all acquired by their labours and good contrivance in that short space of time. The English farmer, when he purchases his farm, finds it already cleared, already fenced, already ditched. His ploughs are excellent; his horses good; his servants humble and subordinate. No wonder indeed that he can perform all the operations with so much neatness and accuracy!

Our present modes of making fences are very bad, though they are the only ones we can possibly make use of. They decay so fast, they are so subject to be hove up by the frost, it is inconceivable the cost and care which a large farm requires in that single article. I have often observed whole lengths of posts and rails raised from the ground in the spring, and the labours of weeks thus destroyed. Often when the frost quits the earth,

81

the stakes of our worn fences are entirely lifted up. Then the riders tumble down, and the strength, the stability they gave them is gone.

These repairs take up, every spring, abundance of time, and, after all, it is impossible to stop up every hole so carefully as to prevent the intrusion of hogs and pigs. Their inclination to mischief and their singular ingenuity in finding out these vacancies are such that, properly speaking, no crops are secured except the fields are surrounded with stone fences. This is a blessing which every country has not. Our sheep will often learn to jump, and no obstacle can possibly prevent them. I have found out, however, one method which entirely puts a stop to their boldness and activity. I carefully cut one of the sinews which passes through their hind fetlocks. The damage done by the hogs is sometimes astonishing. If we yoke them it greatly retards their growth. To prevent them from rooting I cut the two sinews to which their snouts hang. If this simple operation is performed while they are young, for ever afterwards it disables them from doing any mischief with that pernicious instrument. The English farmer, on the contrary, whose fields are surrounded with impenetrable fences, rests secure. He feels not on his mind that concern which so often afflicts the American. When the country becomes older and the price of labour somewhat less we shall likewise be enabled to plant good thorn fences. The American thorn is excellent for that purpose and inexpugnable. I know already many farms that are thus defended. I wish I were able to do the same.

As to labour and labourers,—what difference! When we hire any of these people we rather pray and entreat them. You must give them what they ask: three shillings per day in common wages and five or six shillings in harvest. They must be at your table and feed, as you saw it at my house, on the best you have. I have often seen Irishmen just landed, inconceivably hard to please and as greedy as wolves. These are a few of the many reasons why we can't bring anything to perfection. The few negroes we have are at best but our friends and companions. Their original cost is very high. Their clothing and their victuals amount to a great sum besides the risk of losing them. Our mechanics and tradesmen are very dear and sometimes great bunglers. Our winters are so severe and so long that we are obliged to consume during that season a great part of what we earn in the summer. This is, sir, but a feeble sketch of that great picture I might draw of the amazing inconveniences to which the locality of our situation exposes us.

Last year Mr. ——, the first man in our country, our first judge and assemblyman, received in harvest a large company from the town of ——. He immediately ordered two tables in two different rooms, for he always eats with his work-people. The reapers, perceiving the new distinction which he was going to establish, quitted him after having made very severe reflections, and it was not without great difficulties that he was enabled to finish his harvest with his own people. What would one of your country squires say to this? Whether this gentleman was entitled to the appellation or not, I cannot tell, but sure I am that he possesses fifteen hundred acres of excellent land and [belongs to] one of the most respectable families we have. We should be too happy were it otherwise. And indeed the present constitution of things: our government, modes of religion, our manners, the scarcity of people, the ease with which they may live and have lands of their own,—all these reasons must necessarily tend to subject us to these inconveniences. Better put up with them than with high taxes, encroachment of lords, free passage of hounds and huntsmen, tithes, etc.

Farming in the northern provinces is, therefore, not so advantageous as a European might at first imagine. These are fit only for people who are capable of working; the southern ones for those who have capital and can purchase negroes. I could mention to you a thousand other details, but they would be useless and perhaps tiresome. The proper distinction of ranks in England procures to the rich servants who know their places; to the farmers workmen who are afraid of losing their bread. Very different is our lot. A particular friend of mine who possesses a large farm and mows every year about one hundred and twenty acres of meadow, and keeps one hundred head of horned cattle, sheep, and horses in proportion, came the other day to dine with me. "How happily, how peaceably you live here," he said. "Your farm is not so large as mine and yet brings you all you want. You have time to rest and to think. For my part, I am weary. I must be in the fields with the hired men; nothing is done except I am there. I must not find fault with them or else they will quit me and give me a bad name. I am but the first slave on my farm." Nor is his case uncommon; it is that of every person who tills the earth upon a large scale. This gentleman's farm in Europe would constitute him an opulent man without giving himself any trouble besides a general oversight of the whole.

When I am considering myself thus injudiciously, delineating several of our usages and customs, I blush at the task you have imposed on me and at the readiness with which I have accepted it. There is something truly ridiculous in a farmer quitting his plough or his axe, and then flying to his pen. His hands as well as his mind do not seem well calculated for this new employment. The consequences may be doubly disadvantageous. This may induce me to become careless and remiss in the due prosecution of my daily labour and [the writing] must, when gathered together in your hands, form a strange assemblage of incoherent reflections, trifling thoughts, and useless paintings. 'Tis not from a principle of vanity that I am induced to make these observations, but from a sincere regret that I am not capable of doing better. My wife herself, who has never seen me handle the pen so much in all my life, helps to confound me; she laughs at my folly. What, then, is it that makes me prosecute this theme? Your positive injunctions, my solemn promise, and the desire that you may be enabled to give your friends in Europe a more certain account of our modes of cultivating the earth, as well as of the great advances we must make, and of the inconveniences we labour under.

I hope that in your travels through Virginia you'll find some planter who will inform you of every detail relating to their mode of planting. You'll then possess the two extremes and be better able to judge in what part it will be best for your friends to come and settle. Here we enjoy a happy poverty and a strong health. There riches are attainable, but the necessary intemperance of the climate leads to many diseases which northern farmers are strangers to. The good is always mixed with the evil. The matter is how to choose the least. Were I to begin the world again, I would go and pitch my tent either in a severe climate where the frost is never interrupted by pernicious thaws, or else at the foot of the Alleghenies where they almost enjoy a perpetual summer. Either of these extremes would suit me better than the climate of these middle colonies. Give me either a Canadian or a Mohawk winter, or else none at all.

Nor have I related you the tenth part of the inconveniences to which we are subject. Our country teems with more destructive insects and animals than Europe. 'Tis difficult for us to guard against them all. What man sows must be done here as well as everywhere else at the sweat of his brows, and here he has many more enemies to defend himself from than you have in Europe. The great woods with which our country is replenished affords them a shelter from which we cannot drive them. Such is the nature of man's labours and that of the grain he lives on that he is obliged to declare war against every ancient inhabitant of this country. Strange state of things! First by trials, by fraud, by a thousand artifices he drives away the ancient inhabitants. Then he is obliged to hunt the bear, the wolf, and the fox. The bear loves his apples, often climbs into our trees, and by his weight tears their limbs. The wolves, finding the deer becoming scarce, have learned how to feed on our sheep. The fox, for want of pheasants and partridges, lives on our poultry; the squirrels on our corn. The crows and the blackbirds know how to eradicate it out of the ground, even when it is four inches high. Caterpillars, an awful progeny, sometimes spontaneously arise in some countries and travel in quest of their particular food. Some attack the black oak, on the leaves of which they feed and entirely destroy them. Others attack our grass, eat every leaf, and leave nothing but the bare stalk. Others again spring up from the ground in imitation of the locust and enter into the heart of our corn, blasting the hopes of the farmer. Others climb into our apple trees and, if not prevented, eat all their leaves and buds and blossoms and render a flourishing orchard a sad picture of ruin, sterility, and desolation. At other times innumerable swarms of grasshoppers arise and indiscriminately feed on all they find; grain, grass, turnips, etc. I had once a field of four acres of hemp seven feet high, which they entirely stripped of all the leaves and rendered useless, whereby I lost at least a ton of that commodity.

Man sows and tills, and Nature from her great lap of fecundity often produces those swarms of beings, those great exuberances of life, which seem to threaten us with destruction. If these were general and not transitory, man would soon fall a victim to their devouring jaws, and, small as they are, they become by their numbers powerful agents of desolation. I have heard many people call them the avengers of the Almighty, created to punish men for their iniquities. This cannot be, for they eat the substance of the good and the wicked indiscriminately. They appear in certain districts or follow certain courses which they invariably pursue. What greater crimes do we commit than the Europeans? It is a local evil, and this evil is nothing among us to what you'll observe in the southern provinces. The heat and the moisture of their climates spread everywhere a disposition in matter to form itself into organized bodies. There their fields teem with ten thousand different species with which I am not acquainted. Strange that you should have in England so many learned and wise men, and that none should ever have come over here to describe some part of this great field which nature presents. I have heard several Virginians say that when their wheat is ripe a peculiar sort of winged weevil attacks it in the fields. The heads of this grain seem all alive, and it is with the utmost difficulty that they can save it. When in the barn, it becomes subject to the depredations of another sort [of insect] which, though deprived of wings, is equally terrible in the mischief it causes. Our very peas are subject to the attack of a fly which deposits an egg, imperceptible in the middle of its blossoms. This egg grows with the peas, which serve him as a cradle, but he does not touch them until towards the spring. Then he has acquired a degree of strength sufficient to eat the meat of the two lobes. The fly then bores a hole through which it quits its ancient habitation. The peas, reduced to this hollow state, will grow again, but are unfit for any culinary uses. There is no other remedy but to place them as soon as threshed in an oven half heated. The heat will parch and kill the worms.

Now if you unite the damages which we yearly suffer from all these enemies, to the badness of our fences, to the want of subordinate workmen, to the high price of our labour, to the ignorance of our tradesmen, to the severities of our winters, to the great labours we must undergo, to the celerity with which the rapid seasons hurry all our rural operations, you'll have a more complete idea of our situation as farmers than you had before. Some part of the rich landscape will gradually fail, and you'll soon perceive that the lot of the American farmer is very often unjustly envied by many Europeans who wish to see us taxed, and think that we live too well. It is true that no people feed on better pork and bread, but these are in general dearly earned.

He that is just arrived and sees a fine, smooth plantation with a good house or a flourishing orchard, and hears that the proprietor pays but a small tax, immediately thinks: this man is too happy. His imagination

Various Rural Subjects.

presents him with such images and ideas as are suggested to him by what he has seen in Europe. He sees not that sea of trouble, of labour, and expense which have been lavished on this farm. He forgets the fortitude, and the regrets with which the first emigrant left his friends, his relations, and his native land. He is unacquainted with the immense difficulties of first settlement, with the sums borrowed, with the many years of interest paid, with the various shifts these first people have been obliged to make use of. The original loghouse, the cradle of the American, is now gone, and has made room for the more elegant framed one. Is there no credit to be given to these first cultivators who by their sweat, their toil, and their perseverance have come over a sea of three thousand miles to till a new soil? Thereby they have enlarged the trade, the power, the riches of the mother country.

No, these just ideas seldom enter into the heads of such Europeans or visitors. They come to trade and to get rich and very often at their return do not do us that justice which we deserve. The title of Yankee is given to one province; other contemptuous reflections are made on others. Yet to a philosophic eye, to a heart full of philanthropy, where is that part of the world that can supply an enlightened traveller with more pleasing ideas? The American farmer has his peculiar degree of happiness without which he could not subsist. His toils and situation are such that he cannot afford to pay the taxes of Europe. If he is kept poor, how is he to purchase more lands rough as his own were, and there place his children whom he has taught to work as hard as himself? If he is possessed of but the bare means of subsistence, he must send his children to sea, or to trade, or let them live in idleness. Lands are not purchased for

Eighteenth Century America.

nothing. A man must have a beginning, a certain capital without which he may languish and vegetate simply all the days of his life. Let this European censor quit the sea-shore and go three hundred miles into the wilderness and see how men begin the world. The credit of England enables our merchants to trade and to get rich. The credit and wealth of the fathers enable our children to form new settlements. Were these two sources suspended only for ten years, you would soon see a death of enterprises, a spirit of inaction, a general languor diffuse itself throughout the continent. That bold activity, that spirit of emigration which is the source of our prosperity, would soon cease. I speak not through the narrow channel of a partial American. I speak the language of truth, and I hope that one year of observation will convince you of the propriety of what I have said.

Flourishing as we may appear to a superficial observer, yet there are many dark spots which, on due consideration, greatly lessen that show of happiness which the Europeans think we possess. The number of debts which one part of the country owes to the other would greatly astonish you. The younger a country is, the more it is oppressed, for new settlements are always made by people who do not possess much. They are obliged to borrow, and, if any accidents intervene, they are not enabled to repay that money in many years. The interest is a canker-worm which consumes their yearly industry. Many never can surmount these difficulties. The land is sold, their labours are lost, and they are obliged to begin the world anew. Oh, could I have the map of the county wherein I live; could I point out the different farms on which several families have

Various Rural Subjects.

struggled for many years; [could I] open the great book of mortgages and show you the immense encumbrances, the ramifications of which are spread and felt everywhere,—you would be surprised! Yes, I am sure that the sum total of what is due for the original cost of the land, and what the people owe to each other, would not fall very short of seven hundred[?].

It is vain to say: why do they borrow? I answer that it is impossible in America to till a farm without it. After being possessed of the land one must have a team and a negro. Three or four hundred pounds is but a trifling sum to what is sometimes requisite. It is very true that with industry and health [settlers] will be enabled to pay off the greatest part of these sums in a few years, but life is so full of accidents that out of twelve that begin the world with a debt of three hundred pounds not above six perhaps will be able to pay it all in the first generation. These encumbrances, therefore, descend with the land, aye, even to the third generation. Happy [are they] when their pressure is such that they can be borne without selling the lands! Whoever, therefore, cursorily judges of our riches by the appearance of our farms, of our houses, of our fields, without descending to deeper particulars, judges imperfectly. He should feel the pulse of every farmer, and know whether he is perfectly free.

These are, sir, the great and the enormous taxes which we are obliged to pay, one to another. Our very merchants are obliged to follow the same system. Had it not been for the generous credit of England, how could they have traded? It is a rule which extends itself to every part of this great continent, from the poor, barren fields of Nova Scotia to the slimy plains of the

Eighteenth Century America.

Mississippi. The evil is unavoidable. My father* began the world seven hundred and fifty pounds in debt. He had received from my grandfather very ample beginnings, yet it took him eleven years of the most prosperous industry ere he could call himself a freeman. Nor could he have even succeeded so rapidly but for a legacy of one hundred and fifty pounds which was left him by a relation.* Never was a man who enjoyed the pleasure of owing nothing with more heartfelt joy than he. He and my mother had hitherto toiled night and day. He had taken a solemn vow to buy nothing of English manufacture until he could buy it with his own money, and never before that time had he worn a yard of English cloth. He was perfectly sober and industrious. His wife was prudent, and had it not been for these favourable circumstances, some part of the load must have descended to me. Thank God, I owe nothing, but I can tell you that there are not one hundred besides me in the county who can say that all they have is their own. Are there no praises for, is there no good will due towards a set of men who labour under these excessive burthens, whose toils serve to enrich their mother country? Every bushel of wheat which we raise, every yard of calico, every lock or nail we purchase tend to promote the happiness and the trade of England.

It may appear a very odd sort of speculation, yet I often amuse myself with it: the poor beginner toiling in the woods, peeling the bark of trees to cover his house, stubbing up the heavy ground to produce bread, is very similar and greatly resembles the situation of the English manufacturer. The one works for the other, to supply mutual wants. The odds, however, are in favour

* Crèvecœur may refer here to his wife's family or allude to the average situation of fortune among the farmers.

Various Rural Subjects.

of the American. With good luck and perseverance, he may live to clear his lands of useless wood as well as his title of heavy encumbrances. If he does that, he may then die with a peaceable conscience. He has acted his part as a good American ought to do. He has left an ample provision for his children. Who can wish for more in a country where we have neither bishops, counts, nor marquises? If he leaves them land paid for, and ability to work, they have the most ample inheritance. If it please God that I should live long enough, this will be one day my great happiness, and if I can see [my children] possessed of the proper qualifications requisite to make them good farmers, I shall close my eyes in peace. They won't be apt to say that I have not trained them up to the plough, for I fix them on it, even from the breast.*

But to convince you still further of what I have but imperfectly sketched I will take you to Mr. ———'s office who is our clerk, and there you'll see the many wounds and bleeding places which this county suffers even though it is fifty-three years old. These ulcers generally heal in proportion to the age of the country. It is now much less in debt than it was formerly, and the reason that it owes yet so much money is on account of the many swamps it contains. This may surprise you. They are in general so expensive and difficult to clear that it cannot be done in the ordinary course of husbandry. It is generally done by the acre, and, in order to pay these extraordinary expenses, the proprietors are obliged to borrow money. It is indeed very well laid out. A swamp in five years will repay the cost of clearing. Could these great works be all accomplished, you

* A reference to a fact already mentioned in one of his published letters.

Eighteenth Century America.

would then see how quickly the people would extricate themselves out of all their difficulties. Another reason which keeps us in debt is the multiplicity of shops with English goods. These present irresistible temptations. It is so much easier to buy than it is to spin. The allurements of fineries is so powerful with our young girls that they must be philosophers indeed to abstain from them. Thus one fifth part of all our labours every year is laid out in English commodities. These are the taxes that we pay.

Another is that most of the articles they send us from England are extremely bad. What is intended for exportation is good enough when there are no rival merchants. Their linens and their duffle and their wool cards are much worse now than they were ten years ago. The prosperity of our different counties depends besides on the general qualities of the soil. The more they abound in swamps, the richer they are. It greatly depends also on the genius of the inhabitants. By some chance or other the character of the first settlers imprints a kind of spirit which becomes prevalent by example, and remains ever after the distinguishing characteristic. For instance the county of —— is famous for the litigious spirit of its inhabitants. There the lawyers will have all. The sheriff told me not long since that the whole set of its inhabitants had almost changed in eighteen years; that is, their farms in that space of time were sold in consequence of mortgages unpaid, and they were obliged to remove. That of ——, on the contrary, is remarkable for its peace, tranquillity, and industry. Many of its inhabitants are Dutch, who are so attached to their interest that they never squander any part of it to feed the ravens of the law. I wish we were all like them. Others are remarkable for the goodness of their

94

Various Rural Subjects.

roads and that of their bridges, and so it is throughout the continent. Every province is as different in staple and in the different manners of its inhabitants.

No country ever was so flourishing and happy as to have no poor; there are unfortunate men in all countries. This county is famous for taking good care of those we have. They are placed with some able farmer who feeds and clothes them and receives from the town or precinct from twenty to thirty pounds per annum for their support. We have abundance of roads, and they are repaired not by a tax, which would be better, but by six days' labour of the people. We hate taxes so much that our assemblies dare not venture upon the expedient, though I must confess that I had rather give twenty shillings a year than be obliged to work six days, and these monies properly laid out would do more good. But we cannot expect to enjoy every advantage. I think we have made most rapid strides, considering that the county was but a huge wilderness fifty years ago without a path. You'd be astonished, were I to tell you the extent of its cleared ground, of its meadows, the number of its houses, inhabitants, etc. I have often amused myself with making an estimate of the sum of labour and then comparing it with the original and present value of the land. This fair estimate would be the strongest proof of our industry, an industry which the people of the South cannot boast of, for the evenness and fertility of their land are very superior to ours. There they labour with slaves; here we do everything ourselves. There they enjoy a variety of pleasures and pastimes; here we know of none except our frolics and going to the meeting on a Sunday.

The name "frolic" may perhaps scandalize you and make you imagine that we meet to riot together. Lest

Eighteenth Century America.

you should misunderstand me, give me leave to explain myself. I really know among us of no custom which is so useful and tends so much to establish the union and the little society which subsists among us. Poor as we are, if we have not the gorgeous balls, the harmonious concerts, the shrill horn of Europe, yet we dilate our hearts as well with the simple negro fiddle, and with our rum and water, as you do with your delicious wines. In the summer it often happens that either through sickness or accident some families are not able to do all they must do. Are we afraid, for instance, that we shall not be able to break up our summer fallow? In due time we invite a dozen neighbours, who will come with their teams and finish it all in one day. At dinner we give them the best victuals our farm affords; these are feasts the goodness of which greatly depends on the knowledge and ability of our wives. Pies, puddings, fowls, roasted and boiled,—nothing is spared that can evince our gratitude. In the evening the same care is repeated, after which young girls and lads generally come from all parts to unite themselves to the assembly. As they have done no work, they generally come after supper and partake of the general dance. I have never been so happy in my life as when I have assisted at these simple merriments, and indeed they are the only ones I know. Each returns home happy and is satisfied, and our work is done.

If any of our wives are unable to spin that quantity of flax which was intended, they give out one pound to every one of their acquaintances. The youngsters take the same quantity, which they get spun by their sweethearts. The day is fixed when they all bring home the yarn to the house and receive in return a hearty supper and a dance. Can there be anything more harmless or more useful? The same is done for every species of labour. When my father built his house he had had the stones previously pitched in large heaps, and the winter following he invited upwards of thirty people who came with their sleighs and horses, and brought him in one day upwards of five hundred loads. Had he been obliged to have done that himself, or to have hired it done, it would have cost him more than the house. We generally invite the minister of the precinct who partakes with us of the pleasure of the day, and who sanctifies by his presence the well-meant labours of our people. Thus we help one another; thus by our single toils at home and by our collective strength we remove many obstacles which no single family could do. Many swamps have been cleared in this manner to the great joy of the possessors who were not able to hire the work done.

I could have wished when you were with me that I could have carried you to such an assembly. There you would have seen better what the American farmers are than by seeing them singly in their homes. The cheerful glass, the warmth of their country politics, the ruddy faces of their daughters, the goodness of their horses would give you a more lively idea of their happiness as men, of their native pride as free-holders than anything I could tell you. At these assemblies they forget all their cares, all their labours. They bring their governors and assemblymen to a severe account; they boldly blame them or censure them for such measures as they dislike. Here you might see the American freeman in all the latitude of his political felicity, a felicity—alas!—of which they are not so sensible as they ought to be. Your picture of the poor Germans and Russians makes me shudder. It is, then, to England we

Eighteenth Century America.

owe this elevated rank we possess, these noble appella-
tions of freemen, freeholders, citizens; yes, it is to that
wise people we owe our freedom. Had we been planted
by some great monarchy, we should have been but the
mean slaves of some distant monarch. Our great distance from him would have constituted the only happiness we should enjoy.

The small present of maple sugar which my wife
sends you by this opportunity obliges me to [describe]
to you another pleasurable scene in which I always
spend a week or ten days every spring. In clearing his
farm my father very prudently saved all the maple
trees he found, which fortunately are all placed together in the middle of our woodland; and by his particular caution in bleeding them, they yield sap as plentifully as ever. The common method is to notch them
with an axe. This operation, after a few years, destroys
the tree entirely. That which my father followed is
much easier, and gives these trees wounds which are almost imperceptible. The best time to make this sugar
is between the months of March and April, according
to the season. There must be snow on the ground, and it
must freeze at night and thaw in the day. These three
circumstances are absolutely requisite to make the sap
run in abundance. But as my trees are but a little way
from my house, I now and then go to try them, and, as
soon as the time is come, then I bring all my hands, and
we go to work. Nothing can be simpler than this operation. I previously provide myself with as many trays as
I have trees. These I bore with a large gimlet. I then
fix a spile made of elder through which the sap runs
into the trays. From them it is carried into the boiler
which is already fixed on the fire. If the evaporation is
slow, we are provided with barrels to receive it. In a

little time it becomes of the consistency of syrup. Then it is put into another vessel and made to granulate. When in that state we cast it into little moulds made according to the fancy of the farmer. Some persons know how to purify it, and I am told that there are people at Montreal who excel in this branch. For my part, I am perfectly well satisfied with the colour and taste which Nature has given it. When the trees have ceased to run we stop the holes with pegs made of the same wood. We cut them close to the bark, and in a little time the cicatrice becomes imperceptible. By these simple means our trees will afford sugar for a long time, nor have I ever observed that it impaired their growth in the least degree. They will run every year, according to the seasons, from six to fifteen days until their buds fill. They do not yield every year the same quantity, but as I regularly bleed two hundred trees, which are all I have, I have commonly received six barrels of sap in twenty-four hours which have yielded me from twelve to eighteen [pounds of sugar].

Thus without the assistance of the West Indies, by the help of my trees and of my bees, we yearly procure the sweetening we want; and it is not a small quantity, you know, that satisfies the wants of a tolerable American family. I have several times made sugar with the sap of the birch; though it seldom runs in any quantity, it is sweeter, richer, and makes stronger sugar. These trees, however, are so rare among us that they are never made use of for that purpose. By way of imitating in some respects my provident father, who so religiously saved this small sugar plantation, I have cleared about a half acre of land adjoining it, on which I have planted above seventy young maples, which I have raised in a nursery. As that part of my woods is extremely moist, I propose to enlarge this useful plantation as fast as I can raise trees big enough for transplantation.

II. ENEMIES OF THE FARMER

WHAT! still the same subject? This is really kind; you could not have pitched upon a more proper one for a farmer, [one] with which you know I am best acquainted. Yet, upon a proper recollection, this is the very reason why I am more at a loss. I am afraid of not being able to distinguish the useful from the useless; that which might be worthy your perusal from what might be trifling. To a farmer everything appears important. Besides, what we are familiarly acquainted with does not strike our imagination so forcibly, though necessary to be known, as what we but seldom see. This is the greatest impediment I have to struggle against. This prevents me from arranging my thoughts with that propriety I could wish to possess. You want genuine details of all the benefits we enjoy as farmers; of all the inconveniences to which we are exposed, from birds, insects, animals, from seasons, and climates; of our peculiar modes of living. You wish that I should give you as complete a picture as I am able to draw of our lives and occupations both at home and in the fields. In my preceding letters I have already sketched some of the principal outlines, and without any further ceremony shall proceed on, as my well-meant desire may lead me.

Nor are those which I have mentioned before the only adverse circumstances which we have to struggle with. Many more call for our care and vigilance almost the whole year. Each season brings along with it its

Various Rural Subjects.

pains, pleasures, toils, and unavoidable losses. Often Nature herself opposes us. What then can we do? She is irresistible; I mean the uncertainty of the snows in the winter and the dryness of our summers. It is astonishing how variable the former grows, much more so indeed than formerly, and I make no doubt but that in a few hundred years they will be very different from what they are at present. That mildness, when interrupted by transitory frosts and thaws, will become very detrimental to our husbandry. For though the quantity of snow may diminish, yet it cannot be entirely so with the frost. Our proximity to the horrid mountainous waste which overspreads our north will always expose us to the severe blasts which often nip all our hopes, and destroy the fairest and most promising expectations of the farmer, like a merchant losing his vessel in sight of the harbour. Last spring all my apples dropped in consequence of such an accident, although they were grown to the size of nutmegs. Nor could it be prevented though it was foreseen.

Had my father been as wise as Mr. —— this would not have been the case. This gentleman was very knowing and attentive for a first settler. He planted his orchard on the north side of a hill. This exposure commonly causes the difference of a fortnight in the opening of the blossoms, and this artificial delay always saves his apples. I could wish that [my orchard] had been thus situated, though it is so great an ornament to a farm that most people plant it either on one side of their house or on the other. How naked my settlement would look [were mine] removed! I am surprised, however, that this simple idea has not been more generally extended. The hint, I am sure, was not new, for most people plant their peach orchards in the most northern situation they have, in order to avoid the same inconveniences. You must remember my situation. My loss in apples last year was the greater because of its being the bearing year; for you must know that all our trees (both in the forest and elsewhere) bear but every other year. In a little time I am in hopes to remedy this inconvenience, having planted in the fall a new apple orchard of five acres consisting of three hundred and fifty-eight trees. That of my father was planted in the spring, and by their not bearing at the same time I shall have a yearly supply of apples.

Perhaps you may want to know what it is we want to do with so many apples. It is not for cider, God knows! Situated as we are it would not quit cost to transport it even twenty miles. Many a barrel have I sold at the press for a half dollar. As soon as our hogs have done with the peaches, we turn them into our orchards. The [apples], as well as the preceding fruit, greatly improve them. It is astonishing to see their dexterity in rubbing themselves against the youngest trees in order to shake them. They will often stand erect and take hold of the limbs of the trees, in order to procure their food in greater abundance.

In the fall of the year we dry great quantities, and this is one of those rural occupations which most amply reward us. Our method is this: we gather the best kind. The neighbouring women are invited to spend the evening at our house. A basket of apples is given to each of them, which they peel, quarter, and core. These peelings and cores are put into another basket and when the intended quantity is thus done, tea, a good supper, and the best things we have are served up. Convivial merriment, cheerfulness, and song never fail to enliven these evenings, and though our bowls contain neither the delicate punch of the West Indies, nor the rich wines of Europe, nevertheless our cider affords us that simpler degree of exhilaration with which we are satisfied. The quantity I have thus peeled is commonly twenty bushels, which gives me about three of dried ones.

Next day a great stage is erected either in our grass plots or anywhere else where cattle can't come. Strong crotches are planted in the ground. Poles are horizontally fixed on these, and boards laid close together. For there are no provident farmers who have not always great stores of these. When the scaffold is thus erected, the apples are thinly spread over it. They are soon covered with all the bees and wasps and sucking flies of the neighbourhood. This accelerates the operation of drying. Now and then they are turned. At night they are covered with blankets. If it is likely to rain, they are gathered and brought into the house. This is repeated until they are perfectly dried. It is astonishing to what small size they will shrink. Those who have but a small quantity thread them and hang them in the front of their houses. In the same manner we dry peaches and plums without peeling them, and I know not a delicacy equal to them in the various preparations we make of them. By this means we are enabled to have apple-pies and apple-dumplings almost all the year round.

The method of using them is this: we put a small handful in warm water over night; next morning they are swelled to their former size; and when cooked either in pies or dumplings it is difficult to discover by the taste whether they are fresh or not. I think that our farms produce nothing more palatable. My wife's and my supper half of the year consists of apple-pie and milk. The dried peaches and plums, as being more deli-

Eighteenth Century America.

cate, are kept for holidays, frolics, and such other civil festivals as are common among us. With equal care we dry the skins and cores. They are of excellent use in brewing that species of beer with which every family is constantly supplied, not only for the sake of drinking it, but for that of the bawm without which our wives could not raise their bread.

The philosopher's stone of an American farmer is to do everything within his own family; to trouble his neighbours by borrowing as little as possible; and to abstain from buying European commodities. He that follows that golden rule and has a good wife is almost sure of succeeding.

Besides apples we dry pumpkins which are excellent in winter. They are cut into thin slices, peeled, and threaded. Their skins serve also for beer, and admirable pumpkin-pies are made with them. When thus dried they will keep the whole year. Many people have carried the former manufacture of drying apples to a great degree of perfection in the province of New Jersey. They make use of long ovens built on purpose, and when [the apples are] dried, export them to the West Indies. I have heard many planters say that they received nothing from the continent that was more delicate or better adapted to their climates. For it was transplanting the fruits of our orchards in that state in which they could endure the heat without injury.

In the most plentiful years we have a method of reducing the quantity of our cider and of making it a liquor far superior. I think it greatly preferable to many sorts of wines which I have drunk at ———. We boil the quantities of two barrels into one, in a fair copper kettle, just as it comes from the press, and, therefore, perfectly sweet. Sometimes I have reduced one barrel and a half into one. This is preserved till the summer, and then affords a liquor which, when mixed with a due proportion of water, affords us an excellent beverage. Strangers have often been deceived and have taken it for some kind of Spanish wine. Other people prefer hauling their hogsheads out of their cellars, when it freezes hard. In one night or two the frost will congeal the watery parts. They then draw from whatever remains behind, but this is neither so sweet, nor so palatable as the other; it is too potent.

We often make apple-butter, and this is in the winter a most excellent food particularly where there are many children. For that purpose the best, the richest of our apples are peeled and boiled; a considerable quantity of sweet cider is mixed with it; and the whole is greatly reduced by evaporation. A due proportion of quinces and orange peels is added. This is afterwards preserved in earthern jars, and in our long winters is a very great delicacy and highly esteemed by some people. It saves sugar, and answers in the hands of an economical wife more purposes than I can well describe. Thus our industry has taught us to convert what Nature has given us into such food as is fit for people in our station. Many farmers make excellent cherry and currant wines, but many families object to them on account of the enormous quantity of sugar they require. In some parts of this country they begin to distil peaches and cider, from which two species of brandy are extracted, fiery and rough at first, but with age very pleasant. The former is the common drink of the people in the southern provinces.

However careful and prudent we are, the use of tea necessarily implies a great consumption of sugar. A northern farmer should never pronounce these two words without trembling, for these two articles must be replaced by something equivalent in order to pay for them, and not many of us have anything to spare.

Our summers grow exceedingly dry, and this is a very alarming circumstance. I have seen these droughts so parching that it was dangerous to light our pipes in the fields. If a spark dropped, it would run along from blade to blade and often reach to our fences. As soon as the snow is melted the sun begins to be very powerful. Some years we have no spring. Then we often pass in the space of ten days from the severity of frost to the heat of summer. The surface of the ground dries apace. The frost in quitting the earth uplifts the surface of the ground and detaches the roots of the grain from the soil to which they adhered. This laceration cannot be repaired but by gentle showers. If these are refused, if it thaws in the day and continues freezing at night, the mischief is irreparable. The grain turns yellow and soon dies, a severe mortification for the American farmer, thus to see crops which have escaped all the severities of the winter entirely perish in the spring.

If you unite the casualties of that season—that is, when the snow does not cover the grain, which perishes by the power of the cold—to the parching droughts of the spring, you will easily see what risks our crops run. The stronger the soil the better will the grain resist all accidents, in new grounds particularly. The frequency of these dry springs and summers has had a most surprising effect also on our brooks, wells, and springs. Many of the latter have disappeared, and many of the former have been reduced to almost nothing, since so many swamps have been cleared. Hence these brooks which they feed have failed. I could show you in this county the ruins of eleven grist-mills which twenty years ago had plenty of water, but now stand on the dry ground, with no other marks of running water about them than the ancient bed of the creek, on the shores of which they had been erected. This effect does not surprise me. Our ancient woods kept the earth moist and damp, and the sun could evaporate none of the waters contained under their shades. Who knows how far these effects may extend? Some of our principal rivers, such as the ———, appear to have powerfully felt the consequence of that cause already, nor are our swamps all cleared yet. Fully one-half of them remain in their primeval state.

Nor do the effects of these droughts stop there. They are felt even at a great depth. The first settlers, in digging their wells, only went to what we call the upper springs; those, I mean, which run horizontally, which are obtained at various depths. Almost all these ancient wells, by the droughts of our summer, have failed. I was obliged to have mine taken up and dug until we came to the lower springs, or those which burst upward. They are generally lodged under a stratum of blue clay mixed with gravel. I know nothing more than the simple relation of facts, and to that I confine myself.

As soon as the sun grows warm we are afflicted with mosquitoes, a species of insect which is very troublesome. Were they as large as they are poisonous no mortals could inhabit this country. They breed in ponds, lakes, rivers, and swamps. The whole continent is subject to their stings, but among the northern provinces Nova Scotia is the most overspread with them, owing to its many rivers, sea-coasts, and to that surprising height of tide which runs up the Bay of Fundy, and at its retreat leaves such extensive shores bare. I should assert a truth, should I aver that its present thin population is owing to these insects. Their sting is much more offensive to some persons than to others. Woeful is the appearance of many Europeans I have seen who have been severely stung. Last year a gentleman from Manchester lodged here, and notwithstanding all my care, there happened to be a few of them in his bedroom. Their stings fairly closed his eyes whilst Nature had wrapped them up in sleep. He was blind for above eight hours. Others are totally insensible to their poison. But they are infinitely more troublesome near great lakes and the salt meadows of our maritime counties.

I was once on Lake Champlain, and, perceiving a large tree covered with pigeons, I went ashore in order to kill some of them. I had no sooner landed than I found myself in the thickest atmosphere of them that I had ever seen or felt. Their multiplied and aggregate singings formed not a very disagreeable noise, but if it had been ten times more melodious, who could have remained on that shore, in order to have listened? Glad to find some living flesh that had blood, they covered my face. Far from being able to shoot, I was obliged to exert all my faculties in order to defend myself against these enormous swarms of enemies. I dared not open my eyes and with great difficulty crawled again to my boat, nor did they quit me until several miles from the shore. Who could possibly live there? The lands of ancient Eden could not tempt me to dwell among so many blood-thirsty insects, which seem to be hatched merely to tease the rest of the creation. Near the seashores they are fully as terrible, particularly when the wind is not high enough to drive them away. I think they are of a bigger size than the inland ones. I can't conceive how the people endure them, for it requires a perpetual exercise to drive them away, and very often it is no small labour.

So eager are they to fill themselves with blood that I have sometimes suffered them to alight on my hand and to suck mine quietly. With very little attention I perceived their bellies replenished with the red liquor until they would drop down, unable to fly away. I went some time ago to Mr. ——, who lives near the sea, in order to procure some clams and oysters. The evening I arrived was calm. The air was impregnated with them. My horse could not feed, nor could I rest. Towards night they were succeeded by another brood which we call gnats. They are animalculae just big enough to enter into our pores, and there make a lodgement; no sooner entered than they cause a prodigious inflammation, and a desire of scratching. They are almost invisible. I know nothing in Nature which I can compare them to; they are the smallest class of the stinging insects. What is it that heat and moisture will not create? On a hot sultry day I have often stooped down to consider with attention a shallow puddle of water. The variety of beings which moved on the mud appeared to me infinite. The whole bottom seemed alive. These maritime counties, abounding in salt meadows, teem, besides, with a variety of green and blue flies which attack the cattle, and drive them out of their pastures, sometimes in the woods, at other times in the water where they plunge up to their heads.

From this imperfect sketch you'll easily conceive that if we enjoy some happiness, we are made to pay for it. Yet I must confess that whilst I was there I observed that the people were not so sensible to their stings as I was. My being a stranger entitled me, it seems, to all their regard. The Indians anoint themselves with bears' grease, in order to prevent their punctures, and that is the reason for their being more swarthy than Nature intended them. Mr. —— informed me that a farmer of ——, in order to punish his negro, had thought proper to tie him naked to a stake in one of his salt meadows. He went home, where he staid but twenty-three minutes. At his return he found his negro prodigiously swelled, in consequence of the repeated stings of millions of mosquitoes which he had received. He brought him back to his house, but all his care could not prevent an inflammatory fever of which he died. While there I was obliged to make a smoke in my room, and this expedient prevented me from resting. In the cultivated, opened parts of the country they are not so numerous. The only method made use of in some counties is the smoke, a remedy pretty nearly as bad as the disorder. A large smothered fire is made before the door as soon as the evening comes. I have often seen rings of such fires made, and the cows brought into the middle that the people might milk them. You may judge of the situation of these inhabitants. All new settlements are much more exposed to them, and all new settlers have this additional calamity to struggle with. I would not live in any part of Nova Scotia nor on the Island of St. John for a very valuable consideration. I never should have done, were I to recount to you the many inconveniences and sufferings to which the people of these countries are exposed. I have heard that there were in England baronets of Nova Scotia, but as I have never heard of one residing in that province, I conclude that the mosquitoes have driven them off, as they have done so many other persons. At Annapolis Royal in the Bay of Fundy there is a small garrison in the establishment of which twelve pounds per annum are given to a soldier, in order to keep a constant smoke in the temple of Cloacina.

In most of our swamps we have poisonous vegetables almost as much to be dreaded as the snakes. In clearing them we must carefully avoid the mercury and the water-sumach. The first is a small creeping vine resembling ivy, which adheres either to the pine, oak, or to the maple. It is so exceedingly poisonous that some people are affected by its effluvia in passing twelve feet to the leeward of it, and if burned its smoke will cause the same effects at a greater distance still. It swells the people who are liable to receive its baneful impression, and often brings running sores and scars. The water-sumach is fully as poisonous. A general swelling, particularly of the legs and face, is the inevitable consequence either of touching it or coming near it, except it is to the windward. I had a negro who once lost eleven days' work by imprudently having touched one in order to eradicate it.

We are subjected to a trouble and expense to which, I am informed, you are wholly strangers, and that is to salt our cattle regularly once a week. This is in general done from one end of the continent to the other, but on what principle that necessity is founded, none here can tell. From the horses to the sheep everyone must have a handful given them. It seems that all other American wild animals are equally fond of salt. You have heard of licking-places which have been so long the resort of deer. I am of the opinion that one of the principal causes which brings every year such multitudes of pigeons is not that they visit us on purpose to eat our grains, but only in their progress towards the sea in quest of salt. For during their abode with us two or three times a week they regularly take their flight towards its shores, and as regularly return in twelve hours, except they are caught by the inhabitants of these counties. So great is the necessity of salting our cattle that they will all become wild, restless, and incapable of being kept within the bounds of our farms. The gentlest cows will become intractable. They will shake their heads, loll out their tongues, and plainly ask you for salt. They will not stand in the yard; and hardly give any milk; and even that small quantity will yield no butter. These are facts known to thousands. I relate them to you that I may have the pleasure of hearing some of your philosophical reasons on that subject.

When our hogs are fatting up, we must not forget to mix salt with the crude antimony which we frequently give them. My neighbours say that I am very lucky with my bees, and that they never leave me. Would you believe it? The truth of the matter is that I give them fine salt. You'd greatly wonder to see each of them carrying away a small grain of it in its proboscis. Often our working horses and cattle refuse to drink and to eat. The quickest and best remedy is to give them a handful of salt. This cools them and inspires them with a desire either to eat or drink. Have you never observed near our barn-yards logs of twenty or thirty feet long with the bark peeled? A great number of small cavities are dug twice as big as one's fist. These are every now and then replenished with salt, which the big cattle greedily eat. The young ones and the sheep soon afterwards follow and with care pick up what has been dropped and spend whole hours in licking these places. If any salt has been given them on the ground, their repeated licks will dig small holes in the earth. I have often given it to them in this manner, and each would eat at least a peck of the soil on which I had spilled it. Those farm-

Various Rural Subjects.

ers who live near the salt meadows are obliged to turn both their cattle and their horses on their salt grasses in the spring, which is looked upon as a sovereign remedy for every disorder.

Nor am I going to complain of this want which you have not. For were it not for the attractive power of the salt, what should we do with the dry cattle which we drive to feed on the mountains every spring? The man who takes care of them salts them once a week at one and the same place. By this means he can always bring them together and instead of becoming wild, they are always glad to see him, and assemble all around him whenever he chooses to hold out his hands to them. By this simple means they are kept there as long as the feed is good. By the same expedient each person goes to the mountains and in the fall gathers them together and easily brings them home. It is [done] only [by] alluring the belled one with a handful of salt, and the rest will follow in hopes of having it in their turn. Such, sir, is the simple mechanism by means of which we keep them healthy. We conduct them sometimes thirty or forty miles from home and bring them back.

Thus all countries have their peculiarities, their different customs, and modes of doing perhaps the same thing, all founded on some hidden cause or locality, or climate, or latitude or situation.

Of all the grain which we plant the Indian corn is attended with the greatest labour, is the most profitable, and the most necessary; but at the same time the most subject to accidents from seasons, insects, birds, and animals. It is so superlative a grain that all that live would cheerfully live on that grain if they could. Necessity hath taught us different methods to protect it, and to baffle the combined sagacities of so many enemies.

Eighteenth Century America.

It is no sooner planted than, if the season proves dry, an infinite number of ants will form societies and establish themselves in the very hills in the midst of which the corn is germinating. There they live on the young succulent sprouts which want moisture to rise; and they sometimes attack the grain itself. No sooner is it shot above the ground than it becomes exposed to the rapacity of a black worm which cuts its tender stem a little below the surface of the earth. The same worm will sometimes infest our gardens and make a sad havoc. When I plant cabbages I am obliged to enclose their stems with hickory bark. Its strength and bad taste oblige this worm to desist. The only remedy against the first inconvenience is to stir the hills gently with the hoe. This fills the small cavities the ants have dug and prevents them from being so intent on the destruction of the corn. As for the second, the hills on which the young shoot lies dead must be carefully examined with the finger. The enemy is easily discovered, coiled up near the stem it has fed on, waiting for the coolness of the night to travel on. It is picked up and crushed. This is tedious work, but it must be done. The corn in a little time shoots up again as strong as ever. It has no sooner reached two or three inches above the ground when its greatest enemies, the crows and the blackbirds, come in order to eradicate it by means of their strong bills. Its lobes remain long, entire, and sound. These they dig up as a ready food for their young ones.

With some attention and care the former are easily kept off. Various are our methods. The first is to make a few images by means of bunches of straw shaped like men and dressed with old clothes. These are fixed in various parts of the field. The other is to hang up several pieces of shingles painted black on one side and white on the other, at the end of long threads. The perpetual agitation in which the winds keep them frighten [the birds] away. Another method is to hang two bright pewter plates by means of holes bored in their edges. The rays of the sun reflected from them as they turn greatly resemble the flashes of a gun and have the desired effect. Others try to kill some in the woods and hang them "in terrorem" about their corn-fields. This is not infallible. It is sometimes among crows as it is among men: the calls of hunger are stronger than the fear of punishment. But the most simple and effectual manner to keep them away from our farms as well as the foxes is to dip a certain number of rags in brimstone; then to fix them on short sticks cleft at the top; and to plant them on the ground along the outside fence. They both mistake it for the smell of powder with which they are well acquainted. This will prevent the first from alighting and the second from intruding into our fields and into our poultry-yards. Thus have I often defeated the superior sagacity of Mr. Reynard who is not so well trained as your English ones, yet, as scholars of the same great mistress, are full as sagacious. In the neighbourhood of towns rats have been known to emigrate from them in great numbers and to go to dig the corn out of the hills; or in the fall of the year to climb up its stalks, and prey on the grain. As this is done at night by a great number of keen, intelligent enemies, it is difficult to prevent it, because it is impossible to foresee it.

Nature has placed a certain degree of antipathy between some species of animals, and birds. Often one lives on the other; at other times they only attack each other. The kingbird is the most skilful on the wing of any we have here. Every spring he declares war against all the kites, hawks, and crows which pass within the bounds of his precincts. If they build anywhere on your farm, rest assured that none of those great tyrants of the air will fly over it with impunity. Nor is it an unpleasant sight to behold the contest. Like the Indians, they scream aloud when they go to the attack. They fly at first with an apparent trepidation. They err here and there, and then dart with immense impetuosity and with consummate skill, always getting to the windward of their enemy, let it be even the great bald eagle of the Blue Mountains. By repeatedly falling on him and striking him with their bills, and sometimes by attacking him under the wings they will make the largest bird accelerate its motion, and describe the most beautiful curves in those rapid descents which they compel him to delineate. This amuses me much on two accounts: first, because they are doing my work; second, because I have an excellent opportunity of viewing the art of flying carried to a great degree of perfection, and varied in a multiplicity of appearances. What a pity that I am very often obliged to shoot these little kings of the air! Hunting crows serves only to make them more hungry, nor will they live on grain, but on bees. These precious insects, these daughters of heaven, serve them as food whenever they can catch them.

The blackbird, which you say resembles your starling, visits us every spring in great numbers. They build their nests in our most inaccessible swamps. Their rough notes are delightful enough at a distance. As soon as the corn sprouts they come to dig it up; nothing but the gun can possibly prevent them. Hanging of their dead companions has no kind of effect. They are birds that show the greatest degree of temerity of any we have. Sometimes we poison corn, which we strew on the ground with the juice of hitch-root. Sometimes, after soaking it, we pass a horse-hair through each grain, which we cut about an inch long. These expedients will destroy a few of them, but either by the effect of inspection or by means of some language unknown, like a great many other phenomena, to Man, the rest will become acquainted with the danger, and in two days the survivors will not touch it; but take the utmost pains to eradicate that which lies three inches under the ground. I have often poisoned the very grains I have planted, but in two days it grows as sweet as ever. Thus while our corn is young it requires a great deal of watching. To prevent these depredations some counties have raised money and given a small bounty of two pence per head. If they are greatly disturbed while they are hatching, they will soon quit that district.

But after all the efforts of our selfishness, are they not the children of the great Creator as well as we? They are entitled to live and to get their food wherever they can get it. We can better afford to lose a little corn than any other grain because it yields above seventy for one. But Man is a huge monster who devours everything and will suffer nothing to live in peace in his neighbourhood. The easiest, best, and the most philanthropic method is to break up either our summer fallow or our buck-wheat ground while our corn is young. They will immediately cease to do us mischief and go to prey on the worms and caterpillars which the plough raises. Their depredations proceeded from hunger, not from premeditated malice. As soon as their young ones are able to fly they bid us farewell. They retire to some other countries which produce what they want, for as they neither sow nor plant, it is necessary that either Man or Nature should feed them. Towards the autumn they return in astonishing flocks. If our corn-fields are not then well-guarded, they will in a few hours make great havoc. They disappear in about a week.

At this season another animal comes out of our woods and demands of Man his portion. It is the squirrel, of which there are three sorts, the grey, the black, both of the same size, and the little ground one which harbours under rocks and stones. The two former are the most beautiful inhabitants of our forests. They live in hollow trees which they fill with koka toma nuts, chestnuts, and corn when they can get it. Like man they know the approach of the winter, and as wisely know how to prepare against its wants. Some years their numbers are very great. They will travel over our fences with the utmost agility; descend into our fields; cut down an ear perhaps eighteen inches long and heavier than themselves. They will strip it of its husk and, properly balancing it in their mouths, return thus loaded to their trees. For my part, I cannot blame them, but I should blame myself were I peaceably to look on and let them carry all. As we pay no tithes in this country I think we should be a little more generous than we are to the brute creation. If there are but few, a gun and a dog are sufficient. If they openly declare war in great armies, men collect themselves and go to attack them in their native woods. The county assembles and forms itself into companies to which a captain is appointed. Different districts of woods are assigned them; the rendezvous is agreed on. They march, and that company which kills the most is treated by the rest; thus the day is spent. The meat of these squirrels is an excellent food; they make excellent soup or pies. Their skins are exceedingly tough; they are stronger than eels' skins; we use them to tie our flails with.

Various Rural Subjects.

Mirth, jollity, coarse jokes, the exhilarating cup, and dancing are always the concomitant circumstances which enliven and accompany this kind of meeting, the only festivals that we simple people are acquainted with in this young country. Religion, which in so many parts of the world affords processions and a variety of other exercises, and becomes a source of temporal pleasures to the people, here gives us none. What few it yields are all of the spiritual kind. A few years ago I was invited to one of these parties. At my first entrance into the woods, whilst the affrighted echoes were resounding with the noise of the men and dogs, before I had joined the company, I found a bee-tree, which is my favourite talent. But, behold, it contained also the habitation of a squirrel family. The bees were lodged in one of its principal limbs; the others occupied the body of the tree. For the sake of the former I saved the latter. While I was busy in marking it, I perceived a great number of ants (those busy-bodies) travelling up three deep in a continual succession and returning in the same way. Both these columns were perfectly straight in the ascent as well as in the descent and but a small distance apart. I killed a few which I smelled. I found them all replete with honey. I therefore concluded that these were a set of thieves living on the industrious labours of the others. This intrusion gave me a bad opinion of the vigour and vigilance of the latter. However, as the honey season was not come, I resolved to let them alone; and to deliver them from the rapacity of an enemy which they could not repel.

Next day, accompanied by my little boy, I brought a kettle, kindled a fire, boiled some water, and scalded the whole host as it ascended and descended. I did not leave one stirring. The lad asked me a great many ques-

119

tions respecting what I was doing, and the answers I made him afforded me the means of conveying to his mind the first moral ideas I had as yet given him. On my return home I composed a little fable on the subject which I made him learn by heart. God grant that this trifling incident may serve as the basis of a future moral education.

Thus, sir, do we save our corn. But when it is raised on our low lands, it is subject to transitory frosts, an accident which I have not mentioned to you yet, but as we can foresee them, it is in our power to avoid the mischief they cause. If in any of our summer months the wind blows northwest two days, on the second night the frost is inevitable. The only means we have to preserve our grain from its bad effects on our low grounds—for it seldom reaches the upland—is to kindle a few fires to the windward as soon as the sun goes down. No sooner [does] that luminary disappear from our sight than the wind ceases. This is the most favourable moment. The smoke will not rise, but, on the contrary, lie on the ground, mixing with the vapours of the evening. The whole will form a body four feet deep which will cover the face of the earth until the power of the sun dissipates it next morning. Whatever is covered with it is perfectly safe. I had once some hops and pole-beans, about twenty feet high. Whatever grew above the body of the smoke was entirely killed; the rest was saved. I had at the same time upwards of three acres of buckwheat which I had sown early for my bees. I lost not a grain. Some of my neighbours have by this simple method saved their tobacco.

These low grounds are exposed, besides, to the ravages of grasshoppers, an intolerable nuisance. While young and deprived of wings they may be kept off by

Various Rural Subjects.

means of that admirable contrivance which a negro found out in South Carolina: a few pots filled with brimstone and tar are kindled at nightfall to the windward of the field; the powerful smell of these two ingredients either kills them or drives them away. But when they have wings they easily avoid it and transport themselves wherever they please. The damage they cause in our hemp grounds as well as in our meadows is inconceivable. They will eat the leaves of the former to the bare stalks and consume the best of our grasses. The only remedy for the latter is to go to mowing as soon as possible. The former devastation is unavoidable. Some years a certain worm, which I cannot describe, insinuates itself into the heart of the corn-stalk while it is young, and if not killed by squeezing the plant, it will eat the embryo of the great stem which contains the imperceptible rudiments of our future hopes.

Sometimes our rye is attacked by a small animalcule of the worm kind which lodges itself in the stem just below the first joint. There it lives on the sap as it ascends. The ear becomes white and grainless, the perfect symbol of sterility.

I should have never done, were I to recount to you all the inconveniences and accidents which the grains of our fields, the trees of our orchards, as well as those of the woods are exposed to. If bountiful Nature is kind to us on the one hand, on the other she wills that we shall purchase her kindness not only with sweats and labour but with vigilance and care. These calamities remind us of our precarious situation. The field and meadow-mice come in also for their share, and sometimes take more from Man than he can well spare. The rats are so multiplied that no one can imagine the great quantities of grain they destroy every year. Some farmers more unfortunate than the others have lost half of their crops after they were safely lodged in their barns. I'd forgive Nature all the rest if she would rid us of these cunning, devouring thieves which no art can subdue. When the floods rise on our low grounds, the mice quit their burrows and come to our stacks of grain or to our heaps of turnips which are buried under the earth out of the reach of the frost. There, secured from danger, they find a habitation replenished with all they want. I must not, however, be murmuring and ungrateful. If Nature has formed mice, she has created also the fox and the owl. They both prey on these. Were it not for their kind assistance, [the mice] would drive us out of our farms.

Thus one species of evil is balanced by another; thus the fury of one element is repressed by the power of the other. In the midst of this great, this astonishing equipoise Man struggles and lives.

III. CUSTOMS

I AM glad you approve of my last; I was afraid it might prove tedious. I wanted to have curtailed it, but I knew not what part to lop off lest I should omit some information and repent of my foolish timidity. For the future I will boldly tell you all and leave the future amendment to yourself.

Within the more limited province of our American wives there are many operations, many ingenious arts which require knowledge, skill, and dexterity. In that of dyeing you'd be surprised to see what beautiful colours some families will have in their garments, which

Various Rural Subjects.

commonly are streaked gowns, skirts, and petticoats of the same stuff. This we have borrowed from the Dutch, as well as the art of producing so many colours from the roots and barks of our woods, aided with indigo and alum, the only foreign ingredients we use. I have often, while among the Indians, wished, but in vain, to find out how they dye their porcupine quills with that bright red and yellow which you must remember to have seen on the moccasins I gave you. Nor is the art of their squaws to be despised, when you consider it as it is displayed in the embroidery of their belts, shoes, and pouches, knife cases, etc.

Some families excel in the method of brewing beer with a strange variety of ingredients. Here we commonly make it with pine chips, pine buds, hemlock, fir leaves, roasted corn, dried apple-skins, sassafras roots, and bran. With these, to which we add some hops and a little malt, we compose a sort of beverage which is very pleasant. What most people call health-beer (which is made every spring) would greatly astonish you. I think in the last we made we had not less than seventeen ingredients. The doctors tell us that it is very purgative and necessary; that after the good living and the idleness of the winter it is necessary to prepare ourselves by these simple means for the sweats and the labours of the summer.

It is in the art of our simple cookery that our wives all aim at distinguishing themselves. This wife is famous for one thing, that for the other. She who has not fresh comb-honey, some sweet-meats of her own composing, and smoked beef at tea would be looked upon as very inexpert indeed. Thus these light repasts become on every account the most expensive of any, and as we dine early and work until tea-time, they often are very serious meals at which abundance of biscuits and short-cakes are always eaten. Some people would think it a disgrace to have bread brought on these round tables. Our beef by smoking becomes so compact that we commonly shave it with a plane. The thin, transparent peelings, when curled up on a dish, look not only neat and elegant but very tempting. Thus going to drink tea with each other implies several very agreeable ideas: that of riding sometimes five or six miles; that of chatting much and hearing the news of the county; and that of eating heartily. Considering that our women are never idle but have something to do from one year's end to another, where is the husband that would refuse his wife the pleasure of treating her friends as she has been treated herself?

In the future details which I intend to give you of our modes of living, of our different home manufactures, of the different resources which an industrious family must find within itself, you'll be better able to judge what a useful acquisition a good wife is to an American farmer; and how small is his chance of prosperity if he draws a blank in that lottery! Don't blame us for living well. Upon my word we richly earn it. Were not we to consume all these articles which our farms produce; were they not converted into wholesome pleasant food, they would be lost. What should we do with our fruit, our fowls, our eggs? There is no market for these articles but in the neighbourhood of great towns.

Some Europeans would, on reading these candid details, declare and swear that we deserve to be taxed. May those who thoughtlessly and without any real information advance such a doctrine, come over and be farmers with us one single year. I will then trust to their feelings. This was your early doctrine, too, until you attentively descended into every detail and saw the immense advances we are obliged to make, and the enormity of the price of our labours and the severity of our seasons. You were shocked the first time you saw ditchers and choppers at my table. Like a wise man you soon found that this was but the smallest difficulty which attends our rural operations.

Would you believe that the great electrical discoveries of Mr. Franklin have not only preserved our barns and our houses from the fire of heaven but have even taught our wives to multiply their chickens? The invisible effects of the thunder are powerfully felt in the egg. If, while a hen is hatching, there happens a great storm, not one chicken will appear. (I can express myself but very imperfectly.) To prevent this electrical mischief our wives, without going through a course of lectures, have been taught to place a piece of iron in the bottom of their hens' nests in such a manner that it touches the ground. By what magic I know not, but all the mischief is prevented, and the eggs bring prosperous chickens. Can the name of that distinguished, useful citizen be mentioned by an American without feeling a double sentiment: that of the pleasure inspired by our calling him our countryman, and that of gratitude? Before the erection of his iron conductors, the mischiefs occasioned in Pennsylvania and everywhere else by the thunder annually amounted to a great sum. Now everyone may rest secure. These rods fetch from the clouds (strange to tell) that powerful fire and convey it into the earth alongside the very house which it would have consumed, had it accidentally fallen on its roof. Happy Pennsylvania! Thou Queen of Provinces! Among the many useful citizens thou hast already produced, Ben-

Eighteenth Century America.

jamin Franklin is one of the most eminent of thy sons.

Whilst I was discoursing with you in my last on the many enemies, against the combined instincts of which we had to struggle, I purposely omitted to mention to you several others lest I might appear tedious. Give me leave to resume that subject. You evidently see that I cannot submit to any method. Method appears to me like the symmetry and regularity of a house. Its external appearance is often sacrificed to the internal conveniences.

Our ponds, our lakes, and brooks, with which this country is replenished, abound with enemies which, it is true, touch not our grains, but destroy our fowls. The musquash is the most pernicious on many accounts. Nothing can possibly restrain him. The stoutest and best-made banks cannot resist his instinctive ingenuity. These [animals] undermine and destroy that which has successfully opposed and restrained the fury of the waters. They will pierce them and open a communication for the element in which they swim. They enjoy a double advantage: they can live under water as well as on the earth. The proprietors of the bank-meadows near Philadelphia, and in the county of Salem in West New Jersey, where so much art has been displayed, can well attest the power of their claws. They are the cousin germans of the beavers, and greatly resemble them in their instinct, ingenuity in building, and modes of living. But how different is their conduct! The beavers are the philosophers of the animals; the gentlest, the most humble, the most harmless. Yet brutal Man kills them. I was once a witness to the destruction of one of their associated confederacies. I saw many of them shed tears, and I wept also, nor am I ashamed to confess it.

We abound likewise with otters, and they are very

Various Rural Subjects.

mischievous. At least we call by that name everything through which we lose some small part of our property. We have many species of turtles. Some creep through our woods and are harmless. The gold spotted one is rather an ornament to our ditches. The snapping one is a hideous and very strong animal. Their bills would astonish you, as to their size and strength. I have seen them that weighed forty pounds. Whatever goose or duck swims in their waters is soon pulled down and devoured. These [turtles] are good to eat, and as long as we feed on what would feed on us, that seems to be founded on a just retaliation. Traps of various kinds are laid to catch the otters, and their furs are the only reward they yield.

We have another animal which sometimes makes great havoc among our poultry: that is the skunk. It resembles a black and white small dog. Its mode of defence is very singular: behind it possesses a bladder containing the most foetid and offensive liquor you can possibly conceive. When pursued either by men or dogs it scatters it on its enemies. If it touches the eyes it will cause violent pains. If not, the intolerableness of the smell will turn one's stomach.

We abound with bull-frogs of an enormous size whose deep and sullen voices often startle the unthinking traveller. Common frogs are perfectly harmless. The tree-toads are a species of them; they climb and rest on the limbs of trees. There they live all summer, but on what, I know not. Their notes are not disagreeable. In dry weather they are perfectly silent, and on the approach of rain they sweetly warble their uncouth notes. We always love to hear them sing because they almost infallibly predict the coming of refreshing showers.

Eighteenth Century America.

In the summer our meadows and fields are beautifully illuminated by an immense number of fire-flies,
which in the calm of the evening sweetly wander here
and there at a small distance from the ground. By their
alternate glows of light they disseminate a kind of universal splendour, which, being always contrasted with
the darkness of the night, has a most surprising effect.
I have often read by their assistance; that is I have
taken one carefully by the wings and, carrying it along
the lines of my book, I have, when thus assisted by
these living flambeaux, perused whole pages, and then
thankfully dismissed these little insect-stars. I am told
that a few years ago a Scotch soldier, while he was on
duty at ——, fired at the first he saw, thinking that it
was the flash of an enemy.

We abound with vultures, eagles, hawks, and kites of
many kinds. The best way to preserve our poultry from
their rapacity is to plant elders round our fences. This
serves them as an excellent shelter where they can run.

I have often told you that the philosophy of an
American farmer consisted in doing much with few
hands, in manufacturing in his own family whatever he
may want. This is true in every possible respect. If he
is obliged to purchase many articles, then he works for
others and not for himself; he is but a fool and a slave.
His profits are so inconsiderable that if they are uselessly expended, there remains nothing of his year's
industry.

Our wool, I am afraid, never will be so good as
yours; we have no plains. Sheep in our dry summers are
so destructive to grass that we can't keep many. I have
sixty, and sometimes I think that is a greater number
than my farm can support. Our long winters are very
prejudicial to them. The snow often renders them

blind. We have but one expedient to prevent it, which is to keep some place free from snow where they may see the ground, and give them the limbs of pine-trees, the bark of which they peel and eat. Were it not for the wolves we could turn them out into the woods. It is astonishing how they thrive on wood-feed and how much better their wool becomes. I have often tried the experiment. This feed is certainly stronger and richer than that which our pastures afford.

The best butter in this country is made with the milk of cows that run at large in the woods; it has a more pleasant taste, which a stranger can soon perceive. I intend next fall to send you a firkin that your friends in England may judge whether or not I am right. This is one of the principal advantages which first settlers enjoy. They possess, besides, a certain amplitude of benefits which great cultivated countries have lost. And if they carefully salt their cows at their doors, they are sure that every night they will punctually return home.

The method which is yearly made use of to render the feed of our mountains sweet, tender, and good, is to burn them. You must not imagine that by that operation we consume the trees. No, this operation would ruin us all indeed. For in that case they would become barren and useless. In April the neighbours of each mountain district assemble and, taking the advantage of the wind, set fire to the leaves which lie most contiguous to their fences; and each takes care of his own. Those leaves which fell the preceding fall soon catch. The fire forms itself in a regular line and advances towards the top of the mountains, sometimes with great rapidity. It spreads wherever there are combustibles, etc. This scene viewed at a distance through the trees yields a very pleasing effect in the night. Here the fire, by a sudden puff of wind, is seen to blaze, as it advances with great velocity; there in consequence of some impediment it takes another turn. Now the rarefied air increases the wind, and the wind urges on that fire which at first caused it. Thus on a calm day, when employed in burning great heaps of wood in my swamp, I have been surprised at the tempest I have raised, and the astonishing agitation of the trees whose limbs have often been torn off and have fallen on the ground. As soon as the operation of burning the mountains is over, which sometimes requires many days, it is surprising to see how amazingly quickly every vegetable will spring up. The surface of the earth is rendered perfectly clear. The heat of this transitory fire and the few ashes it leaves greatly accelerate the growth of every shrub and weeds and plants and grass. This is generally the time I visit them when I want to get some snake-root, crow's-foot, Solomon's seal, spignet, etc. I can distinguish them as soon as they appear, and that is the best season of the year to procure them.

Our cattle are sent there some time in May. There they feed all the summer, salted regularly, as I told you before. Everywhere springs abound of the purest water, and everywhere a most benign shade. [There are] very few insects, for you know that our mountains are all covered with the most majestic trees. By the assistance of these three blessings, is it a wonder that in the fall they should return home extremely fat? So would our sheep, too, were it not for the danger of the wolves. Some farmers, to render them still fatter, sow several acres of rye on their low grounds, the second week in September, about two bushels to an acre. They are turned into these rye pastures and into our meadows the latter end of October, when they return from the

Various Rural Subjects.

woods. At first this rye grass, as I may call it, purges them; afterwards you cannot imagine what surprising progress they make. The butchers greatly prefer beef thus fatted to those which are constantly kept in the richest of our meadows.

But we have no foreign market. The limits of our trade do not permit us to send our produce where we might find a ready vent for it. Cattle are so cheap that they are hardly worth raising. Three pence per pound is a great price, which is seldom given. This is a very small fraction, more than three of your coppers. Yet I am astonished that the price of labour does not fall. We abound too much in cattle; every other provision is cheap in proportion. Anyone can board and lodge himself with the most opulent of our farmers for seven shillings a week, that is, something less than four shillings sterling, yet the wages we are obliged to give are enormous. Many times have I given from five to eight shillings per day to a cradler. It is a problem, however, easily explained; it is a contradiction which nothing but the locality of our situation can possibly resolve.

Those people who live near the sea every spring burn their salt-meadows also, that the dead unmowed grass may make room for the new and leave no impediment to the scythe. This operation affords likewise a noble sight. I once saw a body of such meadows consisting of upwards of three thousand acres [burned] in a few hours. The whirlwinds of smoke they produce are of an enormous size and [are] seen at a great distance.

Some of our wives are famous for the raising of turkeys in which, you know, we abound in the fall of the year. The great secret consists in procuring the eggs of the wild sort and then [in crossing] the breed. In that case we are always sure of a hardier and heavier bird.

Eighteenth Century America.

It well repays us for the trouble and care they have cost. I have often killed them that weighed twenty-seven pounds. Pray, are they heavier with you? Here they hate confinement; in the most severe of our freezing nights they will reach the utmost limbs of our highest trees and there boldly face the northwest wind. Does their instinct lead them to such lofty roosts to avoid danger, or because it is not so cold on high as it is nearer the surface of the earth?

You often used to blame us for not taking better care of the breed of our dogs. It would be impossible to amend it. We find that the strength of the climate has the same effect on them as it has on us. In the course of a few generations they become American dogs as well as we American men. Many of them out-run the fox. They never fail to attack the wolf with the greatest fury, nor do they decline encountering the bear. What other accomplishments could we wish them to possess? We neither love nor understand small game.

I once saw a remarkable instance of the sagacity of an Indian dog, which I beg to relate.* Mr. D. W., a distant relation of my wife, lives at the foot of the great mountains; nay, he is the last settler towards the wilderness. [He] possesses both a good mill and a very good farm. While I was there, a child about three years old was missed at ten o'clock in the morning. The neighbourhood was roused; they all marched with the afflicted family in quest of him. In vain did they mention his name a thousand times; no other answer was re-

* This episode has been adapted into French: "Anecdote d'un Chien Sauvage," *Lettres d'un Cultivateur* . . . edit. 1787, t. I, p. 223. In the French version Mr. D. W. is called le Fèvre, is the grandson of a French Huguenot, and lives in the neighbourhood of Wawassing, Ulster County.

turned but by the uncouth echoes of those woods; the search proved vain. I never saw so affecting a scene of distress. After dinner they all returned to the woods; they searched and searched until night came on. The afflicted parents refused to return to the house, and spent the night with many of their friends at the foot of a tree, bemoaning the loss of their poor child.

Next day the search was renewed, but as ineffectually as on the preceding day. Fortunately about one o'clock an Indian, followed by his dog, was seen to go by. He was called in; he expressed a great deal of sympathy at the sad adventure; he immediately demanded the child's shoes and stockings which he made his dog smell; then, taking the house as a center, he described around it a circle of about a quarter of a mile in diameter. Before the circle was completed the dog barked. This happy sound immediately conveyed to the hearts of the afflicted parents some distant hopes of the recovery of their child. The dog followed the scent and barked again. In about a half hour he returned towards the Indian and guided him to a large log where the child lay, half asleep and half [in a faint]. The Indian tenderly brought him home.

Happily his parents were prepared for his reception, for they had been full of hopes from the first time the dog uttered the first sounds. They ran to meet the honest Indian; they embraced their child, their newly-found child; they caught the Indian in their arms; nor did his dog go uncaressed and unthanked. I was by all the time and saw this singular scene in all its gradations. They returned to the house; it was full. By means of some light broth the child recovered, opened his eyes, and began to smile. Alas! one must be a father to participate in all the joys of these parents; to know what they must have felt, and to feel along with them. The Indian had killed a deer which he gave towards the feast; to it Mr. —— added a calf. Upwards of seventy people were entertained there that evening, that memorable evening, and the whole night.

The story soon ran at a great distance, and from a great distance his neighbours and friends all flocked to rejoice with him. The Indian would accept no kind of reward; all he wanted was the skin of his deer. Mr. ——, with great difficulty, made him accept a fine Lancaster rifle. This honest native's name was Tewenissa. Towards evening Mr. —— brought his child into the middle of the yard where everyone was assembled. In a proper talk he thanked the Indian; acknowledged him as his brother; embraced him, and made his child do the same; and earnestly required that his former name of Derick by which he had hitherto been called might be forgot; and that henceforth he should be known under no other than that of his deliverer, Tewenissa. I had never before assisted at such a scene nor partaken of such a feast; it was a feast for the soul as well as for the stomach. Cider, rum, peach-brandy, all that these good people had was profusely poured out in the most pious and grateful libations on this joyful occasion. The honest Indian all this while seemed embarrassed; [Indians] are not used to such noisy scenes. All he said was: "Brother ——, I have done nothing for you but what you would have done for me. It was my dog that did it all. Since you are all happy, I am happy. Since you are all glad, I am glad."

In travelling through our woods and our swamps I have often been astonished at the great quantity of grapes which grow in some particular spots. I verily believe that I have grapes enough some years in my south swamp to make a hogshead of wine, but labour is so dear, and I am so inexpert that I am discouraged from undertaking any new schemes. All the use I make of it, and perhaps it is all it is good for, [is to make] vinegar which is exceedingly strong, indeed. (A scheme was formed by Captain Carver, author of a book of travels through America, for a settlement on the Missouri, where vines abound, and where he was to distil it into brandy to trade with the Indians.)*

Some time ago, as I was walking through my woodland, I found a thrifty sassafras tree about three inches in circumference. Close by there grew a vine twisted round its stem, which appeared to be coeval with its supporter. They seemed to have been the twins of Nature formed at the same time and for each other, a singular circumstance. These spontaneous ideas struck me so much that with infinite care I dug them up and brought them into my garden. Although sassafras will hardly bear transplantation, yet such was my precaution that they both lived, and that very year both bore some small blossoms and fruits. I survey the face of Nature: the plains of Virginia, the swamps of Carolina. I see nothing there equal to this "lusus naturae," to this pleasing assemblage.† You must recollect the fragrance which the blossoms of our wild vine afford. There is none in the southern countries that equals it. They perpetually exhale the most odoriferous smell. I know two thorn-trees not very far from here which are so entirely covered with these vines that neither thorn-leaves nor branches can be discerned; and each makes a most beau-

---

* This is interlineal and seems to have been intended as a footnote.

† This short episode has become in *Lettres d'un Cultivateur* . . . the charming story entitled, "Anecdote du Sassafras et de la Vigne sauvage." *Lettres, op. cit.*, t. I, p. 249.

tiful arbour. Could they be transplanted or purchased from the owners, I'd be extravagant for once. How often have you and I stopped as we travelled along, to inhale these sweet draughts, as you called them, and to snuff up all the perfume they exhaled! Now to the idea of the young blossoming vine, pray add that of the blossoming sassafras which likewise sends forth the most delicate fragrance. Next conceive them united in their stems, the former entwined through all the limbs of the latter, and tell me whether our coarse wintry climate can yield a fairer symbol of southern vegetation, and whether I was not fortunate in procuring so beautifully combined a production. I never look at it with the same indifference as I do at my other trees. I have given it to my daughter Fanny. This gift still enhances the idea and trebles my pleasure.

Next year I intend to send you some of the sassafras's blossoms properly dried. I think their infusion far superior to the Chinese tea. Alas! had the Chinese exclusively possessed the sassafras, we would think it voluptuous to regale on it; but because it grows wild in our woods we despise and overlook it, and, like fools, we poison our bodies, lessen our pockets in purchasing those far-fetched Chinese leaves. Yes, with us it is become an epidemic at which your company no doubt smiles. Everyone drinks tea, from the westernmost settlers in western Florida to the northernmost ones in Canada, and I am sure that is a pretty extensive market. The poorer the people the stronger is the tea they drink. Some have told me that it feeds them,—a strange food indeed! But such is the infatuation of the age, such is the concatenation of events! It was necessary that our forefathers should discover and till this country, in order that their posterity might serve to enrich a parcel

Various Rural Subjects.

of London merchants who though but citizens in England, yet are nabobs in India; who though mighty fond of liberty at home for themselves and their children, yet do not choose that other people should enjoy these great benefits in their Indian dominions. The idea of merchants becoming sovereigns, lords, and tyrants . . . but a poor American farmer must not say all he thinks.

Our cattle are not subject to so many diseases as yours. I am not learned enough to characterize those to which ours are subject. What we call the Spanish staggers is the most dreadful; it is their plague. Some years ago a Spanish vessel was cast away on the coast of Carolina. The hides it contained communicated an infection which had been hitherto unknown. Now and then it breaks out in those provinces, but seldom reaches us. I have heard it asserted that they have begun to inoculate their cattle for this disorder, with what success I know not. A few years ago the proprietors of the great bank-meadows of Philadelphia were wont to fetch lean cattle from there in order to fatten them on their rich bottoms, but the severe losses which the northern people upon that road met with in consequence of the infection made them rise in arms and oppose their passage. Trade has been since interrupted. This is long, but, I hope, not tedious.

IV. IMPLEMENTS

YOUR approbation of my last is an encouragement which I wanted much. Sometimes I despair of finding out anything that may be worth sending over so far. I am obliged to put all my little matters into a sieve; the coarsest and the most useless I throw by, the finest and what I think most valuable I gather together by means of that operation. Upon my word [this] is almost literal. But alas! my sieve, the sieve of an American farmer, is but a poor criterion of what he should write or not write, but I have no other. Happily I am so distant from you that I cannot hear your observations. I do not blush, therefore, as if I were present. By your last you demand of me a detail of our implements of husbandry and of the buildings necessary to constitute a well-established farm. I shall begin with the most useful.

You have often admired our two-horse wagons. They are extremely well-contrived and executed with a great deal of skill; and they answer with ease and dispatch all the purposes of a farm. A well-built wagon, when loaded, will turn in a very few feet more than its length, which is sixteen feet including the length of the tongue. We have room in what is called their bodies to carry five barrels of flour. We commonly put in them a ton of hay and often more. The load is built on shelvings fixed on their sides. A ladder of $\frac{5}{6}$ [sic] stands erect in the front. [The hay is held in place] by means of a boom, one end of which passes through the ladder, and the other end [of which] is brought tight down and fastened to a staple in the hind-most axle-tree. Thus the whole is secured. We can carry twenty-five green oak rails, two-thirds of a cord of wood, three thousand pounds of dung. In short there is no operation that ought to be performed on a farm but what is easily accomplished with one of these. We can lengthen them as we please, and bring home the body of a tree twenty or thirty feet long. We commonly carry with them thirty bushels of wheat and at sixty pounds to the bushel this makes a weight of eighteen hundred pounds, with which we can go forty miles a day with two horses.

Various Rural Subjects.

On a Sunday it becomes the family coach. We then take off the common, plain sides and fix on it others which are handsomely painted. The after-part, on which either our names or ciphers are delineated, hangs back suspended by neat chains. If it rains, flat hoops made on purpose are placed in mortises, and a painted cloth is spread and tied over the whole. Thus equipped, the master of a family can carry six persons either to church or to meetings. When the roads are good we easily travel seven miles an hour. In order to prevent too great shakings, our seats are suspended on wooden springs,—a simple but very useful mechanism. These inventions and [this] neatness we owe to the original Dutch settlers. I do not know where an American farmer can possibly enjoy more dignity as a father or as a citizen than when he thus carries with him his wife and family all clad in good, neat homespun clothes, manufactured within his own house, and trots along with a neat pair of fat horses of his own raising. The single-horse Irish car, with wheels not above two feet high, must appear very inferior to our wagons, and yet several people from that country have told me that the whole internal trade of that kingdom is effected with no other carriages. Exclusive of these middle-sized wagons there are many public ones, driven by six horses, which carry great burthens. In the southern provinces, where the roads are level, they use no other. We generally pay for ours from fifty to sixty dollars. The Dutch build them with timber which has been previously three years under water and then gradually seasoned.

Our next most useful implement is the plough. Of these we have various sorts, according to the soil which we have to till. First, [there is] the large two-handled plough with an English lock and coulter locked in its point. This is drawn by either four or six oxen and serves for rooty, stony land. This is drawn sometimes by two oxen and three horses. The one-handled plough is the most common in all level soils. It is drawn either by two or by three horses abreast, and when the ground is both level and swarded we commonly put upon these a Dutch lock, by far the best for turning up, and the easiest draft for the horses. A team of four oxen is conducted by a lad. If it consists of two horses and two oxen, the boy rides one of the horses, and another lad drives the oxen. Our two and three-horse teams are guided by the man who holds the plough. Lines are properly fixed to the horses' bridles on each side and passed around the plough-handle. The ploughman keeps them straight with his left hand while he guides his plough with his right. Three horses abreast are the most expeditious as well as the strongest team we know of for common land. We cross-plough with two horses, commonly one and a half acres a day. We have, besides, a smaller sort, called the corn-plough with which we till through the furrows, and a harrow proportioned to the distance at which our corn is planted. Our heavy harrows are made sometimes triangular, sometimes square. This last we call the Dutch one. In the rough, stony parts of New England they use no other team but oxen, and no people on earth understand the management of them better. They shoe them with admirable skill and neatness. They are coupled with a yoke which plays loose on their necks. It is fastened with a bow which is easily taken off or put on. They draw by the top of their shoulders.

Besides a wagon, most farmers have an ox-cart, which is fitter to carry heavy stones and large timbers.

Various Rural Subjects.

With these we convey logs to the saw-mills by suspending them under the axle-tree of the cart. A good one, well-shod with iron, costs twenty dollars.

The great objects which an American farmer ought to have in view are simplicity of labour and dispatch. The sun, and the great vegetation which it causes, hurry him along. The multiplicity of business which crowds all at the same time is astonishing. This is the principal reason why we can do nothing so neatly as you do in Europe. Could we fallow our wheat-land in the fall, this would greatly relieve us in the summer. We are, therefore, often obliged to keep double-teams in order to accelerate our operations. What I mean by simplicity is the art of doing a great deal with few hands. For that reason I am extremely fond of ploughing with three horses abreast, because it is a powerful team and requires but one person. I have heard many Europeans blame us for many of our operations. Alas! they censured us before they knew anything of our climate, of our seasons, and the scarcity and dearness of labourers. I think, considering our age, the great toils we have undergone, the roughness of some parts of this country, and our original poverty, that we have done the most in the least time of any people on earth. Call it industry or what you will.

The barn, with regard to its situation, size, convenience, and good finishing is an object, in the mind of a farmer, superior even to that of his dwelling. Many don't care much how they are lodged, provided that they have a good barn and barn-yard, and indeed it is the criterion by which I always judge of a farmer's prosperity. On this building he never begrudges his money. The middle-sized ones are commonly fifty by thirty feet; mine is sixty by thirty-five and cost two hundred and twenty dollars. They are either shingled, clap-boarded, or boarded on the outside. Therein we lodge all our grain, and within many operations are performed, such as threshing, and cleaning of flax and husking the corn, etc. Therein the horses are stabled and the oxen stall-fed. In the summer the women resort to it, in order to spin their wool. The neatness of our boarded floors, the great draught of air caused by the opened doors, which are always made wide enough to permit a loaded wagon to enter, and their breadth afford [the women] an opportunity of spinning long threads, of carding at their ease. Many farmers have several barracks in their barn-yards where they put their superfluous hay and straws. Nor ought the subdivision of these yards to pass unnoticed. They require great judgment, demand attention and expense. All classes of our cattle, our sheep, our calves, must be placed by themselves, and have in each division convenient racks and bars in order to communicate easily from one to another.

Next to a good barn a skilful farmer should have a good hog-pen. The warmer and more convenient it is, the easier will these animals fatten, and the less grain will they consume. We generally place a large yard before them enclosed with posts and rails, where they cast their dung. Dirty as they appear, yet they love a clean habitation. You may remember the care with which mine was erected. Some build them with stones and lime, others with good framed work, others with dovetailed logs. The door hangs like a bell, by which means it is always shut. The floor must be good and tight, for on it the corn is thrown. There are as many holes as there are hogs, and on the outside the great trough is fixed. [The pens] must be well-roofed, because the inferior corn is always placed under it, this being the first grain which is given them.

Next to this is the hen-house. He that carelessly permits his fowls to roost in the adjacent trees will receive very little good from them.

The truly economical farmer has always what we call a shop, that is a house big enough to contain a loom. There, in the weaving season, our wives can either weave themselves, or else inspect the management of the yarn. There we keep also our seasoned timber, our tools. For most of us are skilful enough to use them with some dexterity in mending and making whatever is wanted on the farm. Were we obliged to run to distant mechanics, who are half farmers themselves, many days would elapse, and we should always be behind-hand with our work. Some people have their ovens out-of-doors. This I look upon as very inconvenient, but beginners must do as well as they can. They place them so because they dare not erect them adjoining their log-houses, for fear of the fire. Mine is in the chimney of my negro kitchen. We commonly draw water out of our wells with long sweeps balanced and fixed with an iron bolt in a high forked tree. When the well is deep it is drawn by means of a pulley and two buckets.

Corn-cribs are indispensable because this grain is preserved there longer than anywhere else. You well remember their peculiar structure. Some people are, and all should be, furnished with electrical rods. The best way to place them, in order to save expense, is on a high cedar mast situated between the house and the barn. Its power will attract the lightning sufficiently to save both. Mine is so. I once saw its happy effects and blessed the inventor. My barn was then completely full. I valued it at about seven hundred pounds. What should I have done, had not the good Benjamin Franklin thought of this astonishing invention? Our negro kitchens are always built adjacent to our dwelling houses with a door of communication into the room where we eat, in order that we may inspect whatever passes there; and indeed it is the room which is often the most useful, for all housework is done in it.

Our houses are very different from one another. Each builds them agreeable to his taste and abilities. The common length is about forty-five in front, [having] a passage with a room on each side, and two smaller ones back, and a piazza in front. They are either shingled or boarded and commonly painted.

We are very deficient in gardens, for we have neither taste nor time, and, besides, the labour is too dear. Compare for one minute the additional work to which the American farmer must submit over and above what people of the same class must do in England, admitting that everything else is equal. The very article of firewood is an immense addition, although the wood costs nothing. One year with another I burn seventy loads, this is, pretty nearly so many cords. Judge of the time and trouble it requires to fell it in the woods; to haul it home either in wagons or sleighs, besides recutting it at the wood-pile fit for the length of each chimney.

Every farmer is obliged to make his own ropes. We must all spin our yarn with simple wheels made on purpose, and lay them out-of-doors by means of simple contrivances. We must likewise weave the collars our horses draw with in little frames made on purpose, though we have leather collars for our holidays. I had almost forgot to mention our smoke-houses; without them we could not live. Each family smokes fully one-half their meat, fish, eels; in short, everything we intend to preserve. For, besides the advantage of preservation, it greatly adds to the flavour of our food; it saves it, besides, from the flies. Virginia is the country where they eat the greatest quantity of smoked meat as well as of all other kinds. There they raise their hogs with more facility than we do.

We have another convenience to preserve our roots and vegetables in the winter, which we commonly call a Dutch cellar. It is built at the foot of a rising ground which is dug through, about eighteen feet long and six feet high. It is walled up about seven feet from the ground; then strongly roofed and covered with sods. The door always faces the south. There it never freezes, being under the ground. In these places we keep our apples, our turnips, cabbages, potatoes, and pumpkins. The cellars which are under the houses are appropriated for cider, milk, and butter; meat and various necessaries.

The next building is the bee-house. Some have them elegant; others carelessly leave these insects under the most humble roofs. But as most farmers are not far distant from saw-mills where they can always be supplied with boards and scantlings, I think it unpardonable to leave such industrious little beings so poorly housed as some are in this country. Gratitude alone ought to lead them to a better care of those who are at work for them. But Man is a selfish being.

There are but few people who are at any considerable distance from grist-mills; and that is a very great advantage considering the prodigious quantity of flour which we and our cattle consume annually, for we seldom give them any grain but what is previously ground. I know a miller who has not the command of a very large district who yearly receives fourteen hundred bushels of all kinds of grain, yet his toll is but the twelfth part. Each provident farmer must have, besides all these things, a fanning-mill by means of which he cleans his grain with very little trouble, and even divides the light from the heavy. I have four sets of riddles to mine, each fitted for different sorts of grains. They commonly cost twenty dollars. This is a useful piece of furniture in a barn. He that has them not often loses a great deal of time for want of wind, or else must submit to the labour of fanning. They are most indispensably useful to a northern farmer in order to enjoy the benefit of conveying his grain on the snow to whatever market he may choose. For when the snow falls, it is necessary to take the opportunity it offers, lest a thaw might come.

The vehicles fit for that season are of two kinds very similar to one another. They are in some respects the same: the first is for the pleasure of the family; the other for heavy labour; the one called sleighs; the other sleds. On these latter I have often carried forty bushels of wheat or the biggest log that can be hauled out of the woods, three feet wide by eighteen long. When the snow is good, these sleds cannot be too heavily loaded. It makes no difference in the draught of the horses because the load slides on large iron bars fastened under the runners. The pleasure-sleigh is accommodated with a box handsomely painted, and seats which can easily carry six persons as well as a wagon. 'Tis surprising with what ease and velocity we transport ourselves to a great distance. I have often gone at the rate of twelve miles an hour. For winter with us is the season of festivity. When we are going to any considerable distance we provide ourselves with a globe of pewter which holds two gallons. This is filled with hot gingered cider and placed at the bottom of the sleigh. It keeps our feet warm, and by now and then swallowing a mouthful, we keep the insides warm also.

Our markets in the winter generally are either some stores built on the edges of great rivers, whence the grain is conveyed in the spring to the capital, or else some great bolting-mills where the proprietor purchases it. In the first place we must take our chance for the market of the world; in the second, that chance is fixed by a certain price then received, except we agree to take the current price of such a month. The advantage of the snow simplifies many other operations. When it does not come we severely feel it; the transportation of our grain takes up a great deal of our time in the spring which should be employed in ploughing.

Notwithstanding the experience of so many years, yet it is very extraordinary that almost every winter there are people drowned in crossing our rivers, either on foot or in sleighs. Last winter it was very near being my fate; had it not been for the assistance of my brother-in-law I should have at least lost my two horses. We were going to ——'s, who lives over the river of ——, when in the middle of it [the horses] broke in and sank to their heads. Luckily my sleigh was water-tight, and this gave us an opportunity of jumping off, and fortunately the ice was sufficiently strong to bear us within a few feet of the hole. While I was cutting away the harness, Mr. —— passed a rope with a slip-noose around the neck of one of the horses. We pulled as hard as we could and strangled him. He swelled and immediately rose on the surface of the water. We then easily slipped him up on to the ice, and, cutting the ropes, in a few minutes he came to, and got up. The second was saved in the same manner. As my

147

sleigh was water-tight it still swam. We easily hauled it onto the ice, which was perfectly sound, and, having repaired the mischief, returned back to the shores as quickly as possible. This place had been an air-hole lately frozen over. These holes, however dangerous they may appear, are necessary, for were not it for them, the ice never would be good, at least in running waters. The power of the frost compresses the air so much that it must have a vent somewhere, and by issuing in great quantities at some particular spots, it often keeps the water from freezing all winter. When travelling on the ice one may go to the very edges; there is no kind of danger. These openings are more or less extensive.

Nor are the joys and pleasures of the season confined to the whites alone, as our blacks divide with us the toils of our farms; they partake also of the mirth and good cheer of the season. They have their own meetings and are often indulged with their masters' sleighs and horses. You may see them at particular places as happy and merry as if they were freemen and freeholders. The sight of their happiness always increases mine, provided it does not degenerate into licentiousness; [and this] is sometimes the case though we have laws enough to prevent it. But our magistrates though mostly old, yet are very young in their business. It will take at least one hundred years before our magistracy becomes properly enlightened. Where should the man who daily follows his plough find that spontaneous knowledge which is requisite? Their commissions do not bring along with them the necessary lights and information. These are miracles left to another set of men who by the simple power of the touch receive all they want.

Various Rural Subjects.

It is in this season particularly that the hospitality of the Americans is most conspicuous. The severity of the climate requires that all our doors should be opened to the frozen traveller, and indeed we shut them not, either by night or by day at any time of the year. The traveller when cold has a right to stop and warm himself at the first house he sees. He freely goes to the fire, which is kept a-burning all night. There he forgets the keenness of the cold; he smokes his pipe; drinks of the cider which is often left on the hearth; and departs in peace. We always sleep in these rooms; at least I do, and have often seen mine full when I was in my bed. On waking I have sometimes spoken to them; at other times it was a silent meeting. The reasons which force these people to travel in these dreadful nights is that they may be able to return home the same day. They are farmers carrying their produce to the market, and their great distance from it obliges them to set out sometimes at twelve o'clock. Far from being uneasy at seeing my house thus filled while my wife and I are abed, I think it, on the contrary, a great compliment, when I consider that by thus stopping they convince me that they have thought my house and my fire better than that of my neighbours.

This is, sir, an imperfect sketch of this season, filled with labours as well as the others, but more tempered with pleasures. We then consume the greatest part of what we have earned in the summer, nor can we repine at it. How much happier are we than many other settlers who have no market and can't realize anything on what they raise. Though they might be richer than we are, or living on the best soils, yet they are infinitely poorer; they have not the spirit to enjoy as we have, so that, everything considered, it is all equal. The further from market, generally the better the land, but it costs a great deal to come to that market. We raise much less, but then it costs us but little to convert our produce into money.

I was once at Pa—an,* where several families dwelt on the most fruitful soil I have ever seen in my life. The warmest imagination can't conceive anything equal to it. These people raised what they pleased: oats, peas, wheat, corn, with two days' labour in the week. At their doors they had a fair river, on their backs high mountains full of game. Yet with all these advantages, placed as they were on these shores of Eden, they lived as poor as the poorest wretches of Europe who have nothing. Their houses were miserable hovels. Their stalks of grain rotted in their fields. They were almost starved, not for want of victuals but of spirit and activity to cook them. They were almost naked.

This may appear to you a strange problem. This is representing to you two extremes which you cannot reconcile, yet this relation is founded on fact and reason. This people had not nor could they have, situated as they were, any place where they might convey their produce. They could neither transport, sell, nor exchange anything they had, except cattle, so singularly were they placed. This annihilated all the riches of their grounds; rendered all their labours abortive; rendered them careless, slothful, and inactive. This constituted their poverty, though in the midst of the greatest plenty. They could not build for want of nails. They could not clothe themselves for want of materials which they might easily have procured with their wheat. They were inferior to the Indians. Had they had a market, the scene would have been greatly

* Probably Paxtan, Crèvecœur's spelling for Paxtung.

changed. Neatness, convenience, decency of appearance
would have soon banished that singular poverty under
which they groaned. I stayed five days with them and
could not rejoice enough to think that my farm was so
much more advantageously situated. Happily for this
country we have but few spots among the many which
have been discovered, [from which] the people may
[not] convey what they raise to some markets. But,
you'll say, what could induce people to settle on such
grounds? The extreme fertility of the soil, necessity,
and poverty. This it is, sir, which drives people over the
hills and far away.

LIBERTY OF WORSHIP

IT is astonishing to think how pernicious to the peace of mankind that old maxim has been, that a unity in religious opinions was necessary to establish the unity of law and government, as if law and government could possibly extend to opinions. Yet this has been one of the best established and most respectable maxims of the rulers of the world for many ages, from whence almost all its calamities have proceeded. It is not very long since it has been demonstratively proved that variety, nay, a discord of religious opinions is the true principle on which the harmony of society is established. As in a concert the inharmonious sounds of some instrument tend to promote the accord of the whole, so in society the perfect freedom of mode of worship preserves that peace, that tranquillity which are the triumphs of some countries.

This above all now in the world presents us with the most extravagant latitude of this kind, and yet no country is so happy in every possible respect. It is true that we everywhere seem to be born for error and illusions. But as truth is so difficult to perceive, and appearance may be modified in so many different ways, what matters it which of these inoffensive ways a citizen follows, provided that he loves his country and is a good subject? How do we know whether we have faculties fit to perceive the truth in its unity and in the simplicity of its precepts? In some countries the people think that it resides in symbols, hieroglyphics, splendid ornaments. There pomp chiefly attracts their attention; there ceremonies create respect and promote an artificial venera-

tion. Without being at any pains to investigate anything, without being permitted to ascend to principles,
they may overlook the essence in the variety of parts,
the true object in the shades and ornaments which encompass it. There the love of the marvellous and of the
extraordinary absorbs every other inquiry; they are satisfied. Here, on the contrary, every religious institution
is simpler, entirely divested of any exterior pomp;
everyone reasons for himself and follows the glimmer-
ing of that light which his imagination furnishes him
with. Where is the harm? Everyone is equally happy,
nay, infinitely more. That obstinacy proceeding from
compulsion ceases as soon as that compulsion ceases;
and from turbulent sectaries in Europe they become
here peaceable citizens.

'Tis incredible to what a pitch this indulgence is carried; and 'tis equally surprising how beneficial it has
proved; a happy system of policy, the only one adapted
to replenish an empty continent as well as to tranquillize
the old one. Hence these new modes of government,
which have greatly relieved mankind; and this is the
light which has rendered the era of the Reformation so
remarkable. Like all other human schemes, it was at first
rude, gross, and unpolished. The movements of its new
parts caused a degree of friction which time has since
worn away. Enthusiasm, the child of that era, was better adapted to navigation and discoveries than the old
superstition. Here it led the first settlers, and inspired
them with that courage and constancy which their first
labours required. And if since it has not covered the
earth with sumptuous temples, large monasteries, it has
replenished it with infinite habitations, a numerous people. It has opened for Man a field of industry which the
world wanted much; and now that the great difficulties

are removed, that great principle of action is not so much wanted, 'tis greatly diminished; and in some parts 'tis no more.

It has been succeeded by that spirit of toleration, by that liberal principle which generously allows to others what each wants for himself: a perfect freedom of thought, a latitude of opinion perfectly harmless as to government, which becomes a source of happiness to each individual, to each family, to each district. No other motive, no other system could possibly have replenished the shores of this continent with so many people, and in so short a time. 'Tis true, very opposite motives have led other people to other discoveries. But observe the progress, mark the consequence. They have pulled down, they have destroyed. But have they flourished like these, have they replenished that immense vacuum they caused? No, they barbarously converted fruitful countries into deserts, and a great part of those deserts exhibit to view nothing but the ruins made by the discoverers.

Here not only every community, but every individual worships God as he thinks it most agreeable to Him. Each individual is even allowed, not by virtue of any laws, but by the liberal spirit of the government, to differ from and controvert any of the religious opinions which are here received. This is an amazing indulgence, which, being granted to all, does not in the least disturb the society, but rather serves to unite it even in the most minute of its subdivisions. This is a problem which a great many people in Europe could not comprehend, prejudiced as they are by the ancient manners and customs of the society in which they live.

For instance, a man born of Baptist parents will live and profess the tenets of this sect without ever studying either their propriety or impropriety, and without aiming at any superior refinement. He may for a number of years read and ponder over his Bible, and find the precepts of his sects perfectly agreeable to those particular passages on which they are founded, when a fit of sickness, perhaps a gloomy mood, a fit of idleness, a sudden volition of the mind will lead him to the study of some particular passages, intended, perhaps, to confute some particular doctrines advanced by some ministers whom he had accidentally heard. From this new study he fancies that he has discovered some lights to which his dimmed eyes had hitherto been insensible. This fills him with an idea of perfection to which he immediately wants to direct his steps. Unawed by the decrees of any pontiffs, by inquisitorial timocracy, he boldly follows the new path which he has just found. His conscience, uniting often with his mind, renders the resolution sacred; he cannot deviate; he must begin the new career. Proud of the discovery, he will perhaps promulgate it abroad; he will explain this or that text as he has lately conceived its meaning to be.

He reproaches himself for having so long remained in ignorance, and from that day commences a sort of controversy. But as controversy always implies zeal and ardour, he will feel that zeal and ardour; and the same person who before had been but a passive Christian, following in simplicity and well-meant honesty the precepts he has received in his education, now suddenly enlightened, is surprised at the wonderful change which he, perhaps for want of knowing any other cause, attributes to the particular influence of heaven. This is enough to sanctify his new doctrine, and to justify the steps he takes to promulgate it among his neighbours. They are no politicians; a perfect peace prevails throughout their country. What more innocent subject of conversation can they have? The least opposition— and you may be sure he will meet with abundance— proclaims him a separatist, and perhaps a preacher, if he has abilities enough to persuade others to think as he does. Be not afraid of tumult, sedition, and broils; this is only a simple, harmless schism which will rather amuse than convulse society. Here opens that ancient field once so pregnant with the most poisonous weeds, but now in this tolerating age producing only harmless ones. Here is room for the expansion of a variety of passions mixing themselves with this new religious zeal, but these passions have no bad influence. The great and immense room in which they expand themselves prevents them from producing those evil consequences which opposition and contracted limits formerly occasioned. This is the only philosophical remedy that could possibly have been found to stop that rancour; that malevolence which formerly attended this sort of new system; everyone being indulged with the liberty of systematizing, modifying, and promulgating his opinions. These sorts of innovations have lost all merit; merit which consisted principally in the pleasure of opposition; and was swelled by contradiction.

I remember an instance of this kind which happened not long since in the county of ——, in the person of a friend. He had been bred a Presbyterian. For many years he followed *bona fide* the precepts of this sect, and thought, like all the rest of the congregation, that their mode of worship was the purest and the most acceptable to God. Thus he lived on to the age of forty-seven when he chanced to have a grandson born. His daughter-in-law made some objections to his being baptized. Not that her scruples were founded on any professional abhorrence to this ceremony; but her parents having been Baptists she derived from them some recollection that they had not undergone that ceremony until the age of adult. She recollected, likewise, that she had never been carried to the baptismal font, nor ever been immersed. She was, besides, secretly flattered with the pleasure of proposing a novelty to a family which was Presbyterian. She therefore pretended scruples of conscience.

The husband, young, inexperienced, and tender, laid before his father these difficulties and affectionately mentioned his wife's religious doubts. The well-meaning man struggled against this innovation, which he thought unchristian, and made use of all the arguments generally mustered in support of infant baptism. She replied, and recollecting some of the ancient rudiments of her education, sternly opposed from Scripture this trifling, useless ceremony, which can confer benefit only on those who receive it when of a lawful age and, therefore, capable of knowing the importance of the covenant into which they were entering. Paternal affection overcame religious obstinacy; the old man consented and returned home. Several of the passages his daughter-in-law had quoted returned to his mind; he resolved to study the matter with more carefulness and attention. An inward feeling seems to arise in his breast; imperceptible doubts stagger the validity of his ancient principles. He reads his Bible with redoubled attention; he finds authorities against infant baptism which he had hitherto overlooked; he suddenly awakes to a new set of principles with regard to this religious ceremony; he quits the congregation to which he had hitherto belonged, and attaches himself to that of the

Baptists, not without entering into many controversies with several of his friends and fellow-Presbyterians.

He thinks that he overcame them, and this essay gives him a taste for controversy, a strange taste for a man who hitherto had been acquainted with nothing but the cultivation of his farm. But he does not stop there; he pursues his new studies with unremitted attention. He reads the Bible, now no longer with that spirit of general confidence he was wont. He finds himself suddenly initiated into a vast field, full of intricate scenes. New doubts, new perplexities arise, which he often communicated to me. The new society in which he had enrolled himself was proud of its conquests. He conforms to all its rules, and at last receives the benefits of its immersion in a very cold season of the year, on which he had particularly fixed to enhance his merit. Thus he lived on for two years, a zealous and warm proselyte and the same good man he was before. All the difference I observed in him was that on a Sunday, instead of going east to his former place of worship he travelled west to the new meeting; and surely no change of religious sentiments could be attended with more trifling circumstances.

But behold the restless state of the human mind and the instability of what we vainly call its principles. In the course of his new studies, he discovers contradictions and absurdities among his new brethren. He remonstrated and argued often on these topics with the elders of the congregation. He entered so deeply into this new controversy that he began to neglect his rural business. The pleasure arising from finding out new lights and communicating them to others is often an irresistible one. He endeavoured to divide the new flock to which he had lately attached himself. The dispute grew warmer, and the opponents, according to custom, more obstinate.

One day he invited the elders and deacons of this society to dine with him, and he pressed me to be of the party. He secretly wanted me as favourable evidence in his behalf, but, alas! I was far from wishing to become a witness in a cause in which I understood nothing. I attended, firmly persuaded to remain in perfect silence, and simply to hear this religious altercation. The fate of this controversy, notwithstanding his good cheer, terminated, as most of this kind always do, in recrimination. Each party always retires as fully convinced of the rectitude of its principles, and often more so than before. The part I was obliged to act was for a while both difficult and disagreeable: each party, full of the irrefragability of its arguments, glowing with conscious rectitude, seemed to address me with peculiar complacency and to demand my approbation. But, unwilling to displease, and indeed incapable of passing a definite sentence, I tried to officiate as a mediator. I reminded them of the nature of the dispute, which, different from those founded on worldly concerns, required a great degree of calmness and serious attention. "You seek to enlighten yourselves. Each of you, good men alike, is come here with a lanthorn in your hands in order to compare your lights. This should be done with that caution and mildness which the nature of the dispute, your age, and your candour require. Great vehemence, improper agitation will only serve either to hide or to extinguish them. Consider me, if you please, as a spectator who came here more from the respect I have for you all than in consequence of any knowledge I have of the different points of doctrine which you are examining."

Eighteenth Century America.

They listened not to what I said; their zeal got the
better even of their common civility; they parted but
no longer as brethren; my utmost efforts were useless.
I freely, but in vain, showed them the vanity of all human disputes; attempted to lay before them the necessity of following that standard of rectitude which may
be felt and perceived by each individual exclusive of
all other forms of tenets. Then I attempted to reunite
them, at least in the bonds of their ancient friendship
by means of that communion often practised, by drinking out of the same bowl, by smoking together, that the
commixture and evaporation of smokes might become
an emblem of the banishing of all rancour and malice.
Nothing availed; the new convert separated himself
from the new congregation and set up for himself,
though there was not any other individual in the country that professed the same sentiments.

Next day he went forth in quest of proselytes. The
novelty of his doctrine pleased many who, perhaps indifferent to any particular modes of religion, from re-
moteness of settlement or from neglect, were glad to
have a person coming to their houses in order to rouse
them out of that pristine passiveness in which they
had so long lived. Encouraged by this new essay, he
preached whenever he could find people that would
listen to him. He was well received in many settlements
which were far removed from any public place of worship. This new revolution in his new religion necessarily introduced a new one in his temporal affairs. He
neglected the care of his farm. His negroes, overlook-
ing their duty, followed their master's example; the labours of the field were no longer prosecuted with the
same care and industry. The rest of the family bemoaned in secret the losses which ensued; the master

thought them but insignificant trifles when compared to the more spiritual advantages which he was every day gaining.

The first successes of this self-ordained priest were at first confined to single families. He happened to hear of a new settlement where the people, poor and isolated, had remained hitherto without the benefit of any public worship; they were not able to build any meeting [-house] and, much less, to pay the salary of a minister. All, as is customary, practised in their own houses whatever religious duties they had been taught in the countries from whence they had emigrated; many practised none and lived in that indifference which is so common here. Glad to have some part of the Gospel expounded to them, they received the first tidings of his offers with pleasure and invited him to come among them every Sabbath. He received it with peculiar complacency and attended them most faithfully. Never was there any minister so full of zeal and so ambitious to instruct his flock; and in the sequestered situation [in which] they were placed, they could not receive a greater blessing. They soon became the most faithful disciples; and instead of spending their Sundays at home in gloomy silence or unprofitable, untutored meditation, they had the pleasure of meeting together. They were constrained to clean themselves; the young people had an opportunity of seeing each other; and the institution of Sundays, considered in this temporary light only, is of the utmost consequence.

The relations he gave of his successes were astonishing; he attributed them to the peculiar interposition of God's divine providence. The profound ignorance of his new flock made them admire this new apostle, and they thought that he was superior to anything they ever remembered to have heard. All he told them was conceived in oriental expressions and clothed in vehement language. Soon afterwards, he came to pay me a visit. He glowed with conscious approbation; he related to me all his successes throughout their progressive increase. "How providentially does everything happen in this world," did he say; "how wonderfully linked are all the actions of men! What we vulgarly call chance has insensibly led me to the pitch of happiness I enjoy. For, can a man enjoy a greater share than in opening the eyes of benighted people, in carrying the torch of the Gospel in the gloom of the wilderness? What have I been doing these many years, uselessly employed in the servile labour of the field, an unprofitable occupation compared to that to which I now readily dedicate my time and all my abilities? I have already sown a plentiful crop of good seed; my care and vigilance shall not be wanting to bring it to maturity."

"Though these people are so far removed from any established congregation, don't you imagine that the minister of —— yet looks on them as a distant part of his flock, which, to be sure, he has hitherto most shamefully overlooked because they can pay no part of his salary? Like all other priests, he loves to lord it over. The intrusion of a lay-minister will kindle his clerical wrath; he will counteract all your good works as soon as he is informed of your proceedings."

"What if he does? I can confute all his arguments; nay, I can puzzle him in many texts of the Scripture. I fear him not, and by God's grace I will persevere."

"I am afraid of no mischief, but only that he will try to cover you with ridicule. You do not know perhaps as well as I do the effect of black clothes, and sacerdotal appearance; and though I am sure he knows as little as anybody, yet I am afraid that the very name of a minister will give him such ascendancy as will rob you of all your young successes."

"I fear him not. Don't you remember the sermon he preached the other day on ———. It was enough to ruin the fame of any minister. Ploughman as I am, I really blushed at it. It was as incoherent, senseless jargon as ever I had heard before. The singularity of the text more than any useful doctrine he could adduce from it was the reason for his expounding on it. I am sure he is as strange a genius as ever ascended the pulpit; he is bold, arrogant. He is sure of his salary, and it is what makes him so different a man; when he depended on the voluntary contributions of the people he was meek and lowly."

"I never liked him, for my part. 'Tis very true I join with you in thinking that the people have been deceived in their choice. I can see in him two species of men. When in the pulpit he attempts all the enthusiasm, the rapturous flight of the passionate devotee. He is obscure, hates to touch on morality, always deep in obscure passages. When descended from it, how different! He seems to leave on the cushion those apparent virtues with the few ornaments of that day; none more imperious, more disdainful."

" 'Tis all very true; I know it. An uncle of mine, a man of tender conscience and wanting an explanation of a certain text, went the other day to him for consultation and advice. How did he rebuke him! I am shocked when I think of it: 'Get thee gone, man of ignorance; take care of thy wife and children; mind thy plough and thy scythe.' Why then," I said, "did the congregation fix his salary? Why did they not leave him like all the rest of his brethren to the good will of the flock?

It was done contrary to my advice, I am sure. You see now what the consequence is; old rules should never be altered. The people have a propensity to be always the dupes and the victims of few; the people work and don't think much, but this will teach them better. I will prosecute my plan, however, and by God's grace I am in hopes to bring the people of —— to my way of thinking, which I am sure is the best. What business have they with ordained ministers and salaries and parsonages, etc.?"

For upwards of three years his successes were equal to his utmost wish. The minister of the county did not interfere. The people were poor. They contented themselves with throwing out now and then some few sarcasms which had no effect. Our apostle was rather proud to suffer some few mortifications for the love of God. His zeal was unabated. He was on the eve of being crowned with the summit of his hopes, that is of having a place of worship built for him, when a Baptist minister, travelling like many others to review and vivify the scattered parts of true believers throughout the different colonies, happened to be taken sick in the vicinage. On inquiring of the people concerning their religious state, their situation, etc., he was greatly astonished to hear that they were under the guidance of Mr. ——. The arrogance and presumption of the attempt shocked him greatly. A self-ordination, an intrusion in God's service, and, above all, a mutilated system of obscure doctrines assuming the title of Reformed Baptist, seemed to offer an insult to the church he belonged to, which he could not bear. Immediately on his recovery, he went to the spot; viewed with indignation the materials of that meeting [-house] which was intended to receive the erroneous doctrines of a man who had no right to promulgate them.

In a little time he eclipsed by his eloquence the fame of Mr. ——— and soon buried in oblivion the happy beginnings of our new apostle. He made [the people] sign a paper by which they agreed to receive a lawful Baptist minister to finish the meeting [-house] they had begun; whereby they would be made to forget the erroneous doctrines they had been taught, and receive these pure ones truly derived from the purity of the Gospel. In short, he so thoroughly obliterated all my neighbour's good works that no traces were left of them. He even caused [the people] to be guilty of ingratitude in persuading them to despise the many steps and fatigues Mr. ——— had taken for their sake. So powerful is the ascendancy of the clergy, even in a country where they have so little, and where by the genius of the people and the locality of settlements, it is more likely to diminish than to increase. They were so thoroughly reformed that Mr. ——— found himself without a hearer, without a disciple.

I thought this catastrophe a very fortunate one, as it might perhaps have a tendency to disgust him from these religious toils and persuade him to stay at. home. In the first rancour inspired by this disappointment, he exclaimed against all ministers as wolves in sheep's clothing, against their inutility, and the poor trifling foundation on which their order was established. He showed that our Saviour had never ordained any. In short he revenged himself, as he thought, very amply for his great mortification. Thus finished his successes abroad. Fortune cast him off from her wheel, and left him not the least pretension to begin any new attempts. He amply consoled himself by cherishing the idea that he was still in the right. He voluntarily—nay, cheerfully—excluded himself from all religious societies, and boasted that he was member of a church which was composed of no one but himself. This extraordinary privilege served him as a rich supplement for all his disappointed views. Thus, shepherd and flock, he still persists in maintaining that they are all wrong but himself.

I observed with pleasure that he seemed entirely to forget his former adventure. He returned to his rural occupations with as much activity as ever. His zeal seemed to cool apace, and that cacoëthes of preaching was almost extinguished, though he loved still to talk of his favourite doctrine, when, all of a sudden, he undertook to convert his family. For that purpose he began by degrees to expound to them the meaning of several texts; and regularly preached to them every Thursday, not forgetting to invite as many of his neighbours as he thought had any kind of religious awakenings. In his own house his paternal authority and influence were sure of procuring him hearers if not proselytes; and those that came behaved with a degree of attention which proceeded from respect, but which he took to be the consequence of persuasion. His wife was an Episcopalian, strongly attached to her worship. There was a danger lest this new schism should disturb the peace of the family, but as she possessed a great degree of prudence, she said little and condescended to listen to his long discourses with a patience proceeding from the love of peace. Sometimes I attended these religious meetings, but as I am no worshipper of strange gods, and perfectly satisfied with that form to which I have been bred, this new doctrine had no kind of effect on me. The whole of this new system appeared to be composed of many uninteresting parts enveloped in obscurity of diction, frivolousness of matter. You could perceive an eager desire of persuasion, but that is not always sufficient to convey to the heart those powers which can eradicate ancient prejudices, preconceived opinions. The keenest pencil is not adequate to such vague descriptions of an uninteresting subject; and of all subjects, you are sensible that this must be most disgustingly threadbare. I felt myself perfectly indifferent, and, considering the value I set on my time, often wished I had invented some excuse to have absented myself.

From the little success which attended his new apostolic endeavours among those over whom he had so much authority, there arose a surprising alteration in his mind. He seemed to lose that tenderness and affability for which he was before so conspicuous; he became gloomy, agitated at night. These symptoms were more alarming to his family than all his new religious systems. I often tried to reason him out of this strange vertigo; it was all in vain. At last I thought that vanity was mixed with, and had strongly cooperated in this perversion of his mind.

"What good, pray, do you imagine there can possibly arise, in the mind of those who hear you, from these inductions, from these learned interquotations which you have lavished on them with so much profusion? If you delight in preaching, why don't you explain to them some useful moral subject respecting the common duties of life? These elucidations of subjects which it imports everybody to know would strike and enlighten the tender minds of your children with much more efficacy and success. This would be clearing the path which they are to follow, pointing out the probable difficulties which they are to meet in their intercourse with the world. It is the fruit of the tree you should show them, that important fruit, the possession of which is far superior to any other knowledge. These learned discussions of yours have not this tendency; it is the fruit you should hold forth for the inspection of your hearers. What have we ploughmen to do with the occult property of the timber, with the nature of the caterpillars which feed on its leaves? These refinements are very ill-suited to the taste as well as to the understanding of the generality of mankind. When you instruct your negroes and hired men, do you, pray, waste your time in making dissertations on vegetations and all other occult ways and means by which Nature brings forth the fruits of the earth? No, you content yourself with showing them the theoretical, the useful, the practical, the most advantageous methods of ploughing, harrowing, sowing, dunging, etc. All your lectures on the former philosophical subject would bring you no crop. No harvest would redden in your fields, were you in company with your servants to employ your time in these vain and frivolous researches.

"The principal Christian duties are sublime though simple useful and absolutely necessary. They are unconnected with any forms; they belong equally to all sects. He that was baptized when young is bound by the same rules of justice, mercy, uprightness as he who was plunged at the age of twenty; you should, therefore, teach and enforce them to your hearers. These are the true points, the essential principles on which the purity, the tranquillity of our lives, and even of society, absolutely depend. A man has no need to be learned, to be religiously wise; the code of these laws is simple and fitted for the meanest understanding, adapted to the

Liberty of Worship.

lowest conception. From the enforcement of these moral duties which are the true links of society, a certain, sure, and profitable good will arise; from the former, nothing but cavils, contentions, separations, which, though they disturb not the society we live in, yet do not tend to its improvement as well as to its embellishment so essentially as you might perhaps imagine. Life is spent while we argue, and we remember at last, but sometimes too late, that though we have talked much and read much, yet we have forgotten to act. We are born to labour and not to study. Nature made the soil on which we are and which we till, and to induce us to do this, she surrounded us with wants; but Nature has formed no books. Country farmers, as we are, should, therefore, shun them as the disturbers more than the enlighteners of our minds. Let us peaceably, meekly discharge towards each other those duties which are taught us in the decalogue. Let us with diligence improve this new soil we inhabit; let us, to the best of our power, instruct our children to follow the same simple path; let us teach them by example that sobriety and industry without which they cannot flourish; let us provide for them as our circumstances will permit. This is all we have to do in this world to whatever meeting we may belong; these are the duties of all, and which all must invariably follow if we could wish to be good subjects and good Christians.

"I am, you know, neither preacher nor teacher, yet I am sensible that it requires but very slender abilities to compose sermons to please the ear and to amuse the imagination. But what good would they cause? Some thousands are delivered every year in this province, yet do we see that mankind grows more sober, less contentious? No, because they were intended to promulgate curious but vain theological points which are absolutely unnecessary; because most of our sects think that discourses altogether moral are not popular. Strange perversion! The pulpit of each meeting should be the censor of the neighbourhood and not the promulgator of high controversial lights of which mankind knows nothing, and fit only to amuse idle people in their leisure hours. This is the reason, let me tell you, why so great a part of our inhabitants remain untaught, unacquainted with the primary duties of life. The ministers, instead of clearing up, widening the ancient, useful path pointed out in our Bible, lead their flocks through new and unexplored ways where they are often bewildered and lost; vain theory calculated often to feed the vanity of the teacher more than to instruct the hearers. They should be urged to the practice of moral and, therefore, useful actions. This is all that the Law and the Prophets can teach or require."

"Well, sir, as proof of what you have advanced as a specimen of your ideas, as a sketch of the method you'd pursue, were you in the ministry, I should be very glad [if] you'd compose a sermon, and let it be delivered to the same company which comes to my house. I am still willing to learn and to improve, though I shall not attempt at present to refute you in many reprehensible points you have advanced. All I have to say to Man in my vindication is that I have no sinister views; I mean well. If Man blames me, God, the searcher of hearts, will, I am sure, forgive me."

I may perhaps surprise you when I tell you that I undertook the task he proposed to me. I saw no impropriety in it, and I flattered myself that the mortification which his vanity might inwardly feel would have a greater effect and a stronger tendency to silence him than all the arguments I could possibly make use of. Not that I thought myself master of greater abilities, but I depended on the subject I intended to treat, which being adapted to the comprehension of all, would necessarily become more entertaining and useful.

Agreeable to my promise, I sketched out a few thoughts on that beautiful passage of the Lord's prayer: "and forgive us our trespasses etc." I employed neither study nor learning, yet it had the desired effect. Either my performance appeared to him much superior to his own, or else the keen and irresistible puncture of truth struck him so deep, that he gradually returned to the practice of his former social duties. He preached less often; his former gloom disappeared; he reassumed his former cheerfulness; and although he never would reunite himself to any sect of Christians, he entirely left off teaching and seeking for proselytes. He reacquired the same tranquillity of mind for which he had been so conspicuous. Like a storm which for a while obscures the air and disturbs the atmosphere, when the clouds vanish, the sun shines forth with its wonted lustre.

THE ENGLISH AND THE
FRENCH BEFORE THE
REVOLUTION*

HAVE you never observed what a happy people these latter [the Canadians] were before
their conquest? Notwithstanding the boast of
newspapers, no society of men could exhibit greater
simplicity, more honesty, happier manners, less liti-
giousness; nowhere could you perceive more peace and
tranquillity. Before the last war the character of the Canadians was altogether original and singular: they were
equally removed from the brutality of a savage and the
useless improvements of more polished societies; they
were as different from the natives as from their own
countrymen; they were extremely temperate, happily
ignorant; they possessed a peculiar degree of boldness,
activity, and courage which have led them to the re-
motest parts of the continent. England has found them
the best of subjects. If the influence of religion was
more visible here than in any other of the English
colonies, its influence was salutary; it had here an effect
which one would wish to see everywhere else. For what
else do we expect to gain by the precepts of religion but
less ferocious manners and a more upright conduct?
Badly governed as they were, 'tis surprising to observe
how prosperous and happy they were. They were in a
state of perfect subordination; their government per-

* This essay was in the original a part of the chapter published
earlier in this book under the title, "The Snow Storm as It Affects the
American Farmer." Its title has been supplied by the editors.

172

The English and the French.

vaded everything, yet could not change their opinions. They were as free as men ought to be without contest about freedom. They were bold without being tumultuous; they were active without being restless; they were obedient without slavishness; they were truly a new people respectable for their customs, manners, and habits. To this day the Indians love the name of Canadian; they look upon them to be much more their compatriots than they do the English. Sequestered seven months from the sea by snows and ice, they plunged into the immensity of this continent. Everywhere they lived and associated freely with the natives. Either they more easily imbibed their manners; or else their own were more nearly similar to those of these aborigines; or else they were more punctual in their dealings, less haughty than their neighbours. The struggles of this colony whilst in its infant state are astonishing to read. More than a dozen of times you see the cradle overset, and the infant ready to be devoured by its enemies; and as many times you see it rising superior to the danger.

Had France opened towards it the more philosophic eyes of the year 1776, you'd have seen a nation of Franks rising on Canadian snows, which would have been able to have settled and possessed Acadia, Louisburg, Labrador, the shores of the interior lakes, those huge seas. France overlooked it until it was too late. The very struggle they made during the last war shows what they could have done had they been established on a broader bottom. Now 'tis no longer the same country: the English manners are becoming more and more prevailing; in a few generations they will be no longer Canadians, but a mixed breed like the rest of the English colonies. Their very women were the handsomest

173

on the continent, as is proved by upwards of twenty English officers getting wives at Montreal soon after the conquest. Had they been slaves before, this change would have improved them, but they perhaps were happier than the citizens of Boston, perpetually brawling about liberty without knowing what it was. They were equally secured in the possession of their lands. They loved, though at a distance, the name of a monarch who seldom thought about them. They were united; they were strangers to factions and murmurs and to those evils which disturb society; they were healthy, hardy, subject to no diseases besides old age. Ignorant, they envied not the lot of their more learned, more gaudy neighbours. They ploughed, they fished, they hunted, they discovered new nations. They formed new alliances with the most barbarous nations. They did not spring from felons and banditti; they drew their origin from a purer source, and rather improved their breed by the locality of the new climate under which they lived.

Here they multiplied, unknown to France and to Europe until the demon of politics inspired William Pitt with the idea of continental conquests, exclusive fisheries, exclusive fur trade, a plenum of glory which has so much astonished the world. This very aggrandizement may pave the way to future revolutions. For everything is perpetually revolving; the nearer a state arrives to maturity, the nearer its decline. The very laurel leaves with which William Pitt encircled his sovereign's brow, grew on a soil which may produce shoots of a very different nature, and may exhibit an instance of colonies more philosophically governed indeed, but not the less ambitious. What did the Canadians possess that could inflame the cupidity of the richest people on

The English and the French.

earth? What mines did they work that could make them so eager to enjoy them? These hardy people possessed but a few laborious fisheries; they gathered but a few thousand packs of beavers collected at an expense of fatigues and travels which no European can easily imagine; some wheat, some flour, in which their other provinces abounded; these were all their wealth, which was as limited as their wants. But Massachusetts, New York, Virginia, anxious for dominion, like all other societies, desirous to push their boundaries further, found that the limits of Canada obstructed them. The greatest extent of that colony was supposed by the English to lie towards Labrador and Lake Temiscaming, where no one can live. These colonies clamoured high; they began to talk of the encroachments of their neighbours. (Limitrophe nations are never without such quarrels.) And what were these encroachments, after all, when divested of newspapers' falsehood and misrepresentations?

The hunters and traders of the English colonies happened to meet those of Canada roaming like themselves through these boundless wilds. "How come you here, you rogue of a Frenchman?" "By means of this canoe which has brought me from Montreal, a few miles of land-carriage excepted; and pray how come you here also, you drunken Englishman?" "By means of my legs which have enabled me to climb over the mountains of Allegheny, and I have a better right to come here by land than you have to come here by water; and to convince you of it I'll complain to Major Washington." "You complain and I, at my return home, I will inform our governor, Mr. Duquesne." Sure enough, each told his story. Secretaries went to writing; from writing others went to arms, to war.

Eighteenth Century America.

"Pray, Mr. Englishman, don't you raise at home abundance of everything: rice, indigo, tobacco, pitch, tar, etc.? Don't you trade with all the world, the year round? Don't you possess fifteen hundred miles of sea-coasts? We that are deprived of all these advantages, who live under a hard sky and till a hard soil,—why would not you give us leave to hunt and to travel about just to keep us out of idleness? For, besides that, we have not much to trade with; we are locked up seven months in the year from any communication with the sea."

"Hunt and welcome towards Labrador, Temiscaming."

"What, in that country! Why, there are neither beasts nor birds, and if we even went that way a little too far, the Round-heads would immediately go to Hudson's Bay and complain there that they have seen Frenchmen in their wild territories."

"That is nothing to me. This river, this soil belongs to our people by virtue of the words of Charles the Second, who says that we may go even to the South Seas, if any such there be."

"To the South Seas? I who am a greater traveller than you have never seen any such. All I can tell you is that if I catch you here next year we shall see who is the strongest."

"Very well, neighbour."

The ensuing year, sure enough, Major Washington comes and very civilly kills Captain Jumonville, though clad under the sanction of a flag.* Each party accuses

---

* The incident referred to relates to a skirmish on the Virginia frontier just prior to the outbreak of the French and Indian War. The French had built Fort Duquesne on the present site of Pittsburgh. The French commander sent Ensign de Jumonville with a small party along

The English and the French.

the other of perfidy; God knows who is to blame. But behold the effects of destiny and one of the freaks of fortune. This very Major Washington, the murderer of Captain Jumonville, is the idol of the French. From the banks of the Ohio, in a little stockade, behold him there as a major in 1754, and in 1776 behold him again a generalissimo, the friend and the ally of France. Oh, Virtue! Oh Humanity! and thou, oh Justice! Wert thou painted to us as vain chimeras only or as real objects? Individuals may and must be virtuous; great ministers and rulers may commit crimes without reproach or remorse. From the ashes of Jumonville a Frenchman sees, I suppose, with pleasure the shrub of independence growing up, perhaps to a tall tree, perhaps to remain a bush until some more distant period. In that case a Frenchman could not have died a more useful death for the benefit of his country; his *Manes* are now rewarded by the very hands which dispatched him. Strange concatenation of events! Unfathomable system of things! We know neither causes nor effects, neither beginning nor ending. Success in the conclusion always eclipses the infamy, the perfidy of beginnings.

the headwaters of the Monongahela to the crest of the Allegheny mountains with orders to warn any British he might meet off the territory west of the mountains, such land being claimed by France. Young Major Washington with a small force was ordered into the region by Governor Dinwiddie of Virginia to uphold the English claim to the region. His scouts discovered the camp of Jumonville, and Washington crept up to surprise the French. He says in his journal: "We were advanced pretty near to them as we thought when they discovered us; whereupon I ordered my company to fire. We killed Mr. de Jumonville, the commander of that party with nine others; we wounded one and made Twenty-one prisoners. . . . The *Indians* scalped the Dead, and took most of their arms, after which we marched with the Prisoners and the Guard to the *Indian* Camp, where again I held a Council with the *Half-King*."

THE MAN OF SORROWS*

AMONG this infinite variety and combination of evil equally felt by both parties, some, perhaps, I may select more visible, more affecting [and], therefore, more within my reach. What is wanting in the propriety of the following account will be supplied by the truth of the facts it contains. At peculiar times I cannot resist the force of some thrilling vibrations which suddenly invade my soul when I contemplate some great distress on either side. No country can exhibit more affecting ones than these afflicted provinces. Could I have ever thought that a people of cultivators, who knew nothing but their ploughs and the management of their rural economies, should be found to possess, like the more ancient nations of Europe, the embryos of these propensities which now stain our society? Like a great river, the agitated waves of [which] are now devastating those shores which before they gently surrounded and fertilized, great revolutions in government necessarily lead to an alteration in the manners of the people. The rage of civil discord hath advanced among us with an astonishing rapidity. Every opinion is changed; every prejudice is subverted; every ancient principle is annihilated; every mode of organization, which linked us before as men and as citizens, is now altered. New ones are introduced, and who can tell whether we shall be the gainers by the exchange? You

* This is the original version of an essay which Crèvecœur later adapted into French under the title, "Pensées sur la Guerre Civile, Histoire de Joseph Wilson." A portion of the long introduction has been omitted.

178

The Man of Sorrows.

know from history the consequence of such wars. In every country it has been a field pregnant with the most poisonous weeds, with recriminations, hatred, rapidly swelling to a higher and higher degree of malice and implacability. How many have I seen which it has converted into beasts of prey, often destroying more from a principle of ferocity than from notions of gain! Too many of these vindictive friends on both sides have stained the cause they have espoused.

But why should I wonder at this political phenomenon? Men are the same in all ages and in all countries. A few prejudices and customs excepted, the same passions lurk in our hearts at all times. When, from whatever motives, the laws are no longer respected; when the mechanism of subordination ceases, and all the social bonds are loosened, the same effects will follow. This is now the case with us: the son is armed against the father, the brother against the brother, family against family; the nearer the connection, the more bitter the resentment, the more violent the rage of opposition. What is it then that renders this revolution so remarkable in my eyes? What is it that makes me view some of its scenes with such heart-felt regret? The reason is that before this war we were a regular, sober, religious people, urged neither by want nor impelled by any very great distress.

Oh, that I had finished my career ere our happiness vanished, or that the time of my existence had been postponed to a future and more tranquil period! In an overgrown society similar effects would not raise within me the same degree of astonishment. There the least subversion either of law or trade or government must cause thousands of people to want bread, and those people are ready for the sake of subsistence to commit all the outrages which the spirit of the times or the will of the leaders may dictate or inspire. However, I must remark here that those scenes which exhibit the greatest degree of severity or cruelty are not the work of every day. Forbid it, that human nature should be so universally debased! Nor do they flow from the reflected policy of the times so much as they do from that private rancour which this sort of war inspires, from that spontaneous resentment and irascibility of individuals upon particular occasions. Men in a state of civil war are no longer the same. They cease to view the former objects through the same medium as before. The most unjust thoughts, the most tyrannical actions, the most perverse measures, which would have covered them before with infamy or would have made them dread the omnipotence of heaven, are no longer called by these ancient names; the sophistry of each party calls them policy, justice, self-defence.

Who can live in the midst of this grand overthrow, who can for so many years be a witness to the pangs of this convulsed society without feeling a compunction which must wrench the heart of every good citizen, without wishing to describe some remarkable scenes, if it were only to sympathize with the unfortunate mourners?

Our rulers are very sensible of the impolicy and inexpediency of these severe deeds, but their authority and influence can hardly reach everywhere. I have heard many of them say: "If we are finally victorious, cruelty tarnishes the glory of our achievements; if conquered, we would shudder at the precedent we have given and dread the hour of retaliation." The experience of all revolutions, the uncertainty of all human events must strangely teach them that necessary cau-

The Man of Sorrows.

tion. Alas, let the attempts be ever so wrong or ever so commendable; let war be ever so just or so unjust; the world places its applause only in the success of the enterprise. Success alone is the reward which in the eyes of men glitters and shines; 'tis the symbol of true merit. This is a melancholy proof of the strange fatality which seems to preside over all the actions of men. But I do not pretend to hold this great scale even; I am no politician. I leave with submissive humility the issue of this dispute in the hands of Him who holds the balance of the universe. This problem will be solved like so many others by the strongest. Yet I well know that in great as well as in small undertakings nothing is acquired by too precipitate ardour, which, instead of hastening, often leads into incoherent measures. There is in all schemes a necessary development of effects, a chain of steps which gradually shows maturity at a distance. Too great a velocity of action, running too fast towards fruition without waiting for the accomplishing moment, may lead into erroneous paths. A bold confidence may be the source of arduous deeds, yet it cannot command the event. No one can bring success from the wheel of fortune before it has undergone a certain number of revolutions.

The situation of these people who live on our frontiers is truly deplorable. No imagination can conceive, no tongue can describe their calamities and their dangers. The echoes of their woods repeat no longer the blows of the axe, the crash of the falling trees, the cheerful songs of the ploughman. These happy sounds are changed into mournful accents, deep exclaims; howling of poor orphan children just escaped from the flames, of desolate widows bemoaning the fate of murdered or captivated husbands. Human society presents

181

Eighteenth Century America.

here nothing but tears and groans, and every species of calamity; the most innocent of our blood is daily shed. Some districts, more unfortunate still than the rest, are exposed to the fury of Indian excursions, as well as to the mischief of parties that are sent to protect them. So slender, so impermanent a protection only serves to increase their misfortunes. Their houses become little citadels, often defended and attacked, and, when taken, exhibit the most hideous scenes of blood and conflagrations. These cruel flames are reaching nearer and nearer; nothing can prevent or extinguish them,—no, not even the blood that is shed within their walls. Judge then what ferment, what state of irascibility the minds of people thus situated must be in throughout all these last-settled countries!

Some time ago the beautiful settlement of ——, upwards of a hundred years old, was utterly destroyed. It presented to the eyes a collection of all that the industry of the inhabitants and the fertility of soil could exhibit [which was] most pleasing, most enchanting. Their lands were terminated by the shores of a beautiful river; their houses were all elegantly built; their barns were the most spacious of any in that part of the country; the least wealthy inhabitant raised at least a thousand bushels of wheat a year. Their possessions were terminated by the steep ascent of a great chain of mountains, beyond which no improvements ever can extend. From their bosoms enemies came and laid everything waste. Many sober industrious people were killed, and all they had was destroyed.

Some parties of militia, which had been employed in protecting the contiguous settlements, on their return home were informed that some white people and Indians had, on their way to ——, lodged at a certain

The Man of Sorrows.

man's house, which was described to them. This discovery suddenly inflamed them with the most violent resentment and rage.* Full of the most vindictive sentiment they hastened thither. The man of the house was in his meadows making hay. They instantly surrounded him, and in the most opprobrious language upbraided him with the crime laid to his charge. He solemnly denied it. A strong altercation ensued. Some of the party were resolved to bayonet him instantly, as their friends had been bayoneted before. Their passions were too highly inflamed; they could not hear him with patience or give him an opportunity of justifying himself; they believed him guilty. Their unanimous wish seemed to be that he should confess the crime, a wish founded probably on some remains of ancient justice. He still denied it and appealed to heaven for the truth of his assertions. They disbelieved him, and in the madness of their rage they resolved to hang him by the toes and the thumbs, a punishment which, singular as it may appear, yet has been frequently made use of by the wretches of both parties.

Whilst in this painful suspension he attested his innocence with all the energy he was master of. By this time his wife, who had been informed of the tragical scene, came from her house, with tears gushing in

* In the French version Crèvecœur says: "The militia, assembled within a short time, covered so effectively the neighbouring establishment of Peenpack that Brant and his Indians were obliged to retire. They had left Anaquaga [Ouaquaga] on the eastern bank of the Susquchanna River. One of the detachments of this militia, while returning, was informed that two Indians and a white man had been seen going through the woods east of the Delaware River heading toward New York, entrusted doubtless with bringing there the news of the brilliant expedition which had just been completed; and that these Indians and their guide had lodged at the house of Joseph Wilson known since the beginning of the war as a Royalist."

183

streams, and with a countenance of terror. In the most supplicating posture she implored their mercy, but they rejected her request. They accused her of having participated also in her husband's abominable crime. She repeated her entreaties, and at last prevailed on them to relieve her husband. They took him down after a suspension of six minutes, which will appear a long interval to whoever considers it anatomically. The bitter cries of the poor woman, the solemn asseverations of her husband seemed for a few moments to lull the violence of their rage, as in a violent gale of wind Nature admits of some kind intermission which enables the seaman to bring his vessel to. But all of a sudden one of the company arose, more vindictive than the rest. He painted to them their conflagrated houses and barns, the murder of their relations and friends. The sudden recollection of these dreadful images wrought them up to a pitch of fury fiercer than before. Conscious as they were that he was the person who had harboured the destroyers of their country, they resolved finally to hang him by the neck.

Hard was this poor man's fate. He had been already suspended in a most excruciating situation for not having confessed what was required of him. Had he confessed the crime laid to his charge, he must have been hung according to the principle of self-preservation which filled the breasts of these people. What was he then to do? Behold here innocence pregnant with as much danger as guilt itself, a situation which is very common and is a characteristic of these times. You may be punished to-morrow for thoughts and sentiments for which you were highly commended the preceding day, and alternately. On hearing of his doom, he flung himself at the feet of the first man. He solemnly appealed to God, the searcher of hearts, for the truth of his assertions. He frankly owned that he was attached to the King's cause from ancient respect and by the force of custom; that he had no idea of any other government, but that at the same time he had never forcibly opposed the measures of the country; that his opinions had never gone beyond his house; that in peace and silence he had submitted to the will of heaven without ever intending to take part with either side; that he detested from the bottom of his heart this mode of war which desolated and ruined so many harmless and passive inhabitants who had committed no other crime than that of living on the frontiers. He earnestly begged and entreated them that they would give him an opportunity of proving his innocence: "Will none of you hear me with patience? I am no stranger, no unknown person; you well know that I am a home-staying man, laborious and peaceable. Would you destroy me on a hearsay? For the sake of that God which knows and sees and judges all men, permit me to have a judicial hearing."

The passive character of this man, though otherwise perfectly inoffensive, had long before been the cause of his having been suspected. Their hearts were hardened and their minds prepossessed; they refused his request and justified the sentence of death they had passed. They, however, promised him his life if he would confess who were those traitors that came to his house, and who guided them through the woods to ——. With a louder voice than usual the poor culprit denied his having the least knowledge whatever of these persons, but, seeing that it was all in vain, he peaceably submitted to his fate, and gave himself up to those who were preparing the fatal cord. It was soon tied round the limb of a tree to which they hanged him.

Eighteenth Century America.

As this execution was not the action of cool, deliberate justice, but the effects of mad revenge, it is no wonder that in the hurry of their operation they forgot to tie his arms and to cover his face. The struggles he made as soon as he was suspended; the agitations of his hands, instinctively trying to relieve him; the contortions of the face necessarily attending such a state presented a most dreadful spectacle, which in common executions are hid from the public's eyes. But so irresistible is the power of self-preservation, so high was their resentment, so great their consciousness of his being guilty that these dreadful images conveyed neither horror nor thoughts of mercy to the minds of these incensed people. Whilst they were thus feeding their passions, and whilst unmoved they stood gazing on their departing enemy, Nature was hastening his final dissolution, as evidently appeared by the trembling nerves, the quivering appearance of the limbs, the extension of the tongue. The shades of patibulary death began to spread on his face; the hands, no longer trying to relieve the body, hung loose on each side.

Fortunately at this instant some remains of humanity sprung up in the breasts of a few. They solicited that he might be taken down. It was agreed and done. They next threw cold water on him, and to the surprise of some and the mortification of others he showed some signs of life. He gradually recovered. The first dawn of his returning reason showed what were the objects which had engrossed his last thoughts. He most tenderly inquired for his wife. Poor woman! At a small distance she lay stretched on the ground, happily relieved from feeling the horrid pangs with which the preceding scene must have harrowed up her soul, by having fainted as soon as she saw the fatal cord fixed

186

round her husband's neck. The second part of his attention was attracted by the sight of his children who were crowded at the door of his house in astonishment, terror, and affright. His breast heaved high, and the sobs it contained could hardly find utterance. He shed no tears, for their source had almost been dried up along with those of life. Gracious God, hast Thou then intended that Man should bear so much evil, that Thou hast given him a heart capable of resisting such powerful sensations without breaking in twain?

Again he was commanded to confess the crime he was accused of, and again he solemnly denied it. They then consulted together, and, callous to the different impressions occasioned by so complicated a distress, unwilling to acquit him, though incapable of convicting him, they concluded him guilty and swore that he should die. Some in mercy repented that they had taken him down. Whilst they were employed in fixing on this last resolution, the poor unfortunate man was leaning against a tree. His wife, who had been brought back to life by the same means that had been used with him, sat near him on a log, her head reclined and hid in her hands, her hair dishevelled and loose. On hearing his second final doom, he tenderly and pathetically reproached them with making him pass through every stage of death so slowly, when malefactors have but one moment to suffer. "Why, then, won't you confess that you have harboured our enemies? We have full and sufficient proofs." "Why should I confess in the sight of God that which is not true? I am an innocent man. Aren't you afraid of God and His vengeance?" "God and His vengeance have overtaken you for harbouring the incendiaries of our country." "I have nothing but words to make use of. I repeat it again for the last time:

I am innocent of the accusation." "What say you, men, guilty or not guilty?" "Guilty he is and deserving of death." "Must I then die a second time? Had you left me hanging, now I should be no more. Oh, God, must I be hanged again? Thou knowest my innocence, lend, oh, lend me a miracle to prove it." He shed a flood of tears, and, looking once more toward his children and wife, who remained stupid and motionless, he approached those who were preparing to hang him.

"Stop a while," said the first man, " 'tis the will of these people that you should die and suffer that death which all the enemies of their country so justly deserve. Prepare yourself, therefore; you have ten minutes to make your peace with God." "If I must die, then God's will be done." And kneeling down close by his wife, who kneeled also, he pronounced the following prayer, the sentiments of which are faithfully transcribed, though, through want of memory, clothed in words somewhat different from the original ones: "Gracious God, in this hour of tribulation and of mind and bodily distress, I ask Thee forgiveness for the sins I have committed. Grant me that grace by which I may be enabled to support my fainting spirits, and to quit this world with the confidence of a Christian. Despise not the sighs of my heart, which though sometimes unmindful of Thee in its worldly hours, yet has never been guilty of any gross impiety. The patience with which I have borne my preceding trials, my innocence, my resignation, and Thy divine goodness make me hope that Thou wilt receive me into Thy kingdom. Thou, oh Lord, knowest without the assistance of words the sincerity of my sentiments; to Thee I appeal for the manifestation of my innocence, which unjust men want to rob me of. Receive the repentance of a minute as an atonement for years of sin; Thy incomprehensible mercy and justice, unknown to Man, can do it. Endow me with all the benefits of our Redeemer's cross, the great Pattern of all those who, like Him, untimely perish by the hands of violence. Allowed but ten minutes to live, I seize my last to recommend to Thy paternal goodness my wife and children. Wilt Thou, oh Master of Nature, condescend to be the protector of widows, the father of orphans? This is, thou knowest, the strongest chain which binds me to the earth, and makes the sacrifice of this day so bitter. As Thou hast promised pardon to all men, provided that they also pardon their enemies, I here before Thee cheerfully pardon all my persecutors and those by whose hands I am now going to be deprived of life. I pray that the future proofs of my innocence may call them to early repentance ere they appear before Thy awful tribunal. Forgive me my sins as I forgive the world, and now I go to Thee, the boundless fountain, the great ocean of all created things. Death is but the gateway towards Thee. Oh Lord, have mercy on me and receive my soul."

"You have prayed so well and so generously forgiven us that we must think at last that you are not so guilty as the majority of us had imagined. We will do you no further injury for the present, but it is our duty to send you to —— where, according to law, you may have a fair trial; and there let the law of the land hang you and welcome, if it is found that you deserve it. For my part, I'll wash my hands of you as soon as I have delivered you into safe custody. I wish we had not gone on so precipitately. What say you men?" "Aye, aye, let him go, but mark our words and see if the judges do not completely do what we have done."

With a feeble voice he thanked them and begged

a few minutes to speak to his wife, who with a kind of stupid insensibility and an unmoved countenance, had heard her husband's last sentence and even joined him in prayer. I have no words to describe her joy, for her joy was a mixture of frenzy, of fear, of laughter, of strange expressions. The transition had been too sudden; her nerves, rigidly strained by the preceding scene, were too soon relaxed on hearing the joyful news; it very nearly cost her the loss of her reason. They embraced each other with a tender and melancholy cheerfulness. She ran towards the house whilst he called his children. Poor little souls! They came as quickly as their different strengths permitted them. "What has been the matter, father? We have been crying for you and mother." "Kiss me, my dear little ones, your daddy thought he would see you no more, but God's Providence has spoken to the heart of these people." They all partook of this new and extraordinary banquet in proportion to their ages and understandings. This was a scene which Humanity herself would with peculiar complacence have delineated in all the pleasing hues of her celestial colours. It was indeed so powerfully energetic that it melted all the spectators into a sudden sensation of regret and tenderness, so singularly variable are the passions of men. The most dreadful and afflicting spectacle which the spirit of civil discord could possibly devise was metamorphosed into the most pleasing one which a good man could possibly wish to behold.

Oh, Virtue, thou, then, really existest! Thou, best gift of heaven, thou then secretly residest in the hearts of all men, always ready to repair every mischief and to dignify every action when not repelled by the force of superior vice or passion. [If] I had the pencil of true energy, of strong expression, I would dip it into their

The Man of Sorrows.

best colours; I would discard those which my scanty palette contains.

After a few hours' rest, they carried him to ——, where some time afterwards he had an impartial trial and was acquitted. No government, no set of men can ever make him amends for the injury he has received. Who can remunerate him for all his sufferings, for his patience, for his resignation? He lives, a singular instance of what the fury of civil wars can exhibit on this extensive stage of human affairs. How many other instances, if not similar, at least as tragical might be recorded from both sides of the medal! Alas, poor man, I pity thee. I call thee "poor man" though not acquainted with thy circumstances. I would be meant to conceive by that expression all that sympathy and compassion have of [the] most exquisitely tender and expressive. What a subject for a painter who delights to represent mournful events! What a field for a judge and a master of the passions! A man leaning against a tree, hardly recovered from the agonies of death, still visible in the livid hue and altered lineaments of his face, still weak and trembling, his mind agitated with the most tumultuous thoughts, wracked by the most anxious suspense, hearing his third and final doom. At a little distance his wife, sitting on a log, almost deprived of her reason. At a more considerable distance, his house, with all his children crowded at the door, restrained by amazement and fear from following their mother, each exhibiting strong expressions of curiosity and terror, agreeable to their different ages. I can conceive the peculiar nature of all these colourings, but where would the painter find the originals of these faces who, unmoved, could behold the different scenes of this awful drama?

THE WYOMING MASSACRE*

SOON after my return from this last excursion began the great contest between the mother-country and this. It spread among the lower class like an epidemic of the mind, which reached far and near, as you well know. It soon swallowed up every inferior contest; silenced every other dispute; and presented the people of Susquehanna with the pleasing hopes of their own never being decided by Great Britain. These solitary farmers, like all the rest of the inhabitants of this country, rapidly launched forth into all the intricate mazes of this grand quarrel, as their inclinations, prepossessions, and prejudices led them. [It was] a fatal era, which has since disseminated among them the most horrid poison; which has torn them with intestine divisions; and has brought on that languor, that inter-

* A preceding part of this narrative is concerned with two excursions made by Crèvecœur through the Susquehanna Valley. This portion of his story has been edited and published in the *Yale Review* for April, 1925.

In 1787, Thomas Jefferson wrote from Paris to M. François Soulès: "I am enclosing to you sheets on the subject of Wyoming. I have had a long conversation with M. Creve-cœur on them. He knows well that canton. He was in the neighborhood of the place when it was destroyed, saw great numbers of the refugees, aided them with his wagons, and had the story from their mouths. He committed notes to writing at the moment, which are now in Normandy, at his father's. He has written for them and they will be here in five or six days, when he promises to put them into my hands. He says there will be a great deal to alter in your narration, and that it must assume a different face, more favourable both to the British and Indians. His veracity may be relied on, and I told him I was sure your object was truth. . . ." *Works,* ed. II. A. Washington, II: 102. The title of this essay has been supplied by the editors.

nal weakness, that suspension of industry, and the total destruction of their noble beginning.

Many, however, there were who still wished for peace; who still respected the name of Englishman; and cherished the idea of ancient connection. These were principally settled in the upper towns; the inhabitants of the lower ones were strongly prepossessed with the modern opinions. These latter ill brooked that any-one who had come to settle under their patronage should prove their antagonists, and, knowing themselves to be the strongest party, were guilty of many persecutions,—a horrid policy. Every order was destroyed; the new harmony and good understanding which began to prevail among them were destroyed. Some of the inhabitants of the upper towns fell victims to this new zeal; gaols were erected on these peaceful shores where many sticklers for the old government were confined. But I am not going to lead you through the disgusting details of these scenes with which your papers have been filled, for it would be but a repetition of what has been done from one end of the continent to the other. This new ebullition of the mind was everywhere like one and the same cause; and therefore everywhere produced the same effects.

Many of those who found themselves stripped of their property took refuge among the Indians. Where else could they go? Many others, tired of that perpetual tumult in which the whole settlement was involved, voluntarily took the same course; and I am told that great numbers from the extended frontiers of the middle provinces have taken the same steps,—some reduced to despair, some fearing the incursions with which they were threatened. What a strange idea this joining with the savages seems to convey to the imagination; this uniting with a people which Nature has distinguished by so many national marks! Yet this is what the Europeans have often done through choice and inclination, whereas we never hear of any Indians becoming civilized Europeans. This uncommon emigration, however, has thrown among them a greater number of whites than ever has been known before. This will ere long give rise to a new set of people, but will not produce a new species,—so strong is the power of Indian education. Thus war, tyranny, religion mix nations with nations; dispeople one part of the earth to cause a new one to be inhabited.

It will be worthy of observation to see whether those who are now with the Indians will ever return and submit themselves to the yoke of European society; or whether they will carefully cherish their knowledge and industry and gather themselves on some fertile spot in the interior parts of the continent; or whether that easy, desultory life so peculiar to the Indians will attract their attention and destroy their ancient inclinations. I rather think that the latter will preponderate, for you cannot possibly conceive the singular charm, the indescribable propensity which Europeans are apt to conceive and imbibe in a very short time for this vagrant life; a life which we civilized people are apt to represent to ourselves as the most ignoble, the most irksome of any. Upon a nearer inspection 'tis far from being so disgusting. Innumerable instances might be produced of the effect which it has had not only on poor illiterate people, but on soldiers and other persons bred to the luxuries and ease of a European life. Remember the strong instance of the people taken at Oswego during the last war, who, though permitted to return home, chose to remain and become Indians. The daughters of these frontier people will necessarily marry with the young men of the nation in which they have taken refuge; they have now no other choice. At a certain age Nature points out the necessity of union; she cares very little about the colour. By the same reason and in consequence of the same cause the young Europeans will unite themselves to the squaws. 'Tis very probable, therefore, that fishing, hunting, and a little planting will become their principal occupations. The children that will spring from these new alliances will thoroughly imbibe the manners of the village, and perhaps speak no other language. You know what the power of education is: the Janissaries, though born of Frank parents, were by its impulse rendered the most enthusiastic enemies of the Christian name.

Some time after the departure of these people a few Indians came down under the sanction of a flag to demand their effects, representing that they had been so much disturbed in their huntings that they were not able to maintain so many of them; that, had they their cows and horses, they would give them land enough to raise their own bread. But instead of complying with this just request, in the hour of the utmost infatuation they seized these ambassadors, whipped them, and sent them away. Ignorant, as we suppose them to be, yet this treatment inflamed them to most bitter revenge, and awakened those unguided passions which are so dreadful among this haughty people. Notwithstanding this high insult, the nation sent a second and more numerous embassy than the first. Colonel Dyer, a member of Congress for the province of Connecticut, expostulated with them by letter, and pointed out the injustice and impolicy of their proceedings, but in vain. Though they should have been astonished at a step so new and extraordinary as this second embassy, yet they attempted to seize them. Two only were apprehended and confined; the rest made their escape.

A short time before this the Congress had ordered a body of four hundred men to be raised, in order to cover more effectually the frontiers of this long-extended settlement. The people readily enlisted, and this regiment was soon completed. But what was their surprise and alarm when it was ordered to join General Washington's headquarters! They then, but too late, began to emerge from that state of blindness in which they seemed to have been plunged. They began to fear lest their ill-judged conduct should bring down at last the vengeance of a much larger body of assailants than they could well repel. The absence of this regiment, composed of the flower of their youth, not only left them very much exposed but even seemed to invite the enemy. As they had foreseen it, it hastened the long-premeditated storm which had been gathering. The Europeans who had taken refuge among the natives united with them in the same scheme which had been anteriorly proposed, and set on foot by the commandant of Niagara; they were, therefore, joined by several English officers and soldiers. The whole body of these assailants seemed animated with the most vindictive passions, a sacrifice to which many innocent families as well as guilty ones were doomed to fall. As no bard has as yet appeared to sing in plaintive strains: "Mourn, Susquehanna! mourn thy hapless sons, thy defenceless farmers slaughtered on thy shores!" shall I be excused in following my feelings and in finishing the short ac-

Wyoming Massacre.

count of their final catastrophe as my untutored but
honest impulse directs?

> Oh Man! thou hast made the happy earth thy hell,
> Filled it with cursing cries and deep exclaims;
> If thou delight to view thy heinous deeds,
> Behold this pattern of thy butcheries.

The assailants formed a body of about eight hundred
men who received their arms from Niagara; the whites
under the conduct of Colonel Butler, the Indians under
that of Brant. After a fatiguing march, they all met at
some of the upper towns of the Susquehanna, and while
they were refreshing themselves and providing canoes
and every other necessary implement, parties were sent
out in different parts [of the country]. Some pene-
trated to the west branch and did infinite mischief; it
was easy to surprise defenceless, isolated families who
fell an easy prey to their enemies. Others approached
the New England settlements, where the ravages they
committed were not less dreadful. Many families were
locked up in their houses and consumed with all their
furniture. Dreadful scenes were transacted which I
know not how to retrace. This was, however, but the
prelude of the grand drama. A few weeks afterwards,
the whole settlement was alarmed with the news of the
main body coming down the river. Many immediately
embarked and retired into the more interior parts of
Pennsylvania; the rest immediately retired with their
wives and children into the stockade they had erected
there some time before.

Meanwhile the enemy landed at Lackawanna or
Kingston, the very place where the stockade was
erected. Orders were immediately issued by their com-
manders for the rest of the militia to resort to them.

Some of the most contiguous readily obeyed; distance prevented others. Colonel Butler, seeing they had abandoned their dwellings, proposed to them to surrender and quit the country in a limited time. It was refused by the New England people, who resolved to march out and meet them in the open fields. Their number consisted of five hundred and eighty-two. They found the enemy advantageously situated, but much weaker in numbers, as they thought, than had been reported. This encouraged them; they boldly advanced; and the Indians as sagaciously retreated. Thus they were led on to the fatal spot where all at once they found themselves surrounded. Here some of the New England leaders abandoned them to their evil destiny. Surprised as they were at this bad omen, they still kept their ground and vigorously defended themselves until the Indians, sure of their prey, worked up by the appearance of success to that degree of frenzy which they call courage, dropped their guns and rushed on them with the tomahawk and the spear. The cruel treatment they expected to receive from the wrathful Indians and offended countrymen animated them for a while. They received this first onset with the most undaunted courage, but, the enemy falling upon them with a redoubled fury and on all sides, they broke and immediately looked for safety in flight.

Part of them plunged themselves into the river with the hopes of reaching across, and on this element a new scene was exhibited not less terrible than that which had preceded it. The enemy, flushed with the intoxication of success and victory, pursued them with the most astonishing celerity, and, being naked, had very great advantage over a people encumbered with clothes. This, united with their superiority in the art of swimming,

enabled them to overtake most of these unfortunate
fugitives, who perished in the river pierced with the
lances of the Indians. Thirty-three were so happy as to
reach the opposite shores, and for a long time afterwards the carcasses of their companions, become offensive, floated and infested the banks of the Susquehanna
as low as Shamokin. The other party, who had taken
their flight towards their forts, were all either taken or
killed. It is said that those who were then made prisoners were tied to small trees and burnt the evening of the
same day.

The body of the aged people, the women and children who were enclosed in the stockade, distinctly could
hear and see this dreadful onset, the last scene of which
had been transacted close to the very gates. What a
situation these unfortunate people were in! Each wife,
each father, each mother could easily distinguish each
husband and son as they fell. But in so great, so universal a calamity, when each expected to meet the same
fate, perhaps they did not feel so keenly for the deplorable end of their friends and relations. Of what
powerful materials must the human heart be composed,
which could hold together at so awful a crisis! This
bloody scene was no sooner over than a new one arose
of a very similar nature. They had scarcely finished
scalping the numerous victims which lay on the ground
when these fierce conquerors demanded the immediate
entrance to the fort. It was submissively granted. Above
a hundred of them, decorated with all the dreadful ornaments of plumes and colour of war, with fierce and
animated eyes, presented themselves and rushed with
impetuosity into the middle of the area, armed with
tomahawks made of brass with an edge of steel. Tears
relieved some; involuntary cries disburdened the op-

pression of others; a general shriek among the women was immediately heard all around.

What a spectacle this would have exhibited to the eyes of humanity: hundreds of women and children, now widows and orphans, in the most humble attitude, with pale, dejected countenances, sitting on the few bundles they had brought with them; keeping their little unconscious children as close to them as possible; hiding by a mechanical instinct the babies of their breasts; numbers of aged fathers oppressed with the unutterable sorrow; all pale, all trembling, and sinking under the deepest consternation were looking towards the door—that door through which so many of their friends had just passed, alas! never more to return. Everyone at this awful moment measured his future punishment by the degree of revenge which he supposed to animate the breast of his enemy. The self-accusing consciences of some painted to them each approaching minute as replete with the most terrible fate. Many there were who, recollecting how in the hour of oppression they had insulted their countrymen and the natives, bitterly wept with remorse; others were animated with the fiercest rage. What a scene an eminent painter might have copied from that striking exhibition, if it had been a place where a painter could have calmly sat with the palette in his hands! How easily he might have gathered the strongest expressions of sorrow, consternation, despondency, and despair, by taking from each countenance some strong feature of affright, of terror, and dismay, as it appeared delineated on each face. In how many different modes these passions must have painted themselves according as each individual's temper, ardent or phlegmatic habit, hurried or retarded the circulation of the blood, lengthened or contracted the muscles of his physiognomy.

But now a scene of unexpected humanity ensues, which I hasten to describe, because it must be pleasing to peruse and must greatly astonish you, acquainted as you are with the motives of revenge which filled the breasts of these people, as well as with their modes of carrying on war. The preceding part of this narration seems necessarily leading to the horrors of the utmost retaliation. Happily these fierce people, satisfied with the death of those who had opposed them in arms, treated the defenceless ones, the women and children, with a degree of humanity almost hitherto unparalleled.

In the meanwhile the loud and repeated war-shouts began to be re-echoed from all parts; the flames of conflagrated houses and barns soon announced to the other little towns the certainty of their country's defeat; these were the first marks of the enemies' triumph. A general devastation ensued, but not such as we read of in the Old Testament where we find men, women, children, and cattle equally devoted to the same blind rage. All the stock, horses, sheep, etc., that could be gathered in the space of a week, were driven to the Indian towns by a party which was detached on purpose. The other little stockades, hearing of the surrender of their capital, opened their gates and submitted to the conquerors. They were all immediately ordered to paint their faces with red, this being the symbol established then, which was to preserve peace and tranquillity while the two parties were mingled together.

Thus perished in one fatal day most of the buildings, improvements, mills, bridges, etc., which had been erected there with so much cost and industry. Thus were dissolved the foundations of a settlement begun

Eighteenth Century America.

at such a distance from the metropolis, disputed by a potent province; the beginning of which had been stained with blood shed in their primitive altercations. Thus the ill-judged policy of these ignorant people and the general calamities of the times overtook them and extirpated them even out of that wilderness which they had come twelve years before to possess and embellish. Thus the grand contest entered into by these colonies with the mother-country has spread everywhere, even from the sea-shores to the last cottages of the frontiers. This most diffusive calamity, on this fatal spot in particular, has despoiled of their goods, chattels, and lands, upwards of forty-five hundred souls, among whom not a third part was ever guilty of any national crime. Yet they suffered every extent of punishment as if they had participated in the political iniquity which was attributed to the leaders of this unfortunate settlement. This is always the greatest misfortune attending war. What had poor industrious women done? What crime had their numerous and innocent children committed?

> Where are heaven's holiness and mercy fled?
> Laughs heaven at once at virtue and at Man?
> If not, why that discouraged, this destroyed?

Many accused the King with having offered a reward for the scalps of poor inoffensive farmers. Many were seized with violent fevers, attended with the most frantic rage, and died like maniacs; others sat in gloomy silence and ended their unhappy days seemingly in a state of insensibility; various were the ultimate ends of some of these people.

Towards the evening of the second day a few Indians found some spirituous liquor in the fort. The inhabitants, dreading the consequence of inebriation, repaired

Wyoming Massacre.

to Brant who removed every appearance of danger. After this everyone was permitted to go and look for the mangled carcass of his relation and to cover it with earth. I can easily imagine or conceive the feelings of a soldier burying the bodies of his companions, but neither my imagination nor my heart permit me to think of the peculiar anguish and keen feelings which must have seized that of a father, that of a mother avidly seeking among the crowd of slain for the disfigured corpse of a beloved son, the throbbing anguish of a wife—I cannot proceed.

Yet was it not astonishing to see these fierce conquerors, besmeared with the blood of these farmers, loaded with their scalps hardly cold, still swelled with the indignation, pride, and cruelty, with which victory always inspires them, abstain from the least insult and permit some rays of humanity to enlighten so dreadful, so dreary a day?

The complete destruction of these extended settlements was now the next achievement which remained to be done, in order to finish their rude triumph, but it could not be the work of a few days. Houses, barns, mills, grain, everything combustible to conflagrate; cattle, horses, and stock of every kind to gather; this work demanded a considerable time. The collective industry of twelve years could not well be supposed, in so great an extent, to require in its destruction less than twelve days. During that interval both parties were mixed together, and neither blows nor insults tarnished the duration of this period; a perfect suspension of animosities took place. The scattered inhabitants, who came to take the benefit of the Painter proclamation, all equally shared in the protection it imparted. Some of the Indians looked for those families which were known to have abhorred the preceding tyranny. They found the fathers and mothers, but the young men were killed; they bestowed on them many favours. The horrors of war were suspended to give these unhappy people full leisure to retire.

Some embarked in boats, and, leaving all they had behind them, went down the river towards Northumberland, Paxtung, Sunbury, etc., to seek shelter among the inhabitants of Pennsylvania; others, and by far the greatest number, were obliged to venture once more on foot through the great wilderness which separated them from the inhabited part of the province of New York. They received the most positive assurances that they would meet with no further injuries, provided they kept themselves painted in this long traject. This was the very forest they had traversed with so much difficulty a few years before, but how different their circumstances! 'Tis true they were then poor, but they were rich in hopes; they were elated with the near approach of prosperity and ease. Now that all-cheering, that animating sentiment was gone. They had nothing to carry with them but the dreadful recollection of having lost their all, their friends, and their helpmates. These protecting hands were cold, were motionless, which had so long toiled to earn them bread and procure them comfort. No more will they either hold the plough or handle the axe for their wives and children, who, destitute and forlorn, must fly, they hardly know where, to live on the charity of friends. Thus on every side could you see aged parents, wives, and a multitude of unhappy victims of the times, preparing themselves as well as they could to begin this long journey, almost unprovided with any kind of provisions.

While the faithful hand is retracing these mournful

events in all the various shades of their progressive increase, the humane heart cannot help shedding tears
of the most philanthropic compassion over the burning
ruins, the scattered parts of a society once so flourishing,
now half-extinct, now scattered, now afflicted by the
most pungent sorrow with which the hand of heaven
could chastise them.

For a considerable time the roads through the settled
country were full of these unhappy fugitives, each company slowly returning towards those counties from
which they had formerly emigrated. Some others, still
more unfortunate than others, were wholly left alone
with their children, obliged to carry through that long
and fatiguing march the infants of their breasts, now
no longer replenished as before with an exuberant milk.
Some of them were reduced to the cruel necessity of
loading the ablest of them with the little food they
were permitted to carry. Many of these young victims
were seen bare-headed, bare-footed, shedding tears at
every step, oppressed with fatigues too great for their
tender age to bear; afflicted with every species of misery, with hunger, with bleeding feet, every now and
then surrounding their mother as exhausted as themselves. "Mammy, where are we going? Where is father? Why don't we go home?" "Poor innocents, don't
you know that the King's Indians have killed him and
have burnt our house and all we had? Your uncle Simon
will perhaps give us some bread."

Hundreds were seen in this deplorable condition,
yet thinking themselves happy that they had safely
passed through the great wilderness, the dangers of
which had so much increased the misfortunes of their
situation. Here you might see a poor starved horse as
weak and emaciated as themselves, given them perhaps

by the enemy as a last boon. The poor beast was loaded with a scanty feather-bed serving as a saddle which was fastened on him with withes and bark. On it sat a wretched mother with a child at her breast, another on her lap, and two more placed behind her, all broiling in the sun; accompanied in this pilgrimage of tribulation by the rest of the family creeping slowly along; leading at a great distance behind a heifer once wild and frolicsome but now tamed by want and hunger; a cow, perhaps, with hollow flanks and projecting ribs closed the train; these were the scanty remains of greater opulence. Such was the mournful procession, which for a number of weeks announced to the country, through which they passed, the sad disaster which had befallen them. The generous farmers sent their wagons to collect as many as they could find, and convey them to the neighbouring county, where the same kindness was repeated. Such was their situation, while the carcasses of their friends were left behind to feed the wolves of that wilderness on which they had so long toiled, and which they had come to improve.

HISTORY OF MRS. B.*

An Epitome of all the Misfortunes which can possibly overtake a New Settler, as related by herself.

I WAS born at ——† a very ancient and opulent settlement. My father was the minister of the town; he reared me with the greatest tenderness and care. At seventeen I married. My husband‡ possessed a farm of one hundred and twenty-six acres, but, afraid lest he should not have the means of providing as amply as he wished for children that were not born, (contrary to my advice) he sold it and removed to the county of ——,§ where he purchased a tract of four hundred acres. But even in this first step toward the amelioration of our fortune we met with a severe disappointment which has proved the type of that adversity which we were destined to meet with in the course of our career. My husband was honest and unsuspicious and soon found that he had been cruelly deceived by a villain who pretended that the farm he had sold us was free from any encumbrances. We were obliged to pay upwards of four hundred and twenty-nine dollars, besides an immense deal of trouble for fees, lawyers, and clerks. However,

* This is the original from which Crèvecœur later published in French the *Histoire de Rachel Budd, mère d'une des familles détruites par les sauvages sous la conduite de Brandt & de Butler, sur les rives occidentales de la Rivière Susquehannah en 1778.*

† In the translation the place is indicated as Southampton, Long Island.

‡ In the translation, Benjamin Budd. See *Lettres d'un Cultivateur* . . ., 1787 edition, Vol. I, p. 397.

§ In the translation, Orange County (Crèvecœur's county).

by means of great industry, sobriety, hard labour, and perseverance we retrieved ourselves in a few years. I had then become the mother of eight children, six sons and two daughters. Soon afterwards the asperity of the climate, the roughness of the land discouraged my husband. He heard of the Number 2 scheme and purchase on the shores of the Susquehanna. Captivated with the pleasing report which was everywhere propagated, avidly comparing the fertility of those new grounds with the inferior quality of his own, he early became an adventurer in the scheme which at that time occupied every mind, and was the subject of general conversation. Soon afterwards we sold all we had and removed to Wyoming, as it was then called. We were almost the first who emigrated there. Unspeakable were the fatigues, the hardships we sustained from want of roads, of bridges, from storms of rain and wind, and a thousand other accidents which no tongue can describe, but we were all healthy and felt inwardly happy. Born as I was at ———, you may be sure that I knew nothing of so great, so hideous a wilderness as we had to traverse; I was a stranger to its intricacies and infinite difficulties. For nothing is so easy as to travel on a map: our fingers smoothly glide over brooks and torrents and mountains. But actually to traverse a tract of one hundred miles, accompanied with eight children, with cattle, horses, oxen, sheep, etc.—this is to meet with a thousand unforeseen difficulties.

We arrived at last on that spot so long talked of, and so long promised, on which we were sure to meet plenty, ease, and happiness. The aspect pleased me much. I never could admire enough these extensive plats of admirable grounds which by their grass, the weeds they produced seemed to be the seat of fertility itself. I contemplated with peculiar satisfaction the fair, the placid stream with pebbly bottom, running along these delightful banks. This afforded me a very great contrast when I recollected the stormy ocean near which I had been bred. There we found a few scattered families, poor but as happy as we were. We laboured under the same difficulties and had been impelled by the same motives. We had to think of bread for present subsistence, but that was not to be had. My sons and my husband were obliged to dedicate part of their time to hunting and fishing, else we must have starved. We had a shed to erect, fodder to provide in due time, for the preservation of the stock we had brought along with us. There were the honest cows which, even through the wilderness, had given us milk; there were four oxen which had brought our baggage and the younger children; there was the faithful mare which I had ridden, and there was a score of sheep; they were all part of our household, without the assistance of which we could not subsist. Judge of the fatigues we met with, of the anxiety and earnestness with which we applied ourselves to provide future subsistence for so many mouths. Ah, what a summer that was! And what was worse, I became a mother soon after my arrival. I was the first who added to the population of this country a child, which on that account I called Susquehanna B. A piece of round bark ingeniously fixed by my husband served him for a cradle, and had it not been for this cruel war, he might have lived to have been an opulent farmer, though rocked in so simple a machine.

Three years afterwards we were involved in a quarrel with the people of Pennsylvania. My husband, though a most peaceable man, fell a victim to these disputes and was carried away prisoner to Philadelphia.

Eighteenth Century America.

We lost all our horses and cows, for in these petty wars these movables are always driven off. I was ready to starve, and ashamed to become troublesome to my neighbours. I placed five of my oldest children with the best of them; they began to be able to earn their bread. The oldest was already married and settled thirty miles higher up,* and myself with the second and youngest intended to return to the county of ——† whence we had emigrated. It was then the beginning of winter; the earth was covered with a foot of snow. I was provided but with a single blanket. This snow, which I dreaded so much, proved my kindest support; it kept me warm at night; we must have perished, had it not been for the timely assistance it procured me. I was six days in traversing the long tract which divides Wyoming from the first settlements of ——. My sufferings and the patience with which I bore them would be but trifling objects; I therefore pass them over, though the different images of those calamitous stages are as present to my mind as they were the day I got out of the wilderness.

The following summer my husband procured his freedom. He returned to Wyoming, then called Wilkes-Barre. There he found everything in ruins. He went to see his children. He heard that I was returned to ——, in order to procure horses, without which we could do nothing. After many regrets and many weary steps, he rejoined me. Soon afterwards we plucked up a new stock of courage, bought two horses, and returned to our ruined settlement; and a joyful day it was though we had not a mouthful of bread then. I found my children

---

* In the translation Crèvecœur says, "Quinze milles au-dessous de nous," and in footnote "Mahapeny," *Lettres d'un Cultivatour . . .,* 1787 edition, Vol. I, p. 401.

† In the translation, Orange County, *ibid.,* p. 401.

all healthy and hearty; this was a sufficient feast for a mother. We soon procured plenty of provisions among the neighbours who, less unfortunate than we, began to enjoy a great abundance of everything. We toiled and soon recovered our ancient losses, but the ancient contentions with Pennsylvanians kept us all in suspense and uncertainty. But this was not all: the New England men of the town where we lived were for ever at variance with one another about the boundaries, the divisions of the town. We had no government but what the people chose to follow from day to day, just as passion or caprice dictated. We had, however, everything in plenty, and we looked on these transitory disturbances as evils which would soon cease.

This, however, did not happen so soon as we expected. We loved peace and [owing] to the strong desire of acquiring it, we resolved to remove to Wyalusing, sixty miles up the river; to abandon the labour of three years and to submit ourselves once more to the toils of first settlement. My husband made there a considerable purchase. We thought ourselves far happier as soon as we arrived there. We found the inhabitants satisfied with their lands, with their lots. They spent their time in useful labours and sought to disturb nobody. They were mostly Yorkers, Jersey men, and Pennsylvania High Germans. There lived old G——e, a crafty Indian, who had acquired a love of riches and property, contrary to the general disposition of these people. He had successfully bought several Indian rights and was possessed of upwards of five hundred acres of excellent lands with many houses. He was kind and hospitable. Here we soon lived in affluence. The beautiful grass of this country, the uninterrupted repose we enjoyed made us soon forget our pristine calamities. We thought that we were to be happy for the rest of our days. My husband owned land enough to provide for all children; we wished for no more. Two of them were then married and settled a few miles below towards Wysox. It was a little paradise; not a wrangle or dispute ever tarnished our tranquillity in the space of three years or more.

Congress affairs came, and behold us once more involved in calamities more distressing than any we had as yet met with! What we had hitherto suffered was a sting of bees; we have received the wounds since which came from much more malevolent beings. The great national dispute caused great divisions in the opinions of the people. My two oldest sons unfortunately joined in the most popular one. There was a disunited family, the worst of all evils; this proved a sad heart-breaking to my poor husband and me. The respect many people paid him made him, after a time, interpose in these new disputes, with which we poor back-settlers had nothing to do. The people of these upper towns were settled principally by people called Tories. A secret war was declared against us all by the more populous below. Parties were frequently sent up to apprehend people of this denomination and oblige them to retract their pernicious principles. These operations were never performed without a good deal of plundering under various pretences, sometimes as fines for non-appearance, at other times for the fees of those who were sent up.

This occasioned a new and unforeseen distress among us all. Many banished themselves, and voluntarily abandoned their possessions. The flight of several families intimidated those which remained. They retired also, some one way, some the other. Some young districts just settled were thus depopulated. I think, to the best of my remembrance, that there was not one family left at Standing Stone. They were all frightened; they took wings. Our old Indian sold all his possessions and retired among his countrymen. Happy man, he knew where to find peace! Although we call them wild, we, more civilized, did not know where to go. Would to God we had followed him as he often persuaded us! I would have gone to the extremities of the earth to avoid the broils in the midst of which we lived, and which daily increased.

We were left almost alone; my sons were compelled to enlist in this new sort of warfare. A mother's representation, a father's command had no kind of effect on their hearts. They had in some measure imbibed a good deal of the spirit of the times and thought themselves justifiable in what they did; they were deaf to our remonstrances. The militia-laws, as contrived by the New England people, were extremely severe. There was no middle course to take; one was obliged either to quit the settlement or else to obey. For, as they considered themselves as the founders and legislators, they unhappily thought likewise that they were possessed of the right of establishing their [beliefs] concerning this great dispute as the general one of the whole settlement. My husband and I often trembled at the recollection of all these strange deeds. We foresaw nothing very distinctly, and yet we could sometimes perceive that it might have a longer trail and heavier consequences than most people were aware of.

One day my oldest son brought us by way of present some of the furniture of one of the plundered families. I kicked it out of doors. I would not so much as look at it; I was afraid it would bring us bad luck, of which we had already a sufficient portion. Many at last resisted.

Eighteenth Century America.

Several parties of Indians began to appear, and in one of these encounters my third son was taken. I forgot his principles; I forgave him his past conduct; I shed tears over the unfortunate child, though disobedient. Soon afterwards I heard he was at Ockwackon, and since I have been informed of his being at Niagara on his way to Quebec. Judge of my feelings,—but I am almost grown callous! What a hard destiny for that poor fellow! Now often in my dreams have I followed him through the great tract he had to cross to arrive where he is, traversing the great Ontario, descending the huge rapids of the upper Saint Lawrence. How I have trembled for his life, lest the great tumbling waters, by the least mismanagement of the steersman, should submerge him and all the crew! I have followed him as far as Montreal, emerging from his slavery, and obtaining leave to work with some honest tranquil farmer. Happy shall I be if this part of his fate may reclaim him, and bring him back to my arms an honest man like his father. Dear boy, how many tears hast thou cost thy poor aged mother!

The cruel necessity of the times obliged us at last to quit our favourite habitation; the good opinion they had hitherto entertained of my husband no longer served him as a protection. We bade, without knowing it, an eternal adieu to our house; to those fertile fields which were ploughed with so much ease, and which yielded us such plentiful crops. Thus by the fatality of the times were cut off the reasonable hopes we had conceived of living tolerably easy in our old age and providing amply for each of our children. What a sacrifice we made! We had already lost above one-half of our stock and many other movables.

With the remains we embarked and returned to

History of Mrs. B.

Wilkes-Barre, where we met with but little kindness. They seemed to think us of a suspicious character. As if it mattered much what a couple of old people thought! There we cultivated some little grounds, but, alas! they were not our own. We lived but scantily, and in vain regretted the affluence we had left behind us, an affluence we only enjoyed three years in twenty-nine of hard toils, disappointments, and sufferings. As a woman I made no scruple to speak my mind with my usual freedom and candour. I was condemned by some; by others I was accused of speaking my husband's sentiments, and they began to insult him accordingly. He bemoaned and bemoaned in vain his hard fate. We regretted that ever we should have abandoned Wyalusing. We often thought that it would be better to have remained exposed to every incursion than to the daily mortification of receiving unmerited abuse. I could, methinks, harden myself to the dangers, to the noise, to the perturbations of war, but contumely unmerited, contumely, to an honest mind, is daggers to one's soul. You have no doubt heard of the treatment some Indians of Ockwackon met with. It was blindness itself. Some few well-disposed men saw it in that light, but none dared speak. Alas, how often we lamented our fate! How often we wished us away! But we were now old, now worn down with accumulated fatigues. Our ancient spirits, vigour, and courage were no more. Three of our boys had left us; they were married happily with people who lived higher up.

I shall not tire your patience with repeating what is so well known, our great disaster. The destruction of that great settlement, the death of many hundreds of people are circumstances with which everyone is acquainted. No sooner were we informed of the arrival of

Eighteenth Century America.

the enemy than I hastened with my family to the stockade which had been erected at Kingston, on the opposite side of the river. In getting into the boat, I fell and, unhappily, broke my thigh. Full of the most acute pains, I was carried into the fort and there laid on straw broiling in the sun,—my husband and myself, my daughter, and three young boys. Judge of our consternation and affright! We heard the howling of the Indians, the fire of the musketry, the shrieks of the wounded and dying. I heard and felt more on that day than I thought it possible for a woman to hear, to feel, and to bear. Heaven's arrows were launched against us in all manner of directions, and yet I lived, lived to tell of all this great chain of calamities. Sometimes I am astonished at it. Oh, my God, how thankful was I that my two sons lived at Mahapeny Exeter; they were beyond the reach of the militia commander. This single reflection alleviated all the rest. My poor daughter's husband never returned. She fainted away by my side. But in so great, so general a calamity, when I thought as I did then that my two sons might be in the fray, how could I feel for a son-in-law?

H—e,* the Indian whom I had known before, was among the number of those who entered our fort,—an awful remembrance. He singled out my husband, with whom he shook hands with all the signs of ancient friendship. He immediately asked for our boys; we informed him where they were; he seemed to rejoice. Soon afterwards we were informed that we must all paint ourselves red, and that we must depart from the settlement in five days. Towards the close of the eve-

* The French version of this essay reads: "In our vicinity there lived Job Gelaware [G—e?] and old Hendrique, two respectable *Shawanèses*" [*sic*]. *Lettres d'un Cultivateur* . . ., 1787 ed., Vol. I, p. 405.

216

ning H——e returned again and took my husband along
with him. It proved to him a strange evening, and replete with the strongest impressions of joy and sorrow.
In travelling towards the Indian's tent he was obliged
to pass through the field of battle, where he involuntarily was obliged to view the mangled carcasses of
many of his best friends and acquaintances. He was
ready to faint with anguish and a multitude of ideas
which then crowded on his mind. As soon as he arrived
at the tent, H——e presented him with his two sons
painted red, which prevented him from knowing them
so readily as he otherwise would. They tenderly embraced each other and shed abundance of tears; they
were the tears produced by joy alone. Their joy was
mixed with strange ingredients which you can easily
comprehend. My sons, as well as my husband, had seen
many of their friends lying on the ground. They foresaw the approaching ruin of all their property and the
total destruction of their country. I scarcely can tell of
all these things yet without feeling my heart ready to
break and my eyes full of tears. "Honest brother," said
H——e to my husband, "your house at Wyalusing is not
burnt. Nothing shall be destroyed of what you have. If
you incline to remain, which I wish you would, observe
to keep all your family painted red and wear something
of that colour when you go to the fields. If you prefer
going away, take as many of your things as you can, and
may Kitchy Manitou be favourable to you wherever
you go."

In a few days we procured a canoe and prepared ourselves to go down to Shamokin, towards Pennsylvania.
I would not have remained here among all my departed acquaintances for the most valuable consideration. House, cattle, property,——none of these things ap-

peared now to me of any value. I had lost what I never could regain: the peace of my mind. I cared very little where I went; I was now a poor, helpless, infirm old woman. We soon arrived at Shamokin, but as the settlement is small, we crossed over the river to Northumberland, where we met with all the kindness and hospitality we possibly could expect. But Heaven had not done yet with its frowns. Gracious God, what had we done that we were doomed to meet with so many species of evil? While I was confined to my bed, my husband and one of my sons took the small-pox and died. They died without my being able to see them for the last time. Judge of my situation: to have escaped the fury of such an enemy and thus to die among strangers, unpitied and perhaps unattended! What a singular fate, what peculiar hardships was I born to bear! I had not had the dreadful disorder myself, and they would not let me come near them. Thus was I left destitute, desolate, a cripple deprived of any settlement, my husband and one of my sons dead.

Oh Britain! Little do thy rich inhabitants know of the toils to which we are subjected, and of the sufferings thy mandates have caused. I recommended myself to God and earnestly prayed that He would take me from a world in which I had found so little comfort. Still I had friends and relations, but they were at a great distance. How, in my condition, should I be able to reach them? But after all I had lost, what was it in this world that could give me any concern? I got up and in company with my surviving son and my daughter and her infant we ventured through what they call the lower road, which leads into the cultivated parts of Pennsylvania. We had two horses which had been given us by H——e. However, they were so poor and emaciated that I was obliged often to alight in order to ease them. I scrambled along on my crutches as well as I could, and in these various essays travelled upwards of twenty miles. We had hardly arrived among the inhabitants, when my poor daughter was seized with the distemper which had carried off her father. My hard fortune obliged me to leave her one hundred and twenty miles behind me in the hands of strangers who promised to take good care of her. I took the charge of her infant, nine months old, and with a heart that could not break, I proceeded on my journey until overtaken by a prodigious shower of rain. I stopped at your son's door; he received us with kindness and humanity. My son had left his wife at ———, and had purposely come so far in order to see me safe among my friends. Though I had not then reached them yet, as I found myself among Christians, I insisted on his going back and dismissed him; his own family wanted his presence. But, alas, the measure of my sorrows was not yet filled. The grandchild I had brought with me had suckled his mother too long. He caught the infection and died in my arms and communicated to me the same disorder. I dreaded it not, for I wished to die and have done with so many adverse accidents.

Yet I survived and am almost blind, fitter to descend among those shades which already encompass me than to remain any longer among the living, to which I am become an object of useless pity. My daughter happily recovered and has since rejoined me, but her infant is dead. She has taken a log-house in the neighbourhood of my friends, where we are removed. The industry of my daughter and of my three youngest children, with the extreme kindness of my relations, enable us to live with decency and comfort. Such has been the singular fate, the long peregrination, the total ruin of a family once possessed of three good estates, born and bred of decent parents, endowed with good education; now half destroyed and now reduced to own not a single foot of land.

THE FRONTIER WOMAN*

I MET accidentally not long since an ancient acquaintance of mine, who from the beginning of this war has been a principal actor in these bloody scenes which are seldom attended with any dangers to the aggressor, for everything is done in the night and by surprise.

"I am afraid," he told me, "that I shall not be permitted to die in peace, whenever my hour comes. Even now I never lie down or smoke a pipe alone but a thousand frightful images occur to my mind. Yet when I did those things I felt no more concerned than if I had been girdling so many useless trees." These are his very words. "At times I feel involuntary remorse which oppresses me with melancholy and sorrow. My heart, oh, my heart!" (putting his hand on it) "Sometimes it beats as if it would palpitate its last, and I cannot tell for what."

"I am well in health. The strength of those ancient in-

* By the outbreak of the Revolutionary War settlers had pushed into the Mohawk valley, the Susquehanna valley in New York, and the Wyoming valley in Pennsylvania. A little way to the west of them in the region which is now central New York stood the villages of the Iroquois, among the fiercest fighters of the eastern forest Indians. In the conflict the Six Nations sided actively with the British. In 1777 they suffered humiliations and heavy losses in connection with St. Leger's advance into the Mohawk valley to join Burgoyne. The following year the Indians waged war against the unprotected frontier settlements, and the massacres at Cherry Valley and Wyoming occurred. Many Loyalists participated in these raids. In the following paper Crèvecœur describes the horrors of this war on the border through the words of a Loyalist who has been in the fighting. Crèvecœur published this in French under the title, "La Femme des Frontières" in *Lettres d'un Cultivateur* . . ., 1787 edition, p. 335.

fatuations is now vanished which enabled me to commit those ravages. I dread going to my bed, that bed where I used before to enjoy such an uninterrupted sleep. I feel a mixture of horror and repentance, but what is it good for? What good does it avail those poor people whom we have destroyed? What recompense can I make to the fugitive survivors? By what astonishing power does it come to pass that Man can so thoroughly imbibe the instinct and adopt the ferocity of the tiger, and yet be so indifferent in his faculties and organs? The tiger sheds no blood but when impelled to it by the stings of hunger; had Nature taught him to eat grass, he would not be the tiger. But Man who eats no man, yet kills Man, and takes a singular pleasure in shedding his blood.

"The voices of the many infants I have seen perishing in the wilderness; the curses and imprecations of the desolated fathers; the groans of the afflicted mothers whom I have beheld reduced to a variety of the most distressed circumstance; these are some of the retrospects which distract me.—Ah! that young woman! Because she tried to escape from the Indians whose prisoner she was! That she had never been born! I never should have committed the horrid deed! One single humane action I once did, impelled by—I cannot assign the cause; and this is the only balm which I try to bring to my wounded heart.

"In an excursion which we made to —— our party consisted of twenty-three: five white people and eighteen Indians of the very worst class. We came close to the woods of the settlement about sun-down, but perceived nobody in the fields. We concluded that the people had retired to their houses, of which we counted nine. We divided ourselves in as many companies, so that every house was to be entered at once at the signal of a gun.

"God forbid that I should tell you the history of that attack where there was so much innocent blood shed. I entered that which had fallen to my lot, and the first object I perceived was a woman of a comely aspect, neat and clean. She was suckling two children, whilst at the same time she was rocking the third in a cradle. At the sight of me who was painted and dressed like an Indian, she suddenly arose and came towards the door: 'I know your errand,' she said. 'Begin with these little innocents that they may not languish and die with hunger when I am gone. Dispatch me as you have dispatched my poor aged father and my husband last April. I am tired of life.'

"So saying, with her right hand she boldly pulled the handkerchief from her breast, whilst she still held her two infants with her left, and presented it to me bare. I was armed with my tomahawk and was going to strike when a sudden and irresistible impulse prevented me. 'Good woman, why should I kill you?' I told her. 'If your husband and father are already dead you have suffered enough. God help you.' 'Strike,' she said, 'and don't be faint-hearted. You are only mocking God and me. The rest of your gang will soon be here; this will only serve to prolong my misery. Hark! Hark! the butchers! the villains! Hark to the shrieks of my poor cousin Susy in the next house! Gracious God, why hast Thou thus abandoned me?' She wept bitterly. Motionless, I stood like a statue, my hand uplifted still, my eyes irresistibly fixed on her. My heart swelled; I wept also; I had not shed tears in many years before. 'No, good woman,' said I, 'not a hair of your head shall be touched. Are these three children yours?' 'Two

223

only belong to me,' she answered, 'the mother of the third was killed last April as she was defending her husband who was sick on his bed. The cries of the poor baby who was left alone in its cradle, while its father and mother lay bleeding close by, made me go to its assistance. The neighbours buried them, as soon as they returned from the woods where they had hid themselves, and I have suckled it ever since.' 'And you have suckled it ever since! Live, honest woman, live! Would to God you were at ———, free from any further danger! Let my generosity now serve as a reward for your humanity in making this poor forlorn orphan share the milk of your breast with your own children.' The rest of our people soon rushed into the house with what little plunder they had collected. It cost me a great deal of patience and struggle before I could make them consent that this poor woman should live. Her husband had been a rebel, and no rebel's wife should be spared. Her situation during the barbarous debate was terrible; her fortitude abandoned her. She was seized with the most violent fits, but the dreadful sight which she exhibited as she lay convulsed on the ground, with the shrieks of her children, enabled me to melt my companions into some little transitory humanity.

"What shall I do to get rest, and to restore my mind to its pristine serenity? We had orders for laying everything waste. Read a copy of them and see whether I can be justified before God." I read it. I paused a long while and casting my eyes towards heaven, that heaven where incomprehensible justice and mercy reside, I returned the paper to him. Thus ended our conversation.

Nor are these all the mischiefs caused by these devastations. Their effect is felt at a great distance, even where the danger is not so imminent, like a great storm

Frontier Woman.

on the ocean, which not only convulses it and causes a great number of shipwrecks wherever its greatest violence bursts, but agitates the air so powerfully that it becomes dangerous to the mariners even at a great distance. The various accounts of these incursions have spread a general alarm far and near. The report of these dreadful transactions is even frequently magnified in the various relations of them which circulate through the country. It has set every family a-trembling; it has impressed every mind with the most terrific ideas. Consequently, rural improvements are neglected; the former cheerfulness and confidence are gone. The gloomy, treacherous silence of the neighbouring woods prevents the husbandman from approaching them; everywhere we dread the fire of an invisible enemy from behind each tree. What mode of resistance, what means of security can be devised in so extensive a country? Who can guard every solitary house? He who has been toiling all day to earn subsistence for his family wants rest at night.

I have often persuaded many to retire into the more interior parts of the country,—so much easier is it to give advice than to follow it. Most of them are not able; others are attached to the soil, to their houses. Where shall we go, how shall we fare after leaving all our grain, all our cattle behind us? Some I have seen who, conscious of the integrity of their conduct, had flattered themselves with some marks of predilection; they seemed to comfort themselves with that idea. Poor souls! The same treacherous thoughts have often come into my head. They do not consider the spirit with which this species of war is conducted, and that we are all devoted [to it]. In consequence of this strange infatuation I have lost several relations and friends, one

225

in particular who was possessed of an ample fortune, literate, industrious, humane, and hospitable to a great degree. He was shot through the body as he was fearlessly riding home. As he fell they scalped him and clove his head, and left him in that situation to become a most shocking spectacle to his poor wife. Unfortunate woman! Neither reason nor religion have since been able to convey her the least consolation.

What astonishing scenes of barbarity, distress, and woe will not the rage of war exhibit on this extended stage of human affairs! Pardon my repetitions: these people were so far situated from the theatre of war, so unconcerned with its cause, and in general guiltless, that it is astonishing to see them daily fall as if loaded with every degree of iniquity. But iniquity is not the cause of the calamities we suffer in this world. Neither our insignificance, our lakes, our rivers, our mountains can afford us the least shelter. Our new enemies penetrate everywhere and hardly leave any traces of the flourishing settlements they are hired to destroy. Had a proper moderation, so useful and so necessary even in the most just wars, been prevalent, it would have saved from ruins a great many innocent families. If clemency was banished from the more immediate seat of war, one would have retraced it with pleasure on the extremities. Some part of the whole would have been saved from the general havoc. One would with admiration have observed the benignity of the chastising hand; and, to the praise of its humanity, some thousands of innocent families would have been overshadowed in peaceful neglect, wrapt up in that cloudy recess in which they were situated.

If I have dwelled so long on these inferior calamities and passed over those of the more opulent, more popu-

Frontier Woman.

lous parts of the country, now in ruins, it is because in the latter it is unavoidable. The possessors of rich settlements have friends, connections, and a variety of resources which in some measure alleviate their calamities. But those whom I have been speaking of, we who till the skirts of this great continent, once ruined are ruined indeed; and therefore become objects much more deserving your compassion and pity.

THE AMERICAN BELISARIUS*

JOURNALS, memoirs, elaborate essays shall not fail hereafter to commemorate the heroes who have made their appearance on this new American stage, to the end that Europe may either lavishly praise or severely censure their virtues and their faults. It re-quires the inquisitive eye of an unnoticed individual mixing in crowds to find out and select for private amusement more obscure, though not less pathetic scenes. Scenes of sorrow and affliction are equally moving to the bowels of humanity. Find them where you will, there is a strange but peculiar sort of pleasure in contemplating them; it is a mournful feast for some particular souls.

A pile of ruins is always striking, but when the object of contemplation is too extensive, our divided and wearied faculties receive impressions proportionably feeble; we possess but a certain quantity of tears and compassion. But when the scale is diminished, when we descend from the destruction of an extensive government or nation to that of several individuals, to that of a once opulent, happy, virtuous family, there we pause, for it is more analogous to our own situation. We can better comprehend the woes, the distresses of a father, mother, and children immersed in the deepest calamities imagination can conceive, than if we had observed the overthrow of kings and great rulers.

After a violent storm of northwest wind I never see even a single oak overset, once majestic and lofty, without feeling some regret at the accident. I observe

* A few opening paragraphs have been omitted.

the knotty roots wrenched from the ground, the broken limbs, the scattered leaves. I revolve in my mind the amazing elemental force which must have occasioned so great an overthrow. I observe the humble bushes which grew under its shade. They felt the impression of the same storm, but in a proportion so much the less, as was that of their bulk when compared to that of the oak. I acknowledge that, were I to observe a whole mountain thus divested of its trees by the impulse of the same gale, I should feel a superior degree of astonishment, but, at the same time, my observations could not be so minute nor so particular. It is not, therefore, those great and general calamities to the description of which my pencil is equal; it is the individual object as it lies lowly prostrate which I wish to describe. I can encompass it; I can view it in all situations; and the limited impressions admit within my mind a possibility of retracing them. Reserve this, therefore, for the hours, for the moments of your greatest philanthropy. The enormity may shock you. Here we are more used to it, and, having so many objects to feel for, one is able to feel so much the less for each.

The horror, the shocking details of the following tragedy, 'tis true, show mankind in the worst light possible. But what can you expect when law, government, morality are become silent and inefficacious? When men are artfully brought into a chaos, in order, as they are taught to believe, that they may be raised from their former confined line to a much preferable state of existence? To make use of a modern simile: the action of ploughing seems to be laborious and dirty; numberless worms, insects, and wise republics of ants are destroyed by the operation. Yet these scenes of unknown disasters, of unnoticed murders and ruins happily tend to produce a rich harvest in the succeeding season.

In the township of —— lived S. K., the son of a Dutch father and of an English mother. These mixtures are very frequent in this country. From his youth he loved and delighted in hunting, and the skill he acquired confirmed his taste for that manly diversion. In one of the long excursions which he took in the mountains of —— (which he had never before explored), mixing the amusements of the chase with those of more useful contemplation, and viewing the grounds as an expert husbandman, he found among the wilds several beautiful vales formed by Nature in her most indulgent hours; when, weary with the creation of the surrounding cliffs and precipices, she condescended to exhibit something on which Man might live and flourish,—a singular contrast which you never fail to meet with in the mountains of America: the more rocky, barren, and asperous are the surrounding ridges, the richer and more fertile are the intervales and valleys which divide them. Struck with the singular beauty and luxuriance of one of these spots, he returned home, and soon after patented it. I think it contained about one thousand acres.

With cheerfulness he quitted the paternal estate he enjoyed, and prepared to begin the world anew in the bosom of this huge wilderness, where there was not even a path to guide him. He had a road to make, some temporary bridges to make, overset trees to remove, a house to raise, swamps to convert into meadows and to fit for the scythe, upland fields to clear for the plough, —such were the labours he had to undertake, such were the difficulties he had to overcome. He surmounted every obstacle; he was young, healthy, vigorous, and strong-handed. In a few years this part of the wilderness assumed a new face and wore a smiling aspect. The most abundant crops of grass, of fruit, and grain soon succeeded to the moss, to the acorn, to the wild berry, and to all the different fruits, natives of that soil. Soon after these first successful essays the fame of his happy beginning drew abundance of inferior people to that neighbourhood. It was made a county, and in a short time grew populous, principally with poor people, whom some part of this barren soil could not render much richer. But the love of independence, that strong attachment to wives and children which is so powerful and natural, will people the tops of cliffs; and make them even prefer such settlements to the servitude of attendance, to the confinement of manufactories, or to the occupation of more menial labours.

There were in the neighbourhood two valuable pieces of land, less considerable indeed, but in point of fertility as good as his own. S. K. purchased them both and invited his two brothers-in-law to remove there; generously making them an offer of the land, of his teams, and every other necessary assistance; requiring only to be paid the advanced capital whenever they should be enabled; giving up all pretensions to interest or any other compensation. This handsome overture did not pass unaccepted. They removed to the new patrimony which they had thus easily purchased and in this sequestered situation became to S. K. two valuable neighbours and friends. Their prosperity, which was his work, raised no jealousy in him. They all grew rich very fast. The virgin earth abundantly repaid them for their labours and advances; and they soon were enabled to return the borrowed capital which they had so industriously improved. This part of the scene is truly pleasing, pastoral, and edifying: three brothers, the founders of three opulent families, the creators of three valuable plantations, the promoters of the succeeding settlements that took place around them. The most plentiful crops, the fattest cattle, the greatest number of hogs and horses, raised loose in this wilderness, yearly accumulated their wealth; swelled their opulence and rendered them the most conspicuous families in this corner of the world. A perfect union prevailed not only from the ties of blood, but cemented by those of the strongest gratitude.

Among the great number of families which had taken up their residence in that vicinage it was not to be expected that they could all equally thrive. Prosperity is not the lot of every man; so many casualties occur that often prevent it. Some of them were placed, besides, on the most ungrateful soil, from which they could barely draw a subsistence. The industry of Man, the resources of a family are never tried in this cold country, never put to the proof, until they have undergone the severity of a long winter. The rigours of this season generally require among this class of people every exertion of industry, as well as every fortunate circumstance that can possibly happen. A cow, perhaps, a few sheep, a couple of poor horses must be housed, must be fed through the inclement season; and you know that it is from the labour of the summer, from collected grasses and fodder, this must proceed. If the least accident through droughts, sickness, carelessness or want of activity happens, a general calamity ensues. The death of any one of these precious animals oversets the well-being of the family. Milk is wanting for the children; wood must be hauled; the fleeces of sheep cannot be dispensed with. What providence can replace these great deficiencies?

Happily S. K. lived in the neighbourhood. His extreme munificence and generosity had hitherto, like a gem, been buried, for he had never before lived in a country where the needy and the calamitous were so numerous. In their extreme indigence, in all their unexpected disasters, they repair to this princely farmer. He opens to them his granary; he lends them hay; he assists them in whatever they want; he cheers them with good counsel; he becomes a father to the poor of this wilderness. They promise him payment; he never demands it. The fame of his goodness reaches far and near. Every winter his house becomes an Egyptian granary, where each finds a supply proportioned to his wants. Figure to yourself a rich and opulent planter situated in an admirable vale, surrounded by a variety of distressed inhabitants, giving and lending, in the midst of a severe winter, cloaks, wool, shoes, etc., to a great number of unfortunate families; relieving a mother who has not perhaps wherewithal to clothe her new-born infant; sending timely succour, medicines, victuals to a valetudinarian exhausted with fatigues and labours; giving a milch cow to a desolated father who has just lost his in a quagmire, as she went to graze the wild herbage for want of hay at home; giving employment; directing the labours and essays of these grateful but ignorant people towards a more prosperous industry. Such is the faithful picture of this man's conduct, for a series of years, to those around him. At home he was hospitable and kind, an indulgent father, a tender husband, a good master. This, one would imagine, was an object on which the good genius of America would have constantly smiled.

Eighteenth Century America.

Upon an extraordinary demand of wheat from abroad, the dealers in this commodity would often come to his house and solicit from him the purchase of his abundant crops. "I have no wheat," said he, "for the rich; my harvest is for the poor. What would the inhabitants of these mountains do, were I to divest myself of what superfluous grain I have?" "Consider, sir, you will receive your money in a lump, and God knows when you are to expect it from these needy people, whose indolence you rather encourage by your extreme bounty." "Some do pay me very punctually. The rest wish and try to do it, but they find it impossible; and pray, must they starve because they raise less grain than I do?" Would to God I were acquainted with the sequel of this humane conversation! I would recapitulate every phrase; I would dwell on every syllable. If Mercy herself could by the direction of the Supreme Being assume a visible appearance, such are the words which this celestial Being would probably utter for the example, for the edification of mankind. 'Tis really a necessary relief and a great comfort to find in human society some such beings, lest in the crowd, which through experience we find so different, we should wholly lose sight of that beautiful original and of those heavenly dispositions, with which the heart of Man was once adorned.

One day as he was riding through his fields, he saw a poor man carrying a bushel of wheat on his back. "Where now, neighbour?"

"To mill, sir."

"Pray, how long since you are become a beast of burthen?"

"Since I had the misfortune of losing my jade."

American Belisarius.

"Have you neither spirit nor activity enough to catch one of my wild horses?"

"I dare not without your leave."

"Hark ye, friend, the first time I see you in that servile employment whilst I have so many useless ones about my farm, you shall receive from me a severe reprimand." The honest countryman took the hint, borrowed a little salt and a halter, and soon after appeared mounted on a spirited mare, which carried him where he wanted to go, and performed for him his necessary services at home.

In the fall of the year it was his usual custom to invite his neighbours in, helping him to hunt and to gather together the numerous heads of swine which were bred in his woods, that he might fat them with corn which he raised in the summer. He made it a rule to treat them handsomely, and to send them home each with a good hog, as a reward for their trouble and attendance. In harvest and haying he neither hired nor sent for any man, but, trusting to the gratitude of the neighbourhood, always found his company of reapers and hay-makers more numerous than he wanted. It was truly a patriarchal harvest gathered for the benefit of his little world. Yet, notwithstanding his generosity, this man grew richer every crop; every agricultural scheme succeeded. What he gave did not appear to diminish his stores; it seemed but a mite, and immediately to be replaced by the hand of Providence. I have known Quakers in Pennsylvania who gave annually the tenth part of their income, and that was very great; but this man never counted, calculated, nor compared. The wants of the year, the calamities of his neighbourhood were the measure by which he proportioned his bounty. The luxuriance of his meadows surpassed all belief; I have heard many people say, since his misfortunes, that they have often cut and cured three tons and half per acre. The produce of his grain was in proportion; the blessings of heaven prospered his labours and showered fertility over all his lands. Equally vigilant and industrious, he spared neither activity nor perseverance to accomplish his schemes of agriculture. Thus he lived for a great number of years, the father of the poor and the example of this part of the world. He aimed at no popular promotion, for he was a stranger to pride and arrogance. A simple commission as a militia-captain was all that distinguished him from his equals.

Unfortunate times came at last. What opinion he embraced in the beginning remains unknown. His brothers-in-law had long envied his great popularity, of which, however, he had never made the least abuse. They began to ridicule his generosity, and, from a contempt of his manner of living, they secretly passed to extreme hatred; but hitherto they had taken care to conceal their rancour and resentment. At the dawn of this new revolution, they blazed forth. Fanned by the general impunity of the times, they, in an underhanded manner, endeavoured to represent him as inimical. They prevailed upon the leaders to deprive him of his commission (though fifty-six years of age), and even made him submit to the duties of a simple militiaman. They harassed his son by all the means which false zeal and uncontrollable power—[all] too unhappily—suggested to them. In short, they made themselves so obnoxious as to expose them to every contumely devised by the rage of party and the madness of the times.

As he was a great lover of peace and repose, he obeyed their commands and went forth, as well as his son, whenever ordered. This unexpected compliance became a severe mortification and an insupportable disappointment to his enemies. They became, therefore, more openly outrageous. They began by causing his son to be deprived of a favourite rifle, a rifle that had constantly and successfully contributed to his father's youthful amusements. This outrage the old gentleman could not patiently endure. He seized on the house of the officer who had committed this act of violence. A great dispute ensued, in consequence of which he was cast (into prison) and severely fined. Innumerable other insults were offered to the youth, who, young, bold, and courageous, preferred at last a voluntary exile to so much insult and vexation. He joined the King's troops. This was what had been foreseen, and [was] a part of that plan which had been previously concerted by his brothers-in-law and his other enemies. Thus these people, from the wild fury of the times, contrived the means of S. K.'s destruction, which was to ensure them the possession of his fine estate. This elopement with the doubtful confirmed the preceding suspicions; realized the conjectures of his enemies. Among the more irascible the torch now blazed with redoubled heat. His life was immediately demanded by the fanatical, and his estate secured by the detestable devisers of his ruin.

What a situation for an honest, generous man! Despised, shunned, hated, calumniated, and reviled in the midst of a county of which he was the founder, in the midst of a people the poorest of which he had so often assisted and relieved; pursued and overtaken by his brothers-in-law, whom he had raised from indigence! Gracious God, why permit so many virtues to be blasted in their greatest refulgency? Why permit the radiance of so many heavenly attributes to be eclipsed by men

who impiously affix to their new, fictitious zeal the
sacred name of liberty on purpose to blind the unwary,
whilst, ignorant of Thee, they worship no deity but
self-interest, and to that idol sacrilegiously sacrifice so
many virtues? If it is to reward him with never-fading
happiness, condescend to manifest some faint ray of Thy
design proportioned to the weakness of the comprehension of us, frail mortals and fellow-sufferers, that we
may not despair, nor impious men may arraign Thy eternal justice. Yes, it is virtue Thou meanest to reward and
to crown. The struggle, the contest, the ignominy to
which it is now exposed, the greater disasters which will
soon terminate this scene have some distant affinity with
the suffering of Thy Son, the Moral Legislator, the
Pattern of Mankind.

S. K. bore his misfortunes with a manly constancy.
However, the absence of his son impaired his industry,
and almost put an entire stop to his designs of improvement. He saw but neglected his farm, his fields, his
pastures, and his meadows; the ruinous and deplorable
state in which the country was involved.* His house,
once the mansion of hospitality and kindness, was entered now but by secret emissaries, enemies, committee-
men, etc. The few friends he had left dared not visit
him, for they, too, were struggling with their difficulties; they dared not expose themselves to a declaration
of their sentiments by soothing his oppressed mind, and
comforting him in his adversity. He was taken ill. Nevertheless, militia-duty was demanded and required of
him. He was fined forty pounds for every fortnight he

* This sentence is very awkward through imperfect corrections by
Crèvecœur. The first transcription was: "He saw but he neglected his
farm, the ruinous and deplorable state in which the country was involved overtook his fields, his pastures and his meadows."

had been absent. He recovered and resolved either to cease to be, or else to exist with more ease. He went towards New York, but the guards and other obstacles he met with prevented him from accomplishing his design. He returned, but ere he reached his house, he heard the melancholy tidings that it had been plundered, and that there was a general order for the militia to hunt him through the woods. For a great number of days he had to escape their pursuit from hill to hill, from rocks to rocks, often wanting bread, and uncertain where to hide himself. By means of the mediation of some friends he was at last permitted to return home and remain there on bail. A dejected, melancholy wife, a desolated house, a half-ruined farm, a scarcity of everything struck him to the heart at his first coming, but his sorrow and affliction were all passive. These impressions, however, soon wore away; he insensibly grew more reconciled to his situation. His advanced age, his late sickness, his fatigues had wearied him down; and his mind, partaking of the debility of his body, did no longer view these disagreeable images in the same keenness of light.

This happened in the fall. The following winter some poor people repaired to his house for relief and supplies as usual. "Alas, my friends, committees and rulers have made such a havoc here that I have no longer the means to relieve you. A little hay, perhaps, I may spare, for they have stolen all my horses. Pray, were not you one of those who hunted me whilst I was wild?"

"Yes, sir, I was unfortunately one of them, but I was compelled. I was driven to do it. You know as well as I the severity with which we poor militiamen are treated: exorbitant and arbitrary fines, corporal punishments. Every kind of terror is held out to us. What could I do?"

"I know it, and am far from blaming you, though I greatly lament and pity your situation. Pray, have you been paid for your services against me?"

"No, sir."

"How many days have you been out?"

"Two."

"What! Two days in the woods and you have received no wages? Have neither committees nor captains ever settled that matter yet?"

"No, sir, our services are gratis, and we must, besides, find our victuals, our blankets, and the very ammunition we expend,—we must pay for it."

"I hate, and always did, to see poor men employed for nothing. Take two loads of hay for your two days' work. Will that satisfy you?"

"You were always a good man. God loves you yet though some men are dreadfully set against you."

"Do tell me, would you really have killed me as you were ordered, if you had met me in the woods?" Here the poor man, hiding his face with his hat, shed tears and made no other answer.

The patience, the resignation with which he seemed now to bear his fate, greatly alarmed his enemies. They reproached themselves with the facility with which they suffered him to return and to procure bail; new devices were, therefore, made use of to push him to a final extremity. His determination of thus remaining at home, quiet and inoffensive, might abate that popular rage and malice which were the foundations of their hopes. The keen edge of popular clamour might become blunted; there was a possibility of their being frustrated in their most favourite expectations. They, therefore, secretly propagated a report that he had harboured Indians on their way to New York. No sooner said than believed. Imprisonment, hanging were denounced against him by the voice of the public. This new clamour was principally encouraged by his brothers-in-law, the one now become a magistrate, and the other a captain of the militia.

Finding himself surrounded with new perils, without one friend either to advise or to comfort him; threatened with his final doom; accused of that which, though they could not prove, he could only deny; knowing of no power he could appeal to, either for justice or relief; seeing none but prejudiced enemies in his accusers, judges, and neighbours; he at last determined to join the Indians who were nearest to him, not so much with the design of inciting them to blood and slaughter, as [of finding] a place of refuge and repose. This was what his enemies expected. His house, his farm,—all were seized, even the scanty remains of what had escaped their former avidity and plunder. All was sold, and the house and farm were rented to a variety of tenants until laws should be made to sell the lands.

> Such a house broke!
> So noble a master fallen! All gone! and not
> One friend to take his fortune by the arm,
> And go along with him.

It has been said since that this famed farm has ceased this year to bear as plentifully as usual; that the meadows have brought but little hay; that the grain has been scanty and poor. This is at least the tradition of the neighbourhood. It may be that these inconsiderate tenants neither plough nor cultivate it as it was formerly; that the meadows, late-fed and ill-fenced, have no time to bear a crop; and that in the short space of their lease they refuse the necessary manures and usual care, without which the best land produces nothing.

His wife, alas! has been hitherto overlooked and unnoticed, though you may be sure she has not been passive through these affecting scenes. In all these various calamities which have befallen her family she has borne the part of a tender mother, an affectionate wife. Judge of her situation at this particular and critical moment! The repeated shocks which she has sustained within these three years have impaired the tone of her nerves,—you know the delicacy of the female frame. Though her cheerfulness was gone, the gleamings of hope, the presence of her husband still supported her. This sudden and unexpected blow completed the horrid catastrophe. Soon after his elopement, when the armed men came to seize him, she fainted, and though she has since recovered the use of her limbs, her reason has never returned but in a few lucid intervals. She is now confined to a small room, her servants sold and gone; she is reduced to penury; she is become a poor tenant of that very house which in the better days of her husband's prosperous industry had glowed with the cheerful beams of benevolence. She is now an object of pity without exciting any. When her reason returns, it is only to hear herself and family reviled. "You yourselves have driven my son, my husband away," is all she can say. Could tears, could wishes, could prayers relieve her, I'd shed a flood, I'd form a thousand, I'd proffer the most ardent ones to heaven. But who can stem the tide of Fate? It is the arbiter of kings and subjects; in spite of every impediment it will rise to its preordained height. She lives, happily unknown to herself, an example of the last degree of desolation which can

overtake a once prosperous family, the object of rail-
lery to those who are witnesses of her delirium. It
would have been a miracle indeed, had her senses remained unimpaired amidst the jars, the shocks of so
many perturbations. A Stoic himself would have required the spirit of Zeno to have withstood, placid and
composed, the convulsions of so great a ruin.

One stroke of fortune is still wanting. S. K. in his
flight met with a party of Indians coming towards ——,
which they intended to destroy. He accompanied them,
never ceasing to beg of them that they would shed no
blood and spare the lives of poor innocent farmers. The
deaths of three or four, to which he was witness,
shocked his humane soul. He quitted them and returned
once more towards home, choosing rather to meet his
final doom in his own country than be any longer a witness to the further mischiefs meditated by these incensed people. On his return he was soon informed of
the deplorable state to which his wife was reduced and
of the destruction of his property. He balanced what to
do, as if amidst so much evil there was still a possibility
of choice. Sad, however, was the alternative: whether to
venture and deliver himself up at all hazards, and thus
end the suspense; or whether to live a vagrant, a fugitive in these woods and mountains, with the paths and
intricate ways of which he was so well-acquainted. But
whence was he to procure subsistence? It could not be
by the chase. Was he then to turn plunderer? Weary of
life, he at last found means to inform the rulers of his
return and repentance; but he received no other answer
than what was soon afterwards delivered by the mouths
of the dogs and by the noise of the militia which was
ordered out to search the woods for him. He luckily
escaped their pursuit, but hunger, his greatest enemy,

at last overtook him. He ventured towards a cabin, the tenants of which he had often relieved in their adversity. They gave him some bread and advised him to fly. Soon afterwards, by means of the indiscretion of a child, this mystery of generosity and gratitude was revealed. The aged couple were severely whipped, being too poor to be fined. For a long time he skulked from tree to tree, from rock to rock; now hid on the tops of cliffs, seeing his pursuers below him; now creeping through the impervious ways of marshes and swamps, the receptacle of bears less cruel than his enemies.

Ye angels of peace, ye genii of placid benevolence, ye invisible beings who are appointed to preside over the good, the unjustly persecuted, is there no invisible ægis in the high armouries of heaven? Gently cause one to descend, in order to shield this mortal man, your image, from the imminent danger he is in, from the arrows of malice, from the muskets of his ancient friends and dependants,—all aimed towards him. Whichsoever way he steers, he has to dread the smell of dogs, now become his enemies. Where can he go to escape and live? But if he lives, what life will it be? The goaded mind incessantly represents to itself and compares the ancient days of ease, felicity, tranquillity, and wealth, with the present hours of hunger, persecution, and general hatred; once the master and proprietor of a good house, now reduced to the shelter of the woods and rocks; once surrounded with servants and friends, now isolated and alone, afraid of the very animal which used to be his companion in the chase. Such, however, was the fate of this man for a long time, until, abandoning himself to despair, overpowered by the excess of fatigues, debility, and hunger, he suffered himself to be taken. He was conducted to gaol, where he expected

American Belisarius.

he should not long languish. Mercy was now become useless to him. What good could it procure him, now that his wife was delirious, his son gone, and all his property destroyed? His only remaining felicity was the remembrance of his ancient humane deeds which like a sweet ethereal dew must cast a mist over the horrors of his confinement, and imperceptibly prepare him to appear in that world which blesses the good, the merciful without measure, and has no bitterness for such tenants.

The day of trial soon came, and to his great surprise, as well as to the astonishment of all, he was released on bail and permitted to go to work for his daily bread. Like Belisarius of old, he is returned to live in that small part of his own house which is allotted him for his habitation; there to behold once more the extensive havoc which surrounds him; and to contemplate in gloomy despair the overthrow of his wife's reason and the reunion of all the physical evil that could possibly befall him, without resources and without hope.

Yet he lives; yet he bears it without murmuring. Life seems still to be precious to him; 'tis a gift he has no thought of parting with. Strange! What is it good for when thus embittered, when thus accompanied with so much acrimony, such irretrievable accidents? 'Tis a perpetual state of agony. Better part with it in a heavy, final groan and trust to Nature for the consequence than to drag so ponderous a chain. How much happier the felon, the murderer who at one fortunate blow ends the remembrance of his life and his crimes, and is delivered from chains, putrid holes, and all the other wants of Nature!

Compare now the fate of this man with that of his more fortunate persecutors. I appeal to the enlightened tribunals of Europe, to the casuistical doctors of the colleges of science, to the Divan, to the synods, to the presbyteries, and to all bodies and conventions of men reunited to judge of the various cases which the combined malice of men exhibit on the stage of the world, as well as of the various preventives and punishments designed to check malice and evil deeds. I appeal to the American tribunals on that day when the mist of these times shall be dissipated. I ask them all on what principles can this man be punished? What has he done that can deserve so much severity? The graft, by the virulence of these times, is made to poison the parent stock; the vine is made to corrode the tutelar elm which has so long supported its entwined limbs and branches. 'Tis the jealousy, the avarice, the secret thirst of plunder, sanctified under new and deceiving names, which have found means to vilify this generous citizen, and have set the aspic tongues reviling this innocent man. Can it be? Can this be the reflected work of three years? Yes, it is. But for their demoniacal fury he might have remained at home passive and inoffensive. The produce of his fertile farm might have served to support the cause. But this was not sufficient to satisfy the rage, the malice of an ignorant, prejudiced public.

Are ye not afraid, ye modern rulers, to attract the wrath of heaven, the vindictive fires of its eternal justice in thus trampling under, in thus disregarding the most essential laws of humanity, in thus neglecting the most indispensable ones contained in that code which ought to reign supreme, exclusive of all parties, factions, and revolutions? Is not the deplorable state into which this man and all his family are reduced more than sufficient to atone for the popular offences he is supposed to have been guilty of? Must poverty, lan-

guor, and disease terminate in want, penury, and ignominy a life hitherto pursued on the most generous principles, a life which, contrary to the tenor of yours, has
been so useful, so edifying?

But I am not pleading his cause; I am no biographer.
I give way to an exuberance of thoughts which involuntarily crowd on my mind, unknown to all the world but
its Ruler and yourself. I don't presume that this man
was matchless, devoid of vices and faults. Like all other
men, his cup was no doubt mixed with those ingredients
which enter into the beverage of mortals. It is not the
minutiæ of his life into which I want to descend. This
unfortunate epoch is *that* alone which I want to select
and to describe as a proof of his hard destiny, and as one
of the characteristics of the times in which we live. Yet
I am persuaded that there are several members in Congress and in every province who, moved into compassion at this relation, would shed tears over the ashes of
this ruin; but these men at a great distance direct the
revolution of the new orb. It is the inferior satellites
who crush, who dispel, and make such a havoc in the
paths which it is to follow.

Yet his enemies exult, triumph, and rule. They bear
sway, are applauded, gather every harvest, and receive
every incense which the world can give, whilst he be-
moans his fate, and is obliged to support himself and
his wife. His enemies, now become his masters, were,
before these times, mostly poor, obscure, and unnoticed; great psalm-singers, zealous religionists who
would not have cracked a nut on the Sabbath,—no, not
for any worldly consideration. They were meek, lowly
Christians, always referring every accident to God's divine providence and peculiar appointment; humble in
their deportment, composed in their carriage, prudent

in their outward actions, careful of uttering offensive words; men of plausible countenances, sleek-haired, but possessed at the same time of great duplicity of heart; sly in their common social intercourse, callous,—pushing, with an affected charitable language, from their doors the poor, the orphan, the widow.

I have known some of these country saints to tenaciously detain in gaol some debtors for twelve pounds, which S. K., unknown to everybody, would privately cause to be paid. These are the people who before these times were ostentatiously devout, laboriously exact in their morning prayers, reading, expoundings, etc. These are the men who now in the obscure parts of this country have assumed the iron sceptre and from religious hypocrites are become political tyrants. That affected meekness, that delusive softness of manners are now gone; they are discarded as useless. They were formerly the high road to popularity, applause, and public respect, but this new zeal for their new cause must not, like the ancient one, moulder under the ashes and be afraid of sunshine and of air. It must burn, it must conflagrate; the more violent the flames, the thicker the smoke, the more meritorious. Whilst the unaffected good man, the sincere Christian, who proved his principles by his actions more than by his vain words and his disputations, is reprobated, shunned, despised, and punished, the secret liar, the hidden fornicator, the nocturnal drunkard, the stranger to charity and benevolence are uplifted on modern wings, and obtain the applause of the world which should be the reward of merit, of benefits conferred, of useful actions done.

Surely this points out the absolute necessity of future rewards and punishments. Were not I convinced of it, I would not suffer the rebukes, the taunts, the daily

infamy, to which I have conscientiously exposed myself. I'd turn Manichean like so many others. I'd worship the demon of the times, trample on every law,
break every duty, neglect every bond, overlook every
obligation to which no punishment was annexed. I'd set
myself calumniating my rich neighbours. I'd call all
passive, inoffensive men by the name of inimical. I'd
plunder or detain the entrusted deposits. I'd trade on
public moneys, though contrary to my oath. Oath!
Chaff for good Whigs, and only fit to bind a few conscientious Royalists! I'd build my new fortune on the
depreciation of the money. I'd inform against every
man who would make any difference betwixt it and sil-
ver, whilst I, secure from any discovery or suspicion by
my good name, would privately exchange ten for one.
I'd pocket the fines of poor militiamen extracted from
their heart's blood. I'd become obdurate, merciless, and
unjust. I'd grow rich, "fas vel nefas." I'd send others
a-fighting, whilst I stayed at home to trade and to rule.
I'd become a clamorous American, a modern Whig, and
offer every night incense to the god Arimanes.

LANDSCAPES*

THE following "American Landscapes" are not beneath your attention, though they are the works of neither Salvator Rosa nor Claude Lorrain. They are sketches which, like Chinese paintings, admit draperies and ornaments.

I leave to artists the harmony of shades and brilliance of perspective arrangements. 'Tis not the pompous, the captious, the popular, the ostensible, the brilliant part of these American affairs I want to portray; this is the province of the historiographer, biographer, etc. My simple wish is to show you the vulgar thread of that canvas, once so rude and neglected, the work of low and ignorant artists, but now transmuted into a wide extended surface on which new and deceiving perspectives are represented. 'Tis now surrounded with a superb frame; 'tis now covered with tinsel colours hiding the coarse ligaments and texture beneath. My simple wish is to present you with some of the primary elements and original component parts in their native appearances ere they were artfully gathered, united, new-modelled and polished by our modern legislators. 'Tis not the soaring eagle, rivalling the clouds in height and swiftness, I mean to show you; 'tis only the insignificant egg from which it is hatched. My pencil wants not to sketch the august bird arrayed with majestic feathers; 'tis only the nest in which it was hatched, composed of sticks and twigs cemented with dirt, lined with clay, whence has sprung this new master of the sky.

Such, you know, has always been the turn of my

* Two opening paragraphs have been omitted.

thoughts. 'Tis not in general so much the perspective I admire as the knowledge of this secret from which the deception arises; 'tis not so much the sceneries which attract my attention, as the hidden methods by which they are held suspended, shifted, and alternately presented to my view. Ambition, we well know, an exorbitant love of power and thirst of riches, a certain impatience of government, by some people called liberty, —all these motives, clad under the garb of patriotism and even of constitutional reason, have been the secret but true foundation of this, as well as of many other revolutions. But what art, what insidious measures, what deep-laid policy, what masses of intricate, captious delusions were not necessary to persuade a people happy beyond any on earth, in the zenith of political felicity, receiving from Nature every benefit she could confer, enjoying from government every advantage it could confer, that they were miserable, oppressed, and aggrieved, that slavery and tyranny would rush upon them from the very sources which before had conveyed them so many blessings. Behold then a new source of revolution, a new class of calamity never before experienced. That excess of misrule should rouse a generous people is very natural to conceive; that the avarice of individuals, the cupidity of the republics, the ambition of princes should kindle and promote wars,—we are well acquainted with these veteran causes. Ambition, hypocrisy, enthusiasm are continually travelling from one end of the earth to the other. But this American manœuvre is altogether without a precedent; history affords us no parallel. Feeble, emaciated colonies, ill-governed, cost as much as they are worth. They are the offspring of tyranny; they are excrescences that perhaps may add to the weight, but not to the vigour of the body politic. Those, on the contrary, which, linked by freedom, are supported and upheld by the most rational bonds, those rush towards manhood. They rapidly acquire the strength of nations, and, regardless of every consideration, forgetting the pride, the honour, the safety of ancient connections, they seize the club as they advance; they threaten. A new and unheard-of impunity, grafted on parental indulgence, grows and expands and settles into pertinacity and arrogance. Is this then the state of human nature? Is this the source of things? Premature event! Fatal disposition! My astonishment is boundless when I recollect in a short retrospect the beginning and progressive increase of this unnatural revolt. At present I would choose to consider it as a characteristic anecdote in the annals of mankind, but at the same time the object is so large that I cannot enclose it within the reach of my horizontal vision. 'Tis necessary, for the sake of more explicit details, to view it at different periods, in its beginnings and successive degrees of advancement. These were not an enslaved people whose senses and organs were at the command of a haughty prince. No, these were an immense number of tribes collected together and living on an extensive coast of fourteen hundred miles, who, from their childhood, were bred to censure with the utmost impunity the conduct of their governors and other rulers. Yet these men have insensibly been led through the most flowery path to enter a long career of sorrow and affliction, at the end of which a phantom is exhibited which seems to recede as fast as they advance. No European can possibly conceive the secret ways, the great combination of poisons and subtle sophisms which have from one end of the continent to the other allured the minds, removed every ancient prejudice, and, in short, pre-

Landscapes.

pared the way for the exhibition of this astonishing revolution. From restlessness, from diffidence, from that jealous state in which free men always live, to pass in the course of four years to the implicitness of belief, to passive obedience, is indeed a melancholy proof that if slavery is often extended and cherished by kings, the people, in the hour of infatuation, will sometimes become the artificers of their own misfortunes.

I am now tired of the company of generals, rulers, imperial delegates, modern governors. My predilected province at present is more humble but perhaps not less interesting. I choose now to converse with those vulgar hands, to whom the drudgery of ploughing and scattering the good seed has been committed; seed from which that great harvest is to spring forth, ripening fast for the sole use of the great state reapers. It is not every lung, 'tis not every breast which can bear long unaffected the subtle, the penetrating air of Teneriffe's top, or the exalted crater of Mount Vesuvius. But in my descent I find crevices, as well as a variety of new plants, which afford me some amusement as I proceed downwards. But what if these obscure scenes are scenes without purpose, and exhibit characters without meaning? Great will be my guilt indeed. However, it will be a guilt proceeding from ignorance only and want of proper discernment. Some of these, however, must appear to you very striking and strongly marked. They are the genuine copies of originals such as have presented themselves to my view. If the thoughts are not always clad in the garb of the original words, the reason is that I have attached myself much more to the sentiment, the impression of which forcibly strikes and remains, than to the phraseology and uncouth dialect, to which I am in a great measure a stranger. The faith-

Eighteenth Century America.

fulness of representation, the authenticity of facts, the truth of anecdote, as well as that of the circumstances, which pervade the whole, seem to constitute, however, a sort of merit which I shall one day claim at your hands. These are committed to the bosom of friendship, there to remain until you have made them worthy a witness.

AN AMERICAN PERSPECTIVE
DIVIDED INTO SIX LANDSCAPES

THE several transactions herein represented and comprised in the following scenes begin at seven o'clock in the morning and end at one on the same day. The subject is so diffused throughout, that but a very imperfect idea can be given by way of abstract. Each part must help to elucidate the other. The hypocrisy, slyness, cupidity, inhumanity and abuse of power in these petty country despots are evident and manifest. But to be of genuine American produce, they should be viewed clad under these modish garbs in which they appear, or else they might be taken for that of some other country.

First Landscape: A Deacon's House. Sabbath Morn.

The Deacon unites to the sacred functions of Elder those of Chairman, Colonel, and Commissioner for Selling Tory Estates.

    Beatus, *deacon, etc.*
    Eltha, *his wife.*
    Ruth, *his daughter.*
    Eliphalet, *his son.*
    Philip Rearman, *the Squire.*
    Tom, *the negro.*

Deacon: Do, wife, let the family know that it is time

254

to go to morning prayers. Somehow we have overslept ourselves. The sun is quite high.

Eltha: Come, come, girls; boys, your daddy says 'tis now time to pray. (They all enter the room.)

Deacon: Gracious God, Thou knowest our infirmities. But where is Anthony? I don't see him here.

Eltha: As to that, the poor lad deserves to be excused. He was all night a-Tory-hunting, and did not get home till 'most break of day.

Deacon: Well, well, if so be, let him lie, but 'tis but a poor action indeed that doesn't bring along with it its own rewards. Anyone of you know what luck they have had?

Eliphalet: I have heard him say that he has not had such fun this great while. He likes the light-horse service wonderfully. They have caught old Stubb, who is as deaf as a wall. They challenged him as he was riding by, and as he made no answer, they fired and killed his horse.

Deacon: What have they done with the old wretch?

Eliphalet: They pricked his stubborn flesh pretty well, as he lay on the ground, with their bayonets, and then sent him in irons to the fort.

Deacon: That was well done. These youngsters will really make fine soldiers.

Eliphalet: Next they went to Adam Mill's house, huzzaing all the way. They caught him in his bed by the side of his old wife. They seized all his papers, which were chiefly Continental sheets. They stripped him; then tarred and feathered him till he looked nearly like an owl; and clapped him upon an old jade; and then led him to the Cross-Keys tavern, where they had abundance of diversion. For the honest lads began to gather, and they all hooted and shouted at him till their sides merely ached, as they said. Then they turned him off. They put up his clothes at raffle for the fees and drank merrily on it. The other writings and the money are in the hands of Sergeant Broad-Alley.

Deacon: Why, as to the money, they should have divided it among the company. That is the intention of Congress, I am sure. It looked, however, desperate well to see them so moderate.

Eliphalet: As they passed by What's-his-name's house they killed his dog which kept a-barking; then fired through the doors and windows a fine round volley; and they say that the old Tory and his family were almost scared to death. They say that he went into his cellar and got one of the negroes to hide him in a hogshead.

Deacon: Come, come, we shall hear the rest by and by. Let us proceed in our prayers and return God thanks that He has given us strength to overcome our internal enemies.

(Here he fetches a deep sigh and with a quivering voice he goes on.) Gracious God, pour Thy blessings on Thy favourite people. Make their chosen race to increase and prosper by the influence of Thy heavenly showers. . . .

Eltha: Without interrupting you, my dear, I see somebody a-coming this way.

Deacon: Do then sweep the hearth and spread the bed, while the rest of us do proceed—and enable us to find out and punish those traitors to our cause—

(Somebody knocks)

Come in—who put on the appearance of Whigs and thereby deceive the vigilance of our committees. Ah, ah, Squire, is it you? I did not perceive you before.

Landscapes.

Come, children, you may retire into the kitchen; the Squire and I have somewhat to talk about. Be ye reading in the meanwhile that excellent chapter I just began.

(Exeunt omnes, except Eltha)

Deacon: (With his left hand on his left knee, his right uplifted, his head hanging downwards.)

Well, Squire, it is but talking of some people, as the saying is, and you are sure to see them shortly. My wife and I were a-saying, before you came, how glad I was that you had somehow settled matters with the committee. I sent for you last night to shake hands with you on't.

(He shakes hands with the Squire)

It really does my heart good to see you so fat and hearty,—and pray, how have you fared through all your trials? It was not my fault, you may depend on it. I hope you have nothing in your heart against me.

Squire Rearman: Fared? Sir, hard enough, I can tell you. Your putrid gaols, your cruel turnkeys, your barbarous guards, for ever insulting, teasing the prisoners, —all these render a man's fate ten times harder. I fared so well that I was very near starving.

Deacon: Why! How could that happen? I am sure to the best of my memory I never gave such orders.

Squire Rearman: You know, I suppose, that they took me just after my family had been inoculated; and, under pretence of danger, they would suffer no provisions to come to me. In vain I offered to purchase some of their own. "Suck your paws as your brother bears do," was all the answer I received.

Deacon: Why, that is as true as the Devil is in London. I never did give such orders as those. I wonder what should make them act in that manner.

Eighteenth Century America.

Squire Rearman: What orders they had, I know not. What was wanting in explicitness was supplied and most amply dictated by the fruitful spirit of the times. And really, how can it be otherwise? You have made no provision for the support of those whom you confine. If their friends and relations live at a great distance, great must their distress be until they can be relieved. If they have no friends or connections, they must depend on the charity of the neighbourhood, and that is pretty cold nowadays, you know, Mr. Chairman. Even those that have any humanity left, are obliged to send provisions in a private manner, or else they run the risk of incurring the hatred of the mob, a terrible evil. What, then, must become of poor prisoners thus situated? They can expect nothing from law; it extends its benefits but to the favourers of the new cause. Common mercy is departed.

Deacon: 'Tis hard, I confess. I never knew it was so bad. I am glad truly that you have made shift to overcome this severe trial. I hope you will forget it all and live with us all, as formerly.

Rearman: The horror one meets within those walls, the misery and despair which awaits your victims there, the horrid scenes I have seen there,—all these have made impressions on my mind which I never, never can forget. Oh! that poor young man who died raving, distracted in the midst of us, who begged, but in vain, to be removed where he might enjoy fresh air; who died at last the most cruel death! How can I ever forget him? Every night I see, I hear him still, as soon as I close my eyes. Had we had the same fever, we must all have perished in the same manner.

Deacon: Well, well, as to that and other things, they are unavoidable. The necessary struggles are great and mighty. The billows of the sea in a mighty tempest often shake and tear the resisting shores. I want to know how you came off so well, and by what means you have been able to return home.

Rearman: By the assistance and protection of ——. I found in him a spark of humanity. So much misery, so great a punishment inflicted for mere suspicions shocked him. He became my security, and I stay at home as his prisoner. This is what none of the committee would have ever done for me.

Deacon: That was really fortunate. But how did you escape from —— prison? By what means did you find your way home again?

Rearman: These are mysteries which I can never disclose. Suffice it for you that I have given proper bail and am enabled to remain with my family, from which I have been so long torn. Surely you don't wish it otherwise. The many moments of anxious suspense I have experienced seem to entitle me now to some degree of repose. Although I left all sick with the smallpox, yet from the instant of my confinement I never could be permitted even to hear the least tidings of their health, although but nine miles distant. Confinement, hard fare, obscurity,—all these things, it seems, were not enough.

Deacon: That is really fortunate. I hope you will become deserving of it, but if you will follow my counsel, you will no longer hold —— security. Give it up. Take my word, Squire; you shall be no longer molested.

Rearman: I, give up all my protection! No, sir, on the contrary, I shall repair to his house as soon as the time expires, when I make no doubt to re-obtain a further indulgence to stay at home and cultivate my farm. Have not the committee a field extensive enough to act in without trying to extend it? Thousands obey or rather dread your laws; suffer a poor individual to be scratched out of your list.

I willingly forgive you and the rest of your brethren for what is past, but, at the same time, shall take care how I renounce the favour of a man who, though a stranger to me, yet from motives of the purest generosity has thus relieved me. What else could or should I have done in the few days I lurked at home after my escape from ——? How often was my house surrounded? It seems to me that these people instinctively smelled me as hounds do smell their game. How often false friends, hypocrites, sly emissaries came to my wife under pretence of congratulating her! A less vigilant man than I would have a second time fallen a victim to their fury. Yet I had the courage to hold my ground. I had the dexterity to escape. I could not bear the thoughts of being torn from my family a second time, and leaving them to suffer the stings of that poverty, adversity, and exile which necessarily awaited them. This is what has made me rise superior to the strongest impulses of the human heart; for you know, I suppose, sir, that Tories are men as well as yourself.

Deacon: 'Tis hard, I must needs confess. I am glad to see that you have nothing in your heart against me in particular. I am, you know, but the voice of the people; 'tis they that govern us. The strongest motives force us to follow, nay, to indulge their native inclinations. —— has really nothing to do with the internal management of our county. This interfering of his in your case, I perceive, begins to displease some of our principal people. I do not know how we shall manage this point. 'Tis of more consequence than you think, for you still have friends.

Landscapes.

Rearman: I hope I have, but I am very sure not one of that name is on the committee. Give me leave to tell you that the majority of them have been guided all along by their blind passions much more than by any settled plan of conduct. How have they used —— and ——? Yes, I'll be bold to say that there was not in their proceedings the least show of humanity or even reason. And what amends have they met with, since? Nothing but exorbitant fines, the most unjust assessments. No, sir, expect not that I ever shall pay the committees so great a compliment at the expense of my safety. If this merciful step of —— is unpopular, let the matter be settled with him. Surely you don't mean to make me answerable for it.

Eltha: No, no, my husband has no such thoughts. But you do know how it would make you popular; it would show that you throw yourself into the arms of the country. Our folks would then begin to look on you with better eyes. You do know so well, as my husband and I do, how clever it would look. This affair may take another turn, for what we know; 'tis hard to tell how it may turn out. The chairman, to be sure, has got power, but he can't always do as he pleases. I'd have you, good sir, take notice of that. My husband is too good, and were he to follow my advice, some people would not have to reproach him, as they do, with tenderness of heart. He is so teased that he has no peace in his life.

Rearman: This has been the bait held to me, as well as to many others, from the beginning; I have caught at it many times and have always been duped. Surely you'll allow me that degree of caution which deception naturally inspires. When first the Association was launched forth, how earnestly did you press me to sign it! It was to be the great bond of union which was to unite us all. It was to serve to the weak and unpopular "as a shield against the strong"; this was your expression. Yet, how has it turned out? In all contributions to raise soldiers, in the raising of taxes, in the assessment of teams, forage, etc. I and many others have always been oppressed in the most partial, shocking manner. What is become of your fair promises? It was nothing but delusion. I have signed to please you; I have paid; I have borne everything without a visible murmur. Yet nothing can satisfy your people; nothing can assuage that rancour which they possess, but utter extirpation, banishment, and confiscation. This is now the reward for my passive sufferings, for that long train of oppression and contumely to which, you well know, I have been subjected these three years.

Collected within the bounds of my farms, I have resigned every principle of action into your hands. I have submitted myself to the guidance of fate and hoped for better days. Yet what has my patience, my retirement, my voluntary absence from society deserved? Nothing but contempt, injurious language, and repeated oppression. I have been cruelly confined; put in irons, without hearing, without the least show of reason. I have heard of no evidences deposing against me, and at this very minute I know not what reasons you have had to tear me from my family at the most critical juncture, when my wife and nine children had just received the poison of the small-pox.

Deacon: Why, as to that and all you have said, I could not help it. The good of the cause required it, and the captain that took you has said in my presence many times that he had orders from the government; and, you know, it behooves not inferiors to meddle or inter-

Landscapes.

fere with the conduct of their superiors. What is done over the river, you know, cannot be undone on this side.

Eltha: Why, though I am but a woman, as you may say, yet I can see things pretty plain, and from my wheel cast my eyes all over the county. Though I say it to such a squire, my wheel, to tell you the truth, puts me in mind of our affair. I can't help sometimes wondering how wonderfully the affairs of our county are turned. There is a great difference, Squire, between managing the law as you used to, and passing judgment and pronouncing sentences and sitting on the bench, and the present times. Now is the prophet's turn. Methinks I can see all these things in John's Revelations as plain as I can see my distaff. And, to tell you a plain truth—for I am a plain woman—I have often heard the neighbours say—aye, even those who live within sight of the smoke of your chimney—as how formerly nobody ever went to places of public meetings first and last so punctually as you. There was nothing done up and down the county, not even a road laid out, not a poor bastard put out, but you were at the head and tail on't, as the saying is. Now, Squire, your keeping yourself at home, and washing your hands of all public concerns is an evident demonstration that you dislike them. It does not show well, it does not signify.

Deacon: So I have heard and indeed, myself observed, to tell you the plain truth, that you grew as scarce as gold. Everybody talked; everybody remarked it; and you know that our people are afraid. They are jealous, and there is no knowing sometimes where their suspicions arise from.

Rearman: This never could be the cause of my misfortunes. Many have been taken up and confined for being at all your public meetings, and sometimes pru-

263

dently showing their dissent to a great many things which they did not think altogether proper.

Deacon: 'Tis hard, I confess, but these are mere trifles compared to the good of the cause, a cause which doesn't carry on so much for our sakes as for those of our posterity. 'Tis a bleeding cause, as our minister says of it; therefore sufferings must come from it. This great land of Canaan cannot be purged of its ancient idolators without abundance of trouble. Now the Jews had a much better chance because the Canaanites did not speak the same language. We must guess, and sift, and find out; no wonder if we make mistakes sometimes. However, I am glad you have weathered it. I hope you will now become one of us, and help to defend this country where you were born. What man must that be who turns against the house of his father, and tries to burn these fields which have nourished him so long! A malediction overtake him, I say!

Eltha: So say I. They don't deserve to live except it may be in Guinea with the other slaves of that country.

Deacon: Come, come. Let us forgive and forget. Next time the militia marches, take up your musket and follow us; that will be the best proof you can give.

Rearman: I, take up my musket! Not I! Let those who shine, who rule, who grow rich, who meet every encouragement, go and fight. For my part I am not mad enough to help those who these three years have cut me off from the benefits of society.

Deacon: That won't do either! But to-day is Lord's day. God forbid that I should suffer any wrathful word to defile the sanctity of the day. You must abide by the consequences; that is all I can say. Pray, do you know what is become of your fellow-prisoner, F. M.? I mean him that escaped with you.

Landscapes.

Rearman: He is returned home, sir, I suppose, unless he has been hunted and pursued. For, poor man, he can't endure so much as I can; he has not such a set of nerves. I do not know what fear and despair may induce him to do, but he has told me many times that he wished for nothing more than to remain at home with his family. Have you heard of him lately?

Eltha: Heard of him! Why, don't you know? Come, come, don't plead ignorance; you know it as well as we do ourselves. Why, he is gone to the enemy. He had it always in his heart; it is an old darling scheme of his.

Rearman: You astonish me. He gone, of all men! Well, then he must have met with some new persecution; he must have fallen a second time into the hands of his enemies. He wanted to apply to the Council of Safety, and I believe did do it. Poor man! What he suffered in gaol, I believe, would induce him to run the risk of his life rather than endure confinement again. He must have been forced to it by some new dangers or insults. His age, besides, did not admit of a very active life. His heart now will break in twain to be separated a second time from his wife and children, to whom he is so attached. Oh, could I but repeat what I have heard him say whilst we were both confined! A worthier man never did exist. Though in an obscure station, very few men in the country are there that deserve so much the respect of all. You know him well, sir; is not it so?

Deacon: No matter for what he was, the question is what he is now. However, 'tis all over with him, and I am sorry.

Eltha: Sorry! why, my dear, where did you learn to throw sorrow away in this manner? Keep your sorrow for our poor soldiers that die fighting for us; keep it for the hundreds of our prisoners whom they are wilfully starving in New York. For my part, I have no notion at all to be sorry for any such thing as F. M.'s elopement. He has now confirmed the opinion we had all along entertained of him. He ever was a worshipper of kings. Let him go now and worship his favourite idol, "over the seas and far away," as the song says. For what care we? What he leaves behind him is now become an acceptable offering to his much injured country.

Rearman: Thus it is with thousands whom your barbarous treatment daily converts into enemies. You follow a strange policy, I must confess, but you are not sure of victory yet.

Deacon: Every man to his lot. 'Tis all pre-ordained, as the Scripture says. Yours, sir, has appeared hitherto much happier, but take care how you behave yourself. The arms of the committee can overtake you yet.

Rearman: As a scalded cat dreads the fire, so will I remember the state of probation through which I have passed. I propose to remain at home, wholly passive as before, and to wait for my fate with resignation and fortitude. Your servant, sir.

Deacon: Yours, sir. Remember me to all at home.

Rearman: Ah, sir, this compliment puts me in mind of our old time of peace and concord. 'Tis now out of fashion to remember one another but in the hour of wrath and vengeance. Farewell. (Exit Rearman)

Deacon: Well, my dear, we have been so long conversing with that proud squire that it is almost time to go to meeting. Come, try what haste you can make; get us breakfast as quick as you can.

Eltha: I had a little jaunt to propose to you, to which I could wish you would agree. You won't refuse me, I hope. Do, my dear, come. Shall we go?

Landscapes.

Deacon: Well, what is it? Where is it that you want to go?

Eltha: I long, as much as I did for anything in my life, to go to F. M.'s. I do not know how it is, but I have been dreaming of it all night, and I cannot banish the thoughts from my head. What is it that impels me? I cannot tell. We should not refuse obedience to these impulses. Who knows but they come from above?

Deacon: Oh, fie, fie, wife. This won't do, I am sure. To-day is Lord's day, you know. Who is to set the Psalms and accompany the minister and read the news-paper at the meeting-house door? It will cause, besides, a prodigious misedification. What will the people, the neighbours think?

Eltha: Think! Why, don't they know very well that you have so given up your time to the good of the cause that you have scarce leisure to eat or rest, and that as a chairman, as a colonel, as a commissioner for selling Tory estates, you do not know which way to turn yourself? They will charitably imagine that some particular business belonging to either of these commissions has necessarily called you away. Don't you remember last night there was a talk, just as we were singing our evening Psalms, that some of these pestilential people had risen in the mountains because, forsooth, you had fastened to the ground a half dozen of them the day before. The people, I am sure, will readily excuse you. Somebody will kindly take your place at meeting, and those who for so many years have known you to be so constant an attendant, won't begin to censure you at this time.

Deacon: Why, what is it that urges you so strongly? What do you want to do there? To-morrow, you know, the committee is going to seize all. If you are so inclined, you must come along with us.

Eltha: To-morrow won't do so well. There will be abundance of people. I could wish to see beforehand the good furniture, their bedding, their plentiful cellar, the well-stored granary. I want to see how the woman looks with all her little Tory bastards about her. Do, my dear, do now; I cannot resist it. Who knows—and I am sure you do not know yourself—but these roguish people will sequester something and rob the state of some part of its lawful inheritance? And you are sensible that they have always been the very worst sort of people among us.

Deacon: Well, well, wife, this last reason seems to carry along with it some degree of plausibility. Do you then mention it in that light to the family. I will retire to my Bible while you are getting ready.

Eltha: I will, Colonel. You may be sure we may, besides, sanctify the day and talk, as we go and come, of something about God; and though there will be nobody by that we can edify, thereby the whole good will be unto us. (Exit Deacon)

Eltha: Ruth, Ruthy, do, my child, tell Tom to come to me. Be quick, be speedy. Do you hear?

Ruth: Yes, Mammy. Tom is here at the door, brushing the snow from his feet.

Eltha: Tom, get ready your master's mare and my old jade. We are not going to meeting to-day as he proposed. Some private intelligence he has received obliges him to go another way. Now, Tom, let us see how quick you can do that. Will you have a dram of whisky this morning?

Tom: Tanke you, Misse. Wiseky is good these colde

Landscapes.

weather for negro. Me go, Misse; me have the horses by and by. Masse wante me along?

Eltha: No, Tom, you must stay at home and help the girls to cook and pray.

Ruth: What is that, Mammy, I have heard say—not go to meeting to-day? Why, Mammy, what shall we do? We shall know nothing, neither about the chapter or the Psalms, for, thanks to these plaguy Tories, we cannot go either, as all our other horses have been out all night after them.

Eltha: Make yourselves easy, children; the Lord will forgive us all for once. What we are now doing is for the good of His own chosen cause. 'Tis serving Him to serve His worthy representatives, the Congress. In the meanwhile, that you may not spend your time without gathering a blessing, read the second of Jeremiah and twenty pages of the journal of the Reverend George Whitefield's life. This will be edifying, I am sure, and do you pretty near as much good as though you had gone to meeting.

Ruth: No, not quite, Mammy, I am sure. Why then should all the young fellows and all the young girls attend there so constantly every Sabbath?

Eltha: It must be so to-day, however. You know I never hinder you from going any other time, but to-day your father has particular reasons. Do you hear me?

Ruth: We shall do as you bid us. But before you go, see, Mammy, that you leave us a good dinner. Some of the young people, perhaps, may come to join in our devotions.

Eltha: You know that your father and I have never had any objection to these religious meetings; it promotes a holy sympathy, edification, and proper awakenings. See that you keep good decorum, and, if anybody

269

knocks, mind that they find you with your Bibles in your hands.

Ruth: We shall do so, Mammy. I hope you'll come back before it is dark. We are afraid, you know, since the militia are gone down below.

Eltha: Go then, quick, call the Colonel, and tell him that I am ready.

Second Landscape: On the Road.

On horseback proceeding towards F. M.'s house.

Beatus, *deacon.*
Eltha, *his wife.*
Splash, *militia-lieutenant.*

Eltha: 'Tis really plaguy lucky that this fellow's cowardice has at last driven him off. I wish his good mate, the Squire, had done the same. But at home he will be, and I am really afraid that his stubbornness will enable him to weather it. 'Tis best these rich fellows should go, for they won't fight, and by decamping they leave plaguy good fleeces behind. We want them all, and many more, to raise the credit of our money, and to help us to carry on the war.

Deacon: There you are right, wife; all these quondam gentry are our bitterest enemies, though they dare not declare it. For that purpose I have set the committee of the county upon ways and means to make them scamper, or do worse. I have communicated my plan to the Governor and his council, who mightily approve of it. Did I ever show you, wife, the public thanks I received the other day from ——?

Eltha: Public thanks? As God is my judge, I never have heard a single syllable on it. So much humility, Colonel, is not always good, even to your wife. Really

Landscapes.

I don't understand it. Keep secret from your wife, the flesh of your bones, the ribs of your sides, your second self! Why I am amazed! You know that I have given you many good hints on the pillow which have proved desperate good and serviceable.

Deacon: Hush, hush; speak lower. Look round before you express yourself so freely. When we thus converse together, let us watch and mistrust even the wind that blows.

Eltha: No, no, my dear. None but God hears us from above, and I make no doubt with great complacency. When will that day come, that we shall all enter His new Jerusalem and be as one of His chosen nations, decked in the robes of His Institution, ready to rebuild His temple and make the mounts of His new Sion resound with His praises?

Deacon: God is good; God is great; His mercy is immense. If we serve Him faithfully, I am sure, He tells my heart, that He will reward us with the spoil of our enemies. But, stop, stop. Here comes Lieutenant Splash! Not a word more of this. What news, Lieutenant?

Splash: Nothing very material at present, honourable Colonel, only they say that our folks are a-killing the red-coats by thousands down below. We will hang these Britanneers, see if we don't. Oh, I forgot to tell you that we were like to catch F. M., that great scoundrel. We shot at him a half dozen times, but, as God is my judge, the devil saved him that we might hang him awhile hence. But if we missed him, we surely hit in the head ——, the great thief.

Deacon: What? Have you killed him? Have you really shot him down?

Splash: Aye, aye, have I. Well, Colonel, if it were

not your honour that asked me the question—well, to be sure, not killed him! And why not? As dead as a door-nail. But what a pity that the fellow had been once a lieutenant in our service and a good Whig! I am really sorry that he has thus brought a disgrace on the name.

Deacon: A Whig, did you say? That wants confirmation, I am sure; 'tis very improbable. Now you mention it, I recollect that he never was what you have called him. It is my opinion that [had] he been a Whig, this never could have happened. Why, do you think that, if he had been sincerely one of us, God's divine providence would have thus abandoned him? Believe me, Lieutenant Splash, he was a Tory in his heart. I know it as I do know a great many other things, and I charge you to give him that name wherever you mention him. Besides, let me tell you that you may bring yourself into bad bread by doing otherwise. He was a Tory in his heart, I tell you—that I am sure of—and the committee have agreed to punish the first man who shall call him otherwise.

Splash: Well, Colonel, you'll excuse me. No man but what may fail. I am but an ignorant countryman, that is to be sure. You know better in all things; all the country knows it. I am quite sensible of my error. It would indeed reflect a great, very great blemish on our cause. Let the Tories bear all the iniquity, for they deserve it richly.

Deacon: I know you mean well and, therefore, I excuse you. Which way now?

Splash: To meeting, honoured sir. Any command there?

Deacon: No, tell the people that I shall be there for the afternoon service.

Landscapes.

Splash: I shall not fail. Farewell, sir.
Deacon: Farewell, Lieutenant.

Third Landscape: At a Tavern.

Beatus, *deacon.*
Eltha, *his wife.*
Potter, *landlord.*
Iwan, *a foreigner.*
D. Ecclestone, *an American gentleman.*

While the deacon and his wife proceed on their journey, the scene continues at the tavern.

Eltha, the Chairwoman: Well, landlord, how goes it on to-day? I haven't seen you, no, not I, since my husband tried some Tories in your back-room. Have you got any of that good spiritual you used to have?

Landlord: Why, as to that, Mrs. Chairman, if I may be so bold, I must tell you that since the people are become a lump of clay in the hands of our masters, the juices of the community are become exhausted. And now to talk in conscience, who can afford to sell for ten shillings what one is obliged to give twenty shillings for?

Chairwoman: Aye, aye, that is true in some respects, but in others we may say that it is all for the good of the cause. Every one must contribute something. How should we carry on the war? My good husband, he gives all his time towards it; others give their labour; others some money; others their teams; we must all help. I hope you don't flinch and draw back.

Landlord: As to that and many other things, that is more than true; 'tis evident to the greatest demonstration. But Mrs. Chairman should consider that I spend the best part of my time in doing militia-duty; that I pay heavy taxes—thirty-seven good honest pounds do I

273

now disburse towards Congress instead of fourteen towards the King; that my negro and team is for ever
more a-going. Is not that enough, besides losing so
much on tavern amounts? But though I have taken my
sign down, you are welcome to any little remnant I
have.

Chairwoman: Well, let us taste then. What do you
[think], Colonel, my dear?

Deacon: Why, a little in reason will do no harm, this
cold morning.

Landlord: Here, Mrs. Chairman. I could give no
better to his honour, General Washington, if he was to
pass by.

Chairwoman: It is the true juice of the cane. Oh, how
sweet it smells! Old stores, are they not? Or else you
must deal with the enemy, I am sure. Now tell me
where you got this.

Landlord: Deal with the enemy? Aye, aye, that's to
be sure; and so we do, but after a strange sort of fashion. Our friends to the eastwards have taken some of
their ships, and I have given the Bostonians thirty dollars a gallon for this. Now you understand me.

Chairman Deacon: 'Tis really excellent. What must
I give you for this dram?

Landlord: Give? Why, nothing. I told you that I
kept tavern no longer. You are welcome. Besides, to-
day is Lord's day, and God forbid that I should defile
it with filthy lucre; you are welcome, as I told you
before.

Deacon: I am really glad to see you taking such good
ways; I have been told as how you used to be a pretty
tight churchman. I hope these times will make a good
Christian of you, and teach you to worship as we do,

since your churches are shut up, and your priests have abandoned you all.

Landlord: Why, sir, I always professed myself a Christian and hope I am so still. There is nothing in names that I know of.

Deacon: At times this may do very well, but now we are the favourite Christians, the defenders of liberty, and, if we succeed, you may be sure we shall take care of ourselves. The reapers should enjoy the benefits of harvest, as the saying is. Hard times for poor Tories and churchmen, I must confess; well may they call themselves the militant folks every way. But 'tis the fortune of war; they must grin and bear it. They must become pliable, humour the times, and submit.

Landlord: And so we must, and so we should, and so we do to the best of our power. But it takes time, honorable Colonel, to part with the old stuff and put on new garments. For my part, I always mean well and do the best I can.

Deacon: As people shake off the dust from their feet before they go into meeting, so must you and yours part with their old attachments and prejudices, or else they cannot enter into the New Jerusalem, that new temple of liberty so wonderfully reared in so short a time. Take my word for it: bid farewell to your kings, bishops, and monarchy. But if you still long after the last, you must look toward heaven for the fifth which is there manifested. Though my thoughts are thus, what you have seen concerning monarchy in this world should estrange you from the other.

Landlord: Why, sir, if I might be so bold as to speak my own mind unto you who knows a great deal more than such poor folks as I do, and as to what concerns kings, bishops, and monarchy, is it not under them that we have grown rich and fat? Is it not by their good contrivance that we have become so numerous, that we have so many cleared fields and mowing-grounds, and a fine market for what we raise? What! Would you, Mr. Chairman, impute it as a crime because some people do still revere and respect that form of government from which so much good has arisen, and dared at least respect these new inventions, the usefulness and advantages of which we have never experienced yet? It may be all for the better, and I am sure, for my part, I hope so. But who can tell how the coat will wear, though the cloth may look well?

Deacon: That is all very well said, honest landlord, but yet we must make a good Whig of you and an honest man—do you hear? And we must be sure of your conversion.

Landlord: A Whig, sir? I don't understand that word.

Deacon: Why, have you lived so long and do not know yet what a Whig is? 'Tis a lover of Congress and committees, a lover of his country.

Landlord: And so I do. But why should I wish that our navigable rivers should be converted into a great number of brooks on which our canoes could not swim?

Deacon: Navigable rivers? Brooks? What is the meaning of all this? You shall love the country such as we shall make it for you. Well, to be sure, you Toryfied gentry shall cut and carve for yourselves no such thing. Mourn and bow down; your hope is cut off; you trust in a spider-web. You lean upon an old house, but it is falling. You hold it fast in your heart, we know; but it shall not endure, for it is passing away; the Scriptures condemn you. Well, to be sure, let me hear one word more about your brooks and your rivers!

Landscapes.

Landlord: Mr. Chairman, to be sure, understands the threads of these things better than we poor folks, who have nothing to do with the affairs of the county. For my part, I work and sweat and obey, and I hope the honourable Committee will find no fault with us little ones, who are but herrings in the school.

Deacon: That is well put in for a plaster, but I know full well where the sore lies; the canker is now at your heart. Many and repeated complaints have been made unto me, for all you can say, about your keeping a Tory house. I have always made believe as though it could not be.

Landlord: You have done me justice, good sir; my house was public then. How should I know what sentiments those entertain who resort to it?

Deacon: That is well enough, to be sure, but take care that the people don't talk too much about you. I am their organ, but I am led by their desires; I must please them at any rate. That is between us. Well, landlord, what do you charge for your pint of good spirituals?

Landlord: Not a farthing, honourable Colonel. I am no longer a tavern-keeper, as I told you before; you are heartily welcome.

Eltha: Now, landlord, mind what my husband has told you; 'tis to him you must look, and 'tis him you must please. It will all go well with you if you mind your steps.

Landlord: I shall so, Mrs. Chairman. (Exeunt.)

Fourth Landscape: At the Tavern.

Iwan.
Ecclestone.
Landlord.

Eighteenth Century America.

Aaron Blue-Skin, a new-made squire.

Colonel Templeman.

Three Quakers (tied).

Captain Shoreditch, with a black beard, bushy head, stockings half-way down his legs, and a naked cutlass in his hands.

Six armed militiamen with linsey-woolsey blankets, one end tied over their left shoulders, the other end under their right arms.

Ecclestone: I am right glad the fellow and his doxy are gone. Were there ever seen such scenes of low absurdity and tyranny exercised in so unaccountable a manner over a people who pretended to be so jealous once of their liberties? They have consigned them over to Congress without the acknowledgment even of a pepper-corn.

Iwan: Pooh, these are the very people that are the soonest caught. Only speak to them in their style; make a great fuss about property; talk about encroachments, privileges, etc.; they'll well take you to be their zealous friends and follow you anywhere and everywhere. 'Tis really enough to disgust one of the world and its dependencies to see and trace the conduct of this fellow throughout the meanderings of his pride, ignorance, vanity, consummate hypocrisy. He is a perfect epitome of the times.

Ecclestone: I, who am an American, am as sensible as you. This delegation of power *ad infinitum* from the imperial Congress to these low-lived rulers is intolerable in proportion to the distance of the sovereign, and to the antecedent passions and ignorance of these country chaps. What a devoted people we are that we should be thus suspended between poverty, neglect, and con-

Landscapes.

tempt if we go to New York, and fines, imprisonment, and exile if we stay!

Iwan: 'Tis a shocking circumstance, I acknowledge, but, alas! there is nothing new in all this. Read [in] history, my friend, that the same low, dirty chains lead mankind through all the variations of fate, through all the changes of fortune. We are victims of these two singular powers. What can we do but submit with cheerfulness and resignation? Talking about it only serves to make matters worse.

Ecclestone: 'Tis cursed hard to see, for instance, this fellow, his wife, and the junta dispose of all the social happiness of a county; commit the greatest barbarities, accumulate injustice on injustice, with impunity trample on every law; yet go and worship with an easy conscience. What must that same conscience be? It must be a false guide.

Iwan: Was not it so before these times? Did they not use to juggle and cheat mankind before, in all their dealings and arbitrations? They are the same men raised only five or six feet above the surface of the earth. Their consciences are only modes of thinking, and they have contracted the horrid bias long ago.

Ecclestone: I can't endure their slavish rule. I can't bow and prostrate myself before such wretches, who have perverted every idea of right and wrong.

Iwan: But you must do it. Go home then, and read Seneca, Isocrates; learn to fortify yourself by reason, and run not in despair like a fool; learn to bear the insolence of men. Societies, like individuals, have their periods of sickness. Bear this as you would a fever or a cold.

Ecclestone: How long will this last? This is the question. When the accounts of this mighty revolution arrive in Europe, nothing will appear there but the splendid effects. The insignificant cause will be overlooked; the low arts, this progressive succession of infatuations, which have pervaded the whole continent, will be unknown. The brave, the warlike Americans will be blazoned out as the examples of the world, as the veteran sons of the most rational liberty. Whereas we know how it is: how this country has been trepanned and insensibly led from one error to another, conducted by the glare of false-deceiving meteors.

Iwan: Small causes have generally the most extensive effects; 'tis so all the world over. When you read the resolves of some mighty councils, the edicts of potent kings, you see but the ostensible side of the medal. Could you pervade the little, insignificant cabals of their cabinets, the combination of female influence, the jars of parties, you'd observe the same train; you'd see that it is by the distance, the dense medium through which we little folks contemplate the actions of the great, that we are deceived. We have naturally such respect for grandeur that we are fools enough to think that they are made of other clay. Go learn of our grave-diggers whether there is any difference between the bones of a general and those of the common soldier that used to tremble at the least of his nods.

Ecclestone: That is all very true; that is commonplace talking. But does it not appear to you somewhat strange that there should be no analogy between causes and their effects, and that the chain which links both ends should be invisible to the keenest observer?

Iwan: Not in the least. What connection or similitude, pray, do you find between the acorn and the lofty oak? The few causes which rule the world are derived from the Great One; and if we are so incapable of com-

Landscapes.

prehending anything about it, why should we have the presumption to think that we can follow these threads, these sublime ramifications which pervade both the moral and the physical world?

Ecclestone: I have read with attention of the revolutions of Sweden, of Portugal, of Switzerland, and Holland, and they seem to me to be founded on plain, palpable, distinguished causes. The people were horribly tyrannized; the yoke was too heavy; they agreed to shake it off. The idea is simple.

Iwan: Why is not it the same here? At least they tell you so, and if everybody believes them, it answers the same purpose.

Ecclestone: The people can never believe what they have never felt. I am very sure 'tis not the weight nor the galling of the yoke which has hurried them on in this sorrowful career. 'Tis a multitude of motives adapted to the locality of provinces, which they have artfully reunited into one grand motive. The whole has been gilded by deception, and now forms a singular phantom, to which it is sacrilegious not to pay proper adoration.

Iwan: You are mistaken in the first part of your assertion. The ancient revolutions you have been mentioning had their origin, perhaps, in the same causes: the ambition of a few. But the distance of time, the tinsel of language, the care which the historian has taken to bring on the scene nothing but what is great, conspicuous, and grand, have left the rest behind. Look at the reformation of Russia, for instance. To what cause does it owe the rapid improvements it has made of late, and the conspicuous figure it now exhibits on the stage of the world? Why, to about two grains of poison.

Ecclestone: Two grains of poison! I don't understand you. What connection can you find and trace between two grains of poison and the vast schemes of your immortal Czar?

Iwan: You must remember that his sister, Sophia, who was much more advanced in age than himself, in order to rule alone, thought it political and expedient to give him a dose of poison, which the strength of his constitution enabled him to overcome. Now, an addition of two grains would certainly have dispatched him; and I will have you calculate how many millions to one but that St. Nicholas the Primate and the boyards would still have been the wretched masters of a wretched people. There is myself, for instance. Could you believe the original cause which led me here, you would hardly believe me.

Ecclestone: Did not you come to this country on purpose? Was it not a premeditated plan agreed on by your parents and friends?

Iwan: Not a bit. 'Twas a horse-shoe nail which sent me to England and thence to America.

Ecclestone: Surely you must think me as credulous as a New England man to tell me with a serious face that a horse-shoe nail drove you to this country.

Iwan: I am serious, and have too much respect for you to advance anything but what I can prove.

Ecclestone: Do, then, let us hear this curious anecdote. It is, I believe, the first shoe-nail, since man learnt the art of fabricating them, which has the magical power to send a man from the polar regions across the Atlantic to this new-found land.

Iwan: After my academical studies were finished, I served an apprenticeship with a merchant at Saratov, whose son resided at Archangel,—for which place I was destined also. Going one day to see the marriage of a

Landscapes.

friend, my horse, which had been shod purposely the day before, was severely pricked by a nail. This accident obliged me to hire a hackney one, which proved so bad that I got a very dangerous fall. This determined my father to send me to the bath of Olonets, where I met by mere accident a maternal uncle who had resided in England, to which country he soon after returned and took me along with him. You know the nature of commercial connections: in consequence of new views and schemes, he sent me here where I have lived ever since the most perfect itinerant life. Had I time, I could convince you that from the single circumstance all the shades and variations of my life afterwards flowed with as uninterrupted a connection as the thread of a ball after you have unravelled the intricate beginnings.

Ecclestone: 'Tis really melancholy to see what puppets we are that can't distinguish even the wires that move us on.

Iwan: 'Tis so, and who knows whether we would move at all, could we see to what purpose we are moving? Fate leads the willing, drags the backward on.

Ecclestone: Must I then see my native country conquered by low, illiterate, little tyrants? Must I see the dearest bonds of society torn asunder? All our hopes, our views, our peace, all we had been bred to look on as sacred and useful—must I look upon all these things as indifferent, and passively bear every contumely, suffer every insult, repress the swellings of the big heart, swallow the bitter cup to the last drop, see our famed constitution levelled with the dust, observe the new and imperfect embryo rising out of its dissolved, disunited parts? Must I without either a sigh or a groan, but with a passiveness derived from fatality, worship the pretended saints, veteran Puritans, hair-brained fellows of

283

the East? In the South bend the knee to the little negro lordlings, to haughty, imperious planters who wish to revenge themselves on their native country for the ancient banishment of their forefathers? Must we obey, without repining, their hard rule and overlook all the deceit and disappointment it contains? No, I cannot do it. Let me bleed out of every pore what blood I have, and expire with the pleasing consciousness of having done what I could to prevent it. God grants us no blessing without purchase: health by temperance, harvest by severe labours, riches by industry. Shall not the peace, the glory of the land be repurchased by blows, by struggles, by a well-supported contest?

Iwan: These are laudable sentiments; this is the enthusiasm without which even a peer is unworthy of the name of citizen, and with which the meanest plebeian can become superior to kings. But you can do no more than what you are permitted by your situation and abilities. Who knows but it is irrevocable? In that case you must submit with prudence and not expose yourself in vain; or else you must quit it.

Ecclestone: Quit it! That I shall if this event happen. I will go and hide the shame of being born an Englishman on Terra Australis, in Patagonia, in the most unknown part of the world. Great Britain shall lose the awful name. I shall ever after look upon it as a country lost to the vices of extreme riches, and pray to heaven that some great national misfortune may befall her and reinstate her in all former virtue and energy.

Iwan: The Master of the World alone knows how the event will be. I am not a politician,—and a foreigner, besides. But surely some sort of order, if it is the fruit of fear and coercion, will be better than committee rule, the most detestable of any.

Landscapes.

Ecclestone: I do not know how it is, but if these people succeed, I shall certainly think that this world was made for knaves, hypocrites, and fools.

Iwan: What this world was made for, I am sure I cannot tell. There is rather a degree of impiety in wishing to investigate so sublime a scheme. But in our obscure gropings and strange wanderings, it really appears as if it was even so. For they are the greatest majority, and the greatest number surely should have the greater right in a system where everything depends on force. This is infallibly the case except where the wisdom of the few has set itself in opposition and become superior.

Ecclestone: Sad reflections! Terrific thoughts, big with every bitterness! Poor consolation! Oh, my native country, why did not I die and quit the scene ere our ancient, refulgent sun was eclipsed by these accursed evaporations? To aim at a greater share of political felicity, to make the world believe we were slaves, to make us exchange the silken cords of our ancient government for the rattling chains of our timocracy,—is perhaps the most monstrous instance of perfidy, ingratitude, and successful hypocrisy that ever was exhibited in the world before.

Iwan: This is all very true, but if Providence really interferes in the little quarrels of the ants, which are perpetually busy in rearing and pulling down some part of the mole-hill, who knows but this revolution might have been necessary in order to check the prodigious career of prosperity enjoyed by England? Redden not with anger, but hear me patiently. Who knows but if she had enjoyed the peaceable possession of this country thirty years longer undisturbed, but what she might have had power enough to have ruled the world, and to have collected within her extended arms all its commerce, all its riches, and the influence they bring along with them? The next thing to power, you know, is the inclination to abuse it. Who knows but that the mischiefs that might have ensued would have been far greater, far more extensive, than those you now experience? Could we with our mole-eyes foresee these distant consequences, trace these subsequent dependencies, we might then talk more respectfully of the wisdom of these links of which we now so bitterly complain.

Ecclestone: That is all very well said, but why should every thing be so constituted as to be founded on evil, rise from evil? Poor choice! Sad situation! And so we must think ourselves happy to undergo but seven years' calamity instead of twenty! Why one? Why any? Is not the common chance of diseases, hurricanes, and other natural misfortunes sufficient to keep mankind in remembrance of their dependence, mortality, and of the precarious tenure of their leases?

Landlord: (Hastily coming into the room.) Hush! hush! for God's sake, gentlemen. Let not a word more escape your lips. Be as if you were just come in, weary and tired. Put on your dirty boots, and be as if you knew nothing of me. Here comes N. S. Esq. He is the very inquisitor of these parts; he is a merciless committee-man. The sight of him always makes me shudder. 'Tis said that Mercy and Truth turned their heads from him at the time of his nativity and never looked at him since.

Aaron Blue-Skin: (Enters with a wild, irascible countenance.) Landlord, have you got anything that an exhausted, fatigued man may recruit himself with, this chilly, cold morning?

Landlord: Why, great and good sir, you know that the law has taken my sign down. I don't shut my doors against my friends and acquaintances, but I keep tavern no more. The new law which limits the prices of everything has put it out of my power to entertain folks as I used to.

Aaron Blue-Skin: That is very wrong, my word for it; and I say so. What is more, this is a pure, good stand for the business. I believe you are stiff and stubborn, yet you won't submit as the rest do. The committee, I believe, must take you in hand; they are pure people to bring obstinacy and malice quite low. If they do, depend on't, they will make you as pliant as a glove. I believe you know pretty roundly what they can do. Well, on my word! Taken your sign down to spite your best customers, who were Whigs! Well, really this is defying a power which no one else dares to do within the precincts of the county.

Landlord: What can, what should, what must I do, great and good sir? I wish you'd tell me. If the honourable committee will supply me with a sufficient stock at my price, I shall then entertain them on the old footing. But, good sir, good sir, let not that ruffle you. Whenever your honour goes by and is pleased to stop, you shall always be welcome to such as I have for my own family.

Aaron Blue-Skin: Who are those two strangers eating there? Surely some part of the public is still welcome to your board.

Landlord: As to these two gentlemen, they just came in and merely forced themselves upon me. They said as how they were weary and would go no further without refreshment. I have given them such as I have, and they allow me so much by the hour for the benefit of my fireside; and you know this severe season a tight room and a good fire are more valuable than the best of victuals.

Aaron Blue-Skin: Well, that is really a very impudent way of evading the law and defeating its meaning. What power must legislators have to bind such a set of infamous rascals as we have up and down the country! Charge for the use of his fire, I suppose, as much as the entertainment amounts to! Well, really this is something new, to be sure! The first time I attend the house, I will produce an amendment such as will never want amendment again. I profess, never fear, Mr. Landlord, we shall keep you in our eyes all the time, and by frustrating your sagacity shall defeat that of your fellows.

Landlord: Could the laws be founded but on common justice they would not need of any amendments. But who can afford to lose two-thirds on the retail of everything, and have the house full, besides?

Aaron Blue-Skin: Come, come, sir! I am piping hot from the committee. No sarcasm, no biting reflections, if you please! Not the most distant reflection, to be sure, will allow you to set your poor, pitiful judgment in competition with that of our whole legislative body. Take care that I don't handle you; if I lay my hands on you, it shall be tightly. I promise you that we sent last night thirty-four of your brethren to be fastened to the ground who had not said a fourth part so much; but in consideration of the burley [*sic*] I am willing as a neighbour, besides, to pass over,—but have a care next time! Your name stinks, you know.

Landlord: Good sir, I meant no harm, but when I am a-speaking I can't tell where nor when to stop. My tongue is so used to its ancient declivity it will run off itself, as it were. But you know me very well. Every man has his enemies. God help us!

Aaron Blue-Skin: God help you, pretty fellows! Indeed it is we whom God will and does help every day in enabling us to vanquish our cruel enemies. When our triumph is complete, when these soldiers of Pharaoh have left our land, which they have polluted, you shall see what you shall see: what an orderly set of people we shall make of you all. Look at the Jersey: thanks to their laws and their worthy governor, the very primrose of the continent, they have brought the people to fear and reverence the laws. 'Tis really admirable. I just now voted that for the future no law should pass without a good wedge clapped at the end on't; that whenever any of your qualmish people and your evasive folks make their appearance, some of us may be ready to drive it on and fasten the rascals. In the Jersey aforesaid they never pass a law without enacting that he, they, or she, that shall find fault with the same, shall pay a good stout fine or be imprisoned. That is the matter we want. (He yawns. He strokes and rubs his eyes.) God forgive me, these plaguy Tories have made us intrude on the Sabbath. I do not know how it happened.

Landlord: What! Are you but just come from the committee, Squire Aaron?

Aaron Blue-Skin: Not a half hour ago did we break up.

Landlord: Who are they that have been so severely handled?

Aaron Blue-Skin: Why, there are Squire —— and Major ——, quondam Major, I mean; and there is farmer ——, that proud, rich, old miser; and there is friend Hezekiah, the simple but wealthy Quaker. God knows who the rest were; our clerk may tell. Oh, how it pleases me to bring the pride of these quondam gentry down! This is fulfilling the Bible to a tittle; this is lowering the high and rewarding the low; this is humbling the proud; this is exalting the Christian, the meek man. He, she, or they that fulfil thus the word of God shall be blessed; that is, shall prosper in this world and the next. (He drinks.) Here is, God bless the Congress and damn the popish King. Who says "amen" to it?

Two Strangers: As we belong not to your congregation, we owe you, therefore, no response.

Aaron Blue-Skin: What? Responses? Congregations? Why, you talk like suspected persons. I presume you are Tories travelling towards New York.

Two Strangers: We travel where we want to go. The road is opened, and we know of no difficulty that can stop us. Whenever we meet with guards, if required, we produce our authority which no man dare call in question.

Aaron Blue-Skin: This is the sauciest speech I have heard this great while. I vow, if it were not that the committee is gone to meeting, I'd have you seized and sent to gaol "ipso facto," as the old law used to say. You travel where you please! Well, to be sure, you do not know, I suppose, before whom you are a-speaking; and that I am the very soul and quintessence of a committee-man; and that we are the appointed guardians, the watch-towers of this county, the collective wisdom of the four precincts; and that it is our bounden duty to see and to observe from our high stations everything that passes.

Two Strangers: This all may be, and much more which your modesty prevents you explaining. We are afraid of no man or of no set of men, and as we, by our principles, wish well to all mankind, we have a stock of

Landscapes.

confidence which nothing can alter. Authority is a commodity which is become so common that it is become less valuable than heretofore. There are so many givers of passes and pretenders to power and control that we are extremely cautious of adulterating our general pass by the addition of new and unknown names.

Aaron Blue-Skin: You travel thus under authority, gentlemen?

Two Strangers: That's what we do.

Aaron Blue-Skin: That is another affair. I presume your authority is from the army?

Two Strangers: Yes, sir. Is not it superior to that of committees?

Aaron Blue-Skin: Sometimes we may allow it, but in the administration of our own county we know no superior but God.

Two Strangers: That may be as you say, but as we are not inhabitants of your county we think ourselves not at all amenable to your jurisdiction, as long as we offend nobody, but travel on peaceably.

Aaron Blue-Skin: You are right, gentlemen. By your speech I should take you to be lawyers travelling to headquarters, I suppose?

Two Strangers: Yes, sir, we have heard so much of the Continental army, that we want to go and take a view of these noble defenders of American liberty.

Aaron Blue-Skin: Do tell General Washington that we are preparing ourselves to send him a fine parcel of volunteers, stout lads that turn out for the good of the cause.

Ecclestone: What bounty do you give them in this part of the country?

Aaron Blue-Skin: Bounty! Oh, for shame! The government would be extremely wrong to give them any;

291

it would be putting an affront upon us. But our people, who are naturally generous, club together and make them a purse of about eleven hundred dollars.

Ecclestone: Eleven hundred dollars! Very pretty volunteers, indeed. I hope they are better than those who are a-coming from the eastward; they are old negro boys, lads of all size, etc. . . .

Aaron Blue-Skin: Why, gentlemen, as to that, our stock of young men begins to grow very scarce with us. These lads in a year or two will be grown up; they will be much more pliable and fitter for the great school of arms.

Two Strangers: That may be, but where are the men to do their duty whilst they are growing up?

Aaron Blue-Skin: Enough of them to the southward. 'Tis said that Governor Casewell is a-coming with a powerful number, who bring with them a nation of rice-cakes ready made. Landlord, what have I to pay?

Landlord: Nothing, good Squire, as I told you before.

Aaron Blue-Skin: Why, that is really clever. If the good creature is absolutely so cheap, God bless the law and the law-makers for it. Let us have another tumbler.

Landlord: Here it is, Squire.

Aaron Blue-Skin: Come, honest Tom, won't you pledge me?

Landlord: No, sir, you'll excuse me, I presume to pledge none but my equals; I know what respect I owe to a worshipful committee-man.

Aaron Blue-Skin: Why, as to that, you were a-saying, to be sure, who dares say nay. We committee-men, we can do a great deal; think a great deal; write a great deal; and order abundance of things. But, Tom, never mind it for this time. We are neighbours still. Plague

Landscapes.

on my head! It contains so many things that it's almost ready to burst; it sadly aches. I believe I shall not go to meeting to-day. Can't you lend us a bed for an hour or two?

Landlord: A bed! Nay, two at your service and welcome! But how comes it that you good Christians have so much intruded on the Lord's day? Why did not you finish your business betimes?

Aaron Blue-Skin: Haven't I told you already that the Tories' affairs are so large and so manifold. Transactions of these gentry are to be examined into, so that it takes abundance of time.

Landlord: Generally you don't trouble your head much about evidences. It seems to me that this short method of yours requires but a short time.

Aaron Blue-Skin: That is very true, Tom. We lump it sometimes pretty expeditiously. But then there was waiting for the honourable Chairman; and there was eating supper and smoking a pipe or two and drinking a little whisky toddy and reading the newspapers and examining Governor Johnstone's fine speech—why, all these take abundance of time.

Landlord: That is very true.

Aaron Blue-Skin: And there was hunting of some of the Tories who were lurking in the neighbourhood and were asleep. And there was treating our light-horsemen with a dram apiece, to be sure, for they are really quite smart fellows. They understand surrounding a man's house quite charmingly well and pulling and hauling the Tories out of their beds as well and better than any folks in the world.

Landlord: But, pray, in the midst of all your festivity what did your sober, serious deacon say and do,— he that begins his Sabbath Saturday sundown?

293

Eighteenth Century America.

Aaron Blue-Skin: He was the very merriest of us all, but the poor man was caught one of the very first; his head is so weak. He quitted his chair early in the session; he took a good nap and went home four hours ago. I hope God in His mercy will forgive us all, but upon thinking on it, I must go home. What would folks say to find me abed here? They would swear that I have got drunk here. That won't do either. Farewell, Tom.

Iwan: This is a curious fellow, admirably well-fitted for the time. No wonder he stands so high in the estimation of the people. Profligate yet apparently religious, conceited and stubborn, he can do mischief with all the placidity of a good man and carefully avoid the ostensible parts of the sinner.

Ecclestone: These people have a much easier task to fulfil than what you imagine. Let them but act as their passions guide them; it is only calling the effects of their brutality the good of the cause and pleading in excuse an order of Congress. 'Tis all well, and the suffering world must remain passive and silent.

Iwan: Have these people no idea of reverses? Are they so confident as to think it impossible the scale may turn? For my part, were I in their place I would shudder at the thought and tremble for the hour of retaliation.

Ecclestone: They trust, from the highest to the lowest, to the chapter of events, and seem to have shut their eyes to their soundest policy. They read Montesquieu; better for that man never to have written. You see that he has expended twenty years of his life to very little purpose. The Bible, the "Spirit of the Laws," Seneca's "Morals" are excellent things to furnish us with theo-

294

retical pleasures, and serve to a few as spiritual food. 'Tis too refined for the common herd of mankind.

(Whilst Aaron was getting his horse, who should drop in but Colonel Templeman!)

Colonel: Where now, Squire? I thought you abed and asleep this good while.

Aaron Blue-Skin: For the matter of that, I want it enough, but you must know that when I left the committee this morning, I had to go round by —— house, you know, as it was agreed on; and I had to go and give a peep at ——; and hearing, on my way home, Landlord Bush had taken his sign down, I had a mind to talk to him a little on the subject, and he has sufficiently convinced me for this time. Aren't you coming in? Do alight, Colonel. There are two strangers there; I know not what to make of them. You'd better step in and hear them speak. We may pick up something and teach them good breeding.

Colonel: With all my heart. Is there anything to drink?

Squire: Oh, yes, though the stubborn dog won't sell. But he will give us as much as we want, and that is so much gained from the enemy. (They walk in.)

Colonel: Why, landlord, early at it! I see your business, like a clock, goes on Sundays and holy days.

Landlord: Truly, sir, I follow no business. But people can't leave off yet calling here, and as long as I have anything to eat or drink the honourable committee, above all, are welcome.

Colonel: Well, this will make but poor business at this rate, but am in hope you'll put up your sign again.

Landlord: Not I, Colonel. As long as the new law will take away the means of subsistence by my old sign, I will put up some other and live by some new calling.

Colonel: Law should be respected. There never was a law but what galled at first. You must obey with cheerfulness and seek in perfect obedience that resignation which sweetens everything. Before the chapter of the kings was out we had nothing but will. Now that delegate reigns we have nothing but law.

Landlord: True, sir, but if these laws are the will of a few it comes to the same thing, does it not?

Colonel: No, no! 'Tis the will of a few, it is true, but these few are chosen by ourselves, and their will deserves the respect and attachment of all.

Landlord: How can I respect people with whom I am not acquainted? They say that they are a parcel of lawyers and merchants who are removed to Yorktown. They say that they do just as they please without consulting the people.

Colonel: That is a palpable mistake. They often speak to you through their crises and their resolves.

Landlord: That is true. They now and then address us, whom they call the "good people of America," and no set of beings ever deserved so great a name; but it is only to tell us what they want and to oblige us to furnish it; and they sometimes cause us to be informed of their will by means of the pulpit.

Colonel: Well, but as you never go to our meetings, you never hear anything about it; is it not so?

Landlord: My neighbours tell me on't. That is the same thing, but that is not all. We have so many more masters than we used to have. There is the high and mighty Congress, and there is our Governor, and our senators, and our assemblymen, and there is our Captain of light-horse. God bless him, he never comes here but upon good and lawful errands. And there is you, sir, our worthy Colonel; and there are the honourable committee. And there are, let me see, one, two, three, four, five commissaries who want nothing but our horses, grain, hay, etc., and from whom we never can get any recompense. There is the sergeant of the bate and there is the good squire here present; and there is— I can't tell them all. Why upon my word, put at the end of it the respect we owe to each single law, and you'll find that we poor people have abundance to do, in order to please them all and live.

Colonel: Aye, aye, such refractory folks as you are, such a stubborn set really want bringing down. The time is come when it shall be in our power to make good subjects of you all. I know where the shoe pinches you—

Landlord: That is what you may, and it never pinched nor galled before. Is it a wonder we should shrink a little and wink and blink?

Colonel: You did not know what government was before. We will make a united, strong people of you by and by. A little while longer, and the job will be done.

(Somebody knocks.)

Landlord: Walk in. (Enters Captain Shoreditch heading a party of six militiamen surrounding three Quakers.)

Colonel: Aye, aye, what is this? More pigeons caught?

Captain Shoreditch: Why, honourable sir, I cannot make these men turn out in the militia. Some will come down to us sometimes, but they will neither handle a musket nor touch our victuals. These prisoners pretend to claim some exemption from you. They say that they were at your house last night; that you sent them to me with a message to abate somewhat of their fines, and to let them alone for the present.

Colonel: (Rubbing his head.) I just remember something about it. I am so pestered with this sort of people that I often say or do anything to get rid of them. I am quite sick and tired of these pretended conscientious non-fighting mortals. I have reasoned with them and, for the soul of me, I cannot find in the whole Bible any passages whereon they can build so preposterous a doctrine.

Quakers: Our principles are not new; they are those of a large, numerous society to which they have adhered in the hottest time of persecution. Our forefathers have witnessed them with their lives. Thou should'st consider that these rights, founded on the purest motives of conscience, deserve some respect. The legislature of Great Britain has showed thee an example in our exemption from swearing, etc.

(Soldiers scoffingly deride them. They snatch their hats off, saying: "Rude boors, don't you know that you are speaking to our honourable Colonel?")

Colonel: Pray, gentlemen, do you makest a point of conscience to remain covered before everybody?

Quakers: We make it no point of conscience; it is a custom among our society. Does it offend thee that we should speak to thee covered? Does it add to thy power and honour to see us thus abused by thy soldiers?

Colonnel: I don't care three farthings about it. If you are so attached to your broad-brims, put them on,—and welcome! (The Quakers put on their hats.) But, Captain, tell me in a few words what is the upshot of this people's case. I have quite forgot what I told them last night.

Landscapes.

Captain: Why, honourable sir, they won't train or appear among us when they are ordered.

Colonel: Does not the law fine them?

Captain: Yes, sir, but this seems not to satisfy the people. They insist on their bearing arms.

Quakers: This very Captain of thine who has led us before thee has taken almost everything we had for fines and other penalties. No later than last week he took from our friend, James, an ox worth seventy pounds, as thy money goes, for a fine of ten pounds; yet nothing is returned. Can't we appease thy people without so much plunder? It gives them an example of rapine.

Colonel: That is not the case. The people must be indulged. There is, let me see, besides the fees, trouble, time, advertisements, serving, lawyering, and what not. So the law demands. The rest goes to encourage and support our people. If you'll lie every night by the sides of your wives in whole skins, why, you must expect to pay for it.

Quakers: Then the Lord have mercy on us, if neither law, law-makers, nor rulers of hundreds can protect us, but rather give us up to persecution.

Colonel: Why, don't you know, good people, that you are devoted first and foremost? The law rates you all at ten pounds a year, rich and poor. This, as you may say, for not wearing a button in your hat; and then, let me see, I forget what, besides, for not drafting, not training. Why, we were computing it the other day in the assembly that we shall raise in this state as much as will pay the salaries of our governors and judges, or pretty near the mark.

Quakers: Are then the spoils of an inoffensive sect to feed some parts of thy new rulers? Dost thou then

mean to establish and support thy new government on
wilful, premeditated tyranny and oppression?

Colonel: Tyranny? Oh, no, we don't give it such a
name, by any means. Oppression of such a people as ye
are is no oppression; 'tis an act of justice done to
the rest of the community which you will not help to
defend.

Quakers: Thou wilt never flourish. Follow the example of thy once mother country: encourage every denomination; they are all useful in their way. And keep
them all by gentle means under the benign shadow of
a just and upright government. Then the world will
think indeed that thou art descended from its famed
loins.

Colonel: As to that we shall do as we please. Now
we have got the power, God forbid we should take pattern after its arbitrary rule. The nation of which we are
descended is an old rotten stock full of [dead] and de-
cayed limbs; the white worm is at its roots. Flagitiousness, peculation, venality are arrived there at their utmost pitch. My friends, 'tis an old machine, rusty and
extremely out of repair. It takes so much grease to keep
it a-going that it requires all the substance of the people. Ours, on the contrary, is brighter, simpler; 'tis new
and vigorous.

Quakers: We Friends have nothing to do with the
powers of the world. We submit for conscience sake to
the rulers of the land, but at the same time should wish
that rule were rational, impartial, and mild.

Colonel: Pooh, pooh, you'll fare here as well as anywhere else. Look at your birthplace and cradle, Pennsylvania. Even there you are an oppressed people and
like to lose entirely your ground. How thankful are the
good Presbyterians of that country for all the pains

Landscapes.

your old patron, William Penn, took, the good old soul that he was! We are really the chosen people; we reap the benefits of the Canaanites' labours!

Quakers: Canst thou really imagine a glorious conquest to despoil a harmless set of inhabitants of their lawful inheritance? If the Jews had a title to the possessions of the Gentiles, that title was given them by God who is Master of all. Which of the two dost thee imagine will be recorded by future historians in the most conspicuous manner: our great founder, William Penn, who displayed so much knowledge and ability for the good of mankind, who reared on Justice and Mercy so beautiful a fabric, who introduced into Pennsylvania every distressed European and constituted him his brother, or those who impiously have defaced this noble monument?

Colonel: It is even so. The conquered seldom attract the attention of the world; the conquerors are the people who are talked of. Success is an emanation of the shrine of fortune; 'tis all that the world looks at. Haven't you seen a medal which they say our people are striking there?

Quakers: No, we know nothing of these new things. What dost thou mean by medal?

Colonel: Why, 'tis a round piece, something like a dollar, on which some of our people are represented with rods in their hands driving friend Pemberton and others away. They seem to be loaded with bundles and followed by their wives and children.

Quakers: And where dost thou imagine this poor people must go who have showed to the world such patterns of toleration, who have made that country to flourish as a rose?

Colonel: To Otaheite, to Patagonia, anywhere they

301

please. I fancy they will unite with the Scotch of the Carolinas and the Mertgayees[?] of Virginia; and a pretty company it will be.

Quakers: Would'st thou think proper to discharge us?

Colonel: Discharge you? Why, to be sure. Will you first and foremost take up your muskets and go to fight the red-coats down below? That is the question.

Quakers: Thou know'st well our answer. Why would'st thou then ask a needless question?

Colonel: Well, then, you broad-brims, you must abide by the consequences.

Quakers: We will, most cheerfully. We are not men of blood nor of resistance; we obey this community. When all men must turn fighters, then the plough must stand still; then famine must come. Art thou not afraid of it?

Colonel: Not I; as long as there is bread in the land, I'll get my share on't. The rest must share for themselves, but they say that the southern colonies abound with grain.

Quakers: How shall we fetch it from there, now that our horses and wagons are pressed?

Colonel: Well, then, eat potatoes. That is good enough for those who stay at home.

Quakers: We were brought before thee to obtain and to hear the words of justice. Thou art a ruler, a commander. Who shall administer it unto us, if not thou?

Colonel: If you want justice go to our supreme and inferior courts; there it is retailed. My duty, as well as my inclination, is to make you all fight.

Quakers: Thy new laws excuse us.

Colonel: It does not. Besides, it was a palpable mistake in those that framed it. I know better, and that

Landscapes.

very clause shall be repealed next session. I am law-maker in my own regiment. If you profess yourselves such passive folks, obey them.

Quakers: And is that all the redress we can obtain of thee? God will help us in our distresses if our sins have not rendered us unworthy of His protection. But if thou art determined to sacrifice us all, wilt thou kindly [spare] our wives and children, those innocent creatures who have not yet shared in the guilt of their fathers?

Colonel: Your wives and children shall be bound out to our people. They are able to work, and after they have lost the sight and the remembrance of their fathers' damnable principles, they then will become worthy to become members of our society.

Captain: What is to be done with these people, noble Colonel?

Colonel: Let them even go home. I am sick at the sight of their broad-brims and immovable countenances. You, Quakers, go home for this time, and hold forth in my praise or dispraise as you will. If as pernicious a spirit moved me now as often moves you, I'd send you to the ground. Take care next time! Quakers in the midst of a civil war, and yet pretend to their rights of peace! A most laughable thing, indeed! You may go to the moon and be Quakers there with all my heart, provided God places none else there; and call it New Pennsylvania if you please. There you may have some chance, but here among the other warlike sects of the land,—for shame! Get you gone! A few years more, and you'll be sponged away. Quakers truly! When our cruel enemies are at our door! I shall presently lose my temper. (Exeunt Quakers.)

Captain: I wish, Colonel, you'd give me your final

orders. These folks are really a dangerous example to the rest. "Why should [not] one fight as well as the other?" says one. "Why should that society be exempt from militia-duty?" says the other. "When our independency is established they will be ready enough to come in for their share of the harvest," says the other.

Colonel: I'll tell you what: when you hear any of these Toryfied gentry say the least word disrespectful anyways of our cause, or averse to do their duty, without any ceremony knock them down with the butt of your gun,—do you hear? And then send them away to the gaol. That's my orders.

Captain: I shall so, noble Colonel; I'll make short work of them, I'll warrant. Your servant, Colonel.

(Exit Captain.)

Colonel: I really ask your pardon, gentlemen. Men in my station have really so much plague with Tom, Dick, and Harry, that I am sometimes beside myself. Boy, hand me a coal of fire, this plaguy pipe—By your dress I presume you belong to the army.

Strangers: No, sir, we are going to view it. 'Tis said that it contains more officers than soldiers.

Colonel: Aye, aye, you surprise me. What is become of our soldiers then? I am sure the newspapers don't give an account of many killed.

Strangers: Why, you know how it is: soldiers perish very fast. Some are returned home, some deserted, and a good many [were] cut off last campaign.

Colonel: And how do you know?

Strangers: Why, sir, we were at the battle of Brandywine where we saw a good many fall. We met even General Washington in the utmost distress of mind,

Landscapes.

praying to heaven for some friendly ball to put an end to his pains. Night, however, saved them.

Colonel: Why, this is not the account we have had of it. However, there are men enough in the country. Liberty can't be purchased too dearly. New recruits, I suppose, will be wanted.

Strangers: They are sending them from the East as fast as they can.

Colonel: Do they? Indeed these people are always ablest. They began the revolution and it is on their vigour and strength we must ultimately depend.

Strangers: Why should you pay them so great a compliment at the expense of your own state?

Colonel: We are a smart people too, that is sure, but we have unfortunately so many disaffected persons; and [so are] some of our principal families. We are not so knotty and united as they are there.

Strangers: As to that, Colonel, it is a misfortune under which every state labours, and I cannot conceive how you'll remedy this great evil.

Colonel: As to that, we are much divided in our opinions. Some there are who are for crushing, banishing everything that is not consonant. I and many more are for palliating, for consolidating our new society by all the means in our power. War and other accidents have weakened us already sufficiently. Why should we [be] severe for ever? These maxims, however, I am sorry to say, prevail among a minority only.

Two Strangers: A pity 'tis. Your new laws and governments would become more respectable at home and abroad, and the character of non-persecution would procure friends and well-wishers. What a pity that so noble an enterprise should be contaminated with so much mischief and evil!

Eighteenth Century America.

Colonel: That is true. I have often shed tears over it and blushed within myself that the foundation of American liberty should have been laid in oppression and injustice. Yet zealous as I am, I must needs confess it. God forgive us, what can men do in which they don't mix some strong native poison?

Two Strangers: Had the first legislators and movers of this American scheme thought as you seem to do, America would have triumphed before now. Their justice and humanity in the support of their own cause compared to the cruelty, injustice, arrogance, and flagitiousness of the E. Am. [*sic*] which in the same manner we lament.

Colonel: Things cannot be helped at present. I am in hopes the contest won't be long now. Surely the people of England will get tired of feeding and paying soldiers and officers who do nothing. Our connections with Europe are such, and such is the nature of our cause, that all nations wish us well. The opening of this grand mart, or the alternative of shutting it for the sole use of the selfish English,—this consideration alone, united with our successes, makes me confident that Providence sees our progress with complacency.

Iwan: This is grounding hopes on too presumptuous a foundation. Both parties have been very much to blame, as all the judicious part of the world knows. For my part, I am so much the humble servant of events that I am determined to wait the issue and live if possible like Atticus, shaking hands with both parties.

Ecclestone: That is impossible, at least to a native. I easily can conceive that the feelings of a foreigner cannot be so keen.

Iwan: I beg pardon; if you mistrust my zeal, I am sure you don't mistrust my probity.

Landscapes.

Colonel: Come, come, you are both honest men and see the same object with different eyes. Let us wait with patience the grand issue; 'tis not your wishings or my wishing that will turn the scale. Whenever you return this way again I should be glad you'd call at my house; your talk is sober and clever.

Two Strangers: We shall so, Colonel. Farewell to you.

Colonel: The same to you. (Exeunt strangers.)

Colonel: Landlord, who do you think they are?

Landlord: Upon my word, I do not know. They seem to be clever gentlemen. They never were here before that I know of.

Fifth Landscape: Francis Marston's House.

Beatus, *deacon.*
Eltha, *his wife.*
Mrs. Aurelia Marston.
Family of children.
Nero, *the negro of the house.*
Peter Marston, *a young lad.*
Major Popino.

Colonel [Deacon]: Oho, I say, my lad, is your mother at home?

Young Marston: Where should she be, now that our poor father is shot and murdered by your orders? What do you [want] more, for God's sake?

Eltha: Come, come. Lads must not spruce up quite so high neither. Well, really, Mr. Lad, do you know who we are? Is your mother at home or is she not?

Nero: (Just come up with an alarmed countenance.) Yes, yes, Massa; Misse at home and all the little family. Misse been crying all night. 'Tenant Plash stope here last night and told her as how Massa, poor

307

Massa was shote, and that he himself had crak'd his brains after he felle down and just quivered* him a little with leaves. Misse is sickly and I, too. Massa, what your Hona please to have?

Chairman: Come, come; leave off crying. Go in and inform your mistress that my wife and I are come to bring her good tidings.

(In comes Mrs. Marston with a child in her arms, four daughters, and the lad.)

Mrs. Marston: What can the Colonel demand of me on this day? Do you mean to rob me of that rest which the oxen and the beasts of burthen enjoy this day?

Colonel: Madam, I am like Eliphaz, the Temanite, Job's friend. We are come, on the contrary, to commune with you and assuage your pains. Even my wife wanted to share with me the pleasure of bringing you the glad tidings. Your husband has escaped the pursuit of our people below, and is safe arrived in New York.

Mrs. Marston: God be praised! But is it true, sir? Perhaps you mean to increase still more my woes and feed on the object which a desolated family presents you. 'Tis duty, it seems, to spread misfortunes far and wide. But can it be your inclination to glut yourself on the objects, individuals, on which they happen to fall? Since you were talking of Job's friend, what Zophar says is that the triumph of the wicked is but short and the joy of the hypocrite but for a moment. Do you really come on purpose, and is it really so, that my husband is safe?

Colonel: You know, Madam, that I never swear. What proofs then must I give you? My word of old has been and is to this day proof enough.

* Probably negro dialect for "covered."

Landscapes.

Eltha: It shows really bad to be received with so much diffidence, and to see suspicions, fears, and terror spread over all those faces.

Mrs. Marston: We are so used to being treated as enemies, to be cut off from every share of compassion and feelings.

Colonel: Enemies, Madam? To be sure the law does not mean that we should show you much mercy; that I will allow.

Mrs. Marston: Poor unhappy man! How many are they who have longed for his blood, that they might glut themselves on his property!

Colonel: Now you are talking of property puts it into my mind to suppose that you know that to-morrow the Board of Commissioners is going to sell all you have, [it] being forfeited to the use of the state by the elopement of your husband.

Mrs. Marston: Sell all I have! How should I fish out of your political abyss such a thought as this? Must I, then, and my children, starve or go a-begging?

Colonel: Aye, aye, and to that and a great many other things the law says it, and the law must be obeyed.

Mrs. Marston: I am not deceived. I expected the very worst that could possibly befall me, and I am ready to submit to my fate. Let us, Mr. Chairman [hear] the whole of it. Would you not please to sit down, you and your wife? Or have I already lost all right and title to what this house contains? (The chairman takes a chair and reads in the Bible.)

Mrs. Chairman: As to that it is but precarious, indeed. However, you hide nothing. You may look at it all until to-morrow, three to six p. m. Upon the whole I am glad to see you so well-prepared. We must try to do something for you and your little ones. I cannot en-

Eighteenth Century America.

Colonel: Do, pray, let us hear what this great matter is. Are you insulted, are you abused? There is the precinct; there is the county; there are the united committees of the county. You must apply to them; they replace all other authorities.

Martha: Committee! That name conveys to my brains the most horrid smell; 'tis the most offensive sensation I can receive. 'Tis from them I have received all my distresses and misfortunes, and God in heaven is silent. He lets them hang the innocent, persecute the poor, the widows, the naked orphans.

Eltha: Good woman, you should know before whom you speak: this is the chairman of the committee.

Martha: This the man of the chair! 'Tis you then who have done me all this mischief; 'tis you who have reduced me into despair and reduced me into affliction and poverty lower than ere was a poor living soul reduced. Gracious God, why dost Thou suffer these rulers to plunder the widows and their children, and call their rags their country's inheritance,—a miserable one, which to feed and pamper a few, leaves hundreds desolate, a prey to death and despair? And you are the chairman! Do me justice then,—but, alas, they say you are deaf and blind to remonstrances.

Colonel: What would the woman be at? Why accuse me thus? I know you not, neither the beginning nor the ending of your story. You are mad.

Martha: Does not the sight of me make you recollect some late transactions? Is there nothing in you that vibrates and palpitates as in other men? Is everything tight and rigid? Do you fear neither God nor His judgments? How do you expect mercy at His hands when you show none to no one for His sake?

Colonel: If you won't declare who you are, what it

at last fired at him twice by the sleigh, while he had this very infant in his arms. This it is which obliged him at last to quit his own house. Can you reasonably expect that a slave of some sensibility, as a great many are, could live with his master's intentional murderer?

Chairwoman: Mam, you are too high. You must come down; your pride must have a downfall. Lower your top-gallants, as the saying is. That fellow must be sold. In that case what is it to you who buys him?

Mrs. Marston: Oppression rather inflates me; misfortunes animate me. How else should I bear their weight? What precaution have I need to take? You have insulted and treated my husband worse than a slave these six months. You have hired myrmidons to hunt him, to kill him if possible; if not, to threaten setting fire to his house that he might fly to save it; and that, by flying, his extensive estate might become a sweet offering to the rulers of this county. Now you are going to strip me and his children of all we possessed, and pray, what can you do more?

Chairwoman: You have forgot, I suppose, the kind proposition I have been hinting to you just now. You should at least acknowledge favours when certain folks mean to confer them.

Chairman: Come, come, no pride, I desire. Let it be all done in lowliness and meekness.

Chairwoman: That is true, my dear; we all know it. But can common flesh bear such ingratitude?

Mrs. Marston: The amount of your favours I do not well understand. Do you mean to compound with me, do you mean to tamper with your law, or do you really mean and wish that mercy should silence tyranny for a while?

Eltha: What signify so many questions? The thing

you know is this and nothing more: your husband has been inimically inclined from the beginning. He may plead his oath of office, but the just demands of his country are far superior. They bind us at the day of our nativity; all others are more recent, less ancient, and far less respectable. His fate has not overtaken him for nothing. Remember, good Mam, if you please, the right of the conquerors. How did the Jews behave to the Canaanites? Do you think that they offered them gowns and linen and some gammons in mere compassion? No, not they; they took all because the law commanded it.

Mrs. Marston: I understand you, I believe. If you want to feast your eyes on what I have, if any part of my furniture or clothing attracts your attention, I suppose that you have but to speak or perhaps to will, and the things are yours.

Chairwoman: Why, to be sure, to speak within the compass of possibilities, you are right, for you know well that my husband has got the power.

Mrs. Marston: Aye, aye, that ineffable word, power. I know full well all its extensive meaning. 'Tis like the New England drams: they have no kind of effect except they produce intoxication. If you'll please to follow me, I will endeavour to satisfy not only your curiosity but whatever other passion may come uppermost. You are sure of this, that impunity awaits you both in this world as well as in the next; in this as wife of a chairman, in the next as that of a deacon.

Mrs. Marston's Daughters: (crying) What, Mammy, are we going to lose all our gowns and shifts and petticoats, that we have spun ourselves and dyed, according to your rule, with so much care? Must we lose all we have?

Chairwoman: And why not, pray? The sin of Adam

overtook all his descendants, and so must the sin of the Squire, your father. We won't leave you in your naturalibus, don't be afraid.

Mrs. Marston: Come, dear children, I wish you'd withdraw. We must all submit, and your tears and reflections behind me quite disarm me of my fortitude. Go into the other room till I call you. (Exeunt children.)

Chairwoman: Pretty good advice, truly, and in answer to what you were saying before, although you mean to joke, yet I'd have you know that there is a good deal of truth in it. Do let us see that sweet teapot that I have heard so much of.

Mrs. Marston: Here it is, Madam. 'Tis remarkable for nothing but for being made in England with crowns of Charles the Second, as you see, artfully soldered together. My grandfather brought it from Britain, that renowned native land, which you so fervently curse and hate.

Chairwoman: Upon honor 'tis a sweet thing. Pity it should go out of the family, but your family is, as it were, divided and annihilated. What will you do with it? However, I'll take it away to save it from the inventory.

Mrs. Marston: Do! So be it with yourself, but put yourself in my situation and feel for me.

Eltha: My daughter, Judith, was a-mentioning the other day—poor child, she had no bad thoughts in so doing—a very handsome purple gown, a large cloak, and a new-fashioned bonnet. Pray, where are they?

Mrs. Marston: Did not your daughter, Judith, think then of my daughter Julia? To tell the truth I have nothing fashionable. I and my daughter wear nothing but what is solid, decent, and substantial, becoming the condition of independent American farmers.

(Here sighing involuntarily, and restraining the tears from gushing out of her eyes, she empties several large chests of drawers.)

Eltha: Extravagant indeed! What, so much of everything! You must have been a costly wife. It has been flood with you, and the ebb should take place and let out some of your long accumulated stores.

Mrs. Marston: 'Tis the fruit of my industry and that of my daughters. My husband gave us every fourth cheese, every third firkin of butter, and all the honey of our stores, and a few calves. With these well-earned perquisites I decently clad the family with Sunday clothes. The rest we spin, we dye, we weave ourselves in this house. Can you find any great harm?

Eltha: This is really a beautiful quilt. These shoes with the buckles, I believe, will suit my daughter's foot admirably well. She is about being married; these things will come in good time.

Mrs. Marston: Would you as a mother encourage her to wear the spoil of fraud and tyranny? Would she enter the pale of matrimony decked with the plunder of the desolated family, of the banished husband, the oppressed wife, the orphan children? An't you afraid that she would entail a curse, though latent, in that very womb which [is] to bear her and her husband the source of future joys? Would you [not] be afraid that some evil destiny would attend children born under such fatal omens?

Eltha: This is all a matter of simple opinion, as I may say. I take it to be rather a matter of triumph; the daughters of Israel were never ashamed to wear the golden bracelets which their youth brought from the field.

Mrs. Marston: Excellent doctrine, Madam. The Old Testament affords you abundance of such proofs, but if you have a mind to be merciful, open the New.

Eltha: Pshaw, woman, that is no excuse. Both are conjoined together and give us one set of laws and precepts. The latter is well enough for you bigoted church people.

Mrs. Marston: Then take, ravish, and plunder. Glut yourself, but I beg you'll carry your insults no further.

Eltha: Well, then, put up together these things which I have set apart. Let your wench wrap them up together that I may carry them home. A proper compensation, a certain degree of indulgence you may expect, if I have any influence over my husband.

Mrs. Marston: Any way you please. But what do you think the pious man will do, he who is now sanctifying the day in the next room by reading the Bible?

Eltha: As to that, he has a certain rule which he reconciles with his conscience and the duty he owes his country. I am but a woman; this is not the first time that such cases have come before him.

Mrs. Marston: Excellent evasion! Admirable sophistry!

Colonel: (Reënters the room, sanctified and demure.)

Eltha: Well, Colonel, my dear, are you ready to go? I have viewed what I thought most proper to be removed out of the sight of the other commissaries, lest they should imagine that so much wealth was ill-got.

Colonel: Wife, if you mean well, I am satisfied. I will suffer no transaction anyways fraudulent. Our bleeding country wants everything that can strengthen

it and relieve it from the burdens under which it labours. I am but the executor of laws, and they must be
obeyed.

Mrs. Marston: I am sure, sir, you don't execute them
for nothing. You pay yourself well for your trouble, I
know it; and it is this which inflames your patriotic zeal
to so high a pitch. Remember that the world was created round to convince us that therein nothing is stable
and permanent. The time may come when you could
have wished to have felt for the misfortunes of others,
but your heart is callous. How you can reconcile the
profession of so much religion with the execution of so
many evil deeds, I know not.

Colonel: I shall not enter with you into any such dis-
quisition. Where the crime lies, the lawful revenge
should take place. Your husband from the beginning
has been a supporter of the oppressive acts of Parliament, that venal body which wants freedom at home
and loves to spread tyranny abroad. They have not to
deal with the inhabitants of Bengal, I promise you. Mr.
Marston has been, in short, exceedingly inimical and a
bad man in the true sense of the word.

Mrs. Marston: You have so subverted the course and
order of things that no one knows what is a bad man in
your new political sense; but in spite of modern defini-
tion the true meaning of that word stands yet on its old
foundation. A bad man is he, sir, who tears up the bowels of his native country; who subverts its best laws;
who makes tyranny, informing, injustice, oppression of
every kind the cause of God; who arrests people without cause; imprisons them for whole months and seasons without hearing or inquiries; and leaves them to
languish under the accumulated weight of want, despair, and disease. A bad man, sir, is he who, when he

Landscapes.

had it in his power to prevent it, suffered an innocent young man to perish in a suffocating gaol, panting for breath, burnt and scorched by the most excessive fever; and yet would not release him. A bad man is he who sternly denied the most earnest solicitations of an unfortunate aged couple, imploring on their knees that their child might be removed. Such deeds you must remember. What cause can you serve when you support it by such systems?

Colonel: Madam, Madam, you go too fast. Hoity-toity! Neither general nor private reflections! I see that you are pointing them to me. My hands were tied by the committee; I could not help it.

Mrs. Marston: Well, well, sir, the horrid deed is committed; the innocent young man removed out of your clutches. God, I hope, will reward him.

Colonel: And so He will your husband whom I have so long indulged. I might a year ago have thrown him into gaol; the breath of my lips was sufficient. Yet I suffered him to remain; I overlooked his night visitors, his correspondents. I am obliged to let the law descend on his head. And now he has joined our cruel enemies, he is civilly dead, and when overtaken, hard will be his fate; no mitigation can be introduced.

Mrs. Marston: No man ever behaved with more prudence, but it was that very prudent conduct of his which shocked you and yours. You never ceased laying snares for him, swelling the public report till he was put on the list, sent to gaol. While there you never brought him to trial. All the messages you sent him were that if he had a mind to disprove himself guilty, he had nothing to do but to take up his musket and go into the field. Did you want that he should attempt impossibilities to redeem himself, and betray his con-

317

science? Did you really expect that a man of his age, a magistrate, a person once respectable to all and respected even by you, whom he has often indulged, should herd with your soldiers and fare as they do? The fate he has met with is the supreme wish of his heart; I can prove it.

Colonel: No irascibility, I pray. He is gone; he has pronounced sentence on himself; and fate cannot redeem him.

Mrs. Marston: What could he do less than what he has done? A clay-fabricated animal would have done the same. He has sacrificed his repose to that of his family. He broke his fleet-prison and came here with the view of imploring a trial, and that he might remain either on security or otherwise peaceably on his farm. But, no, that would not have answered the excellent purposes.

Colonel: As his wife, you are necessarily prepossessed. You do not see things in the same impartial light which men in my station do view it. Bitter as the pill is you must swallow it. What can I do? I cannot dry up all the tears which perfidy to our cause will make people shed. This is but the beginning of their sorrow, but so great is their attachment to the English government that to it they will sacrifice everything in the world.

Mrs. Marston: Irony, deceit, and mock-hypocritical show of mercy are your distinguishing characteristics, and that is the reason that you have been placed at the helm of this county. Permit me once more to recapitulate to you some of his proceedings. Compare them with yours. It shall not be recrimination nor a claim of justice; 'tis but a simple satisfaction which I cannot, and I hope you won't, refuse me.

Colonel: It will be vain, Madam. If we intended to

Landscapes.

have heard any preaching to-day, we might have gone to town and heard that of our worthy minister.

Mrs. Marston: I preach not. I simply repeat facts, the recollection of which is too much for the frailty and common nerves of a woman to bear.

Chairwoman: You know, it seems, full well my husband's good nature and patience, and you mean to abuse them. We merely came to inform you as how your husband was safely arrived. We meant it as a comfort, and behold, here is the return! Like a Tory who, bred and nourished by the milk of this country, yet aims at stabbing it and plunging the dagger in its breast! But, Mam, lest you might hurt your longing, pray, go on.

Mrs. Marston: Everything is strangely perverted; black is become white, and white is become black. Blush thou, oh Justice, oh thou fair Truth, fly, quit this terrestrial abode; go beyond the reach of these pervert rulers; we are no longer worthy of you! Yes, my husband as well as a great many more have been driven to seek shelter far, very far from their homes and families. Last April, poor man, he was hurried to gaol after having been seized from my side at twelve o'clock at night. With all the aggravated insults that brutal militia could invent, through dirt and mire and darkness he was hurried to gaol, where he was kept three months. I was not permitted to see him, nor could he be [informed] during all this time of the state of his children. Next he was fastened to another man as unfortunate as himself and thus sent on foot to N. W. on a hot sultry day, without the least compassion save what he met with along the road from people who, remembering his better days and his former hospitality, secretly shed tears over his hard fate and relieved him with meat and drink. Not being able to reach the destined place of em-

319

barkation he and his mate begged each a horse,—which was granted. With what derision they were both uplifted from behind, thus obliged to ride chained! Your wild, your profligate guard soon afterwards fired a gun and frightened the horses, which brought to the ground the two unfortunate objects, thus abandoned to popular fury. In the fall my husband broke his arm, and the other [suffered] several terrible contusions. Next they were married in a wagon to N. W., and from thence carried by water to their fleet-prison. There he was for three months longer without hope of ever regaining his liberty. He made his escape and returned here. He applied to J. W., who promised protection and a final release. He took some steps to effect these good purposes. You heard of it—I know precisely when—and to defeat these benevolent purposes and prevent him from sharing the fate of his companion, Squire Rearman, who had somehow slipped through your fingers, you sent at different times a party of men headed by your son Anthony. He, after lurking about the house a considerable time, spied my husband at last, leaning over his sleigh with his child in his hand. They fired two rifles at him and missed him. This atrocious deed made him imagine that the offer of protection he had received from J. W. was but delusive and calculated to lead him on. "If J. W. proves a traitor, a bad man," said he, "after all his humane actions, I have nothing more to do than to leave you. When I am gone they will swear that I am gone from choice. God hears me and bears witness that I'd rather stay with you here than go to New York where I cannot subsist and do anything." These are his words. He marched through the woods. Next night his oppressed heart would not give him the means of proceeding any further. He returned,.

determined to wait his fate. Unfortunately some of your gang perceived him. They sent word that if he did not quit in three hours, the whole should be in flames. He roused himself up once more and with streaming eyes and a bleeding heart he bade me farewell. Yet this is the man you proclaim a traitor. He would have been a traitor to himself had he stayed any longer. 'Tis for my sake and that of his children, 'tis to preserve these buildings and what they contain that he quitted. Can you in the face of that pure sun, can you say he went away out of choice?

Colonel: This all may be as you have represented it, though some parts about my son, Anthony, I will never believe. But what can I do? Had I shown him any favours, the people, whose confidence I possess, might immediately have suspected me; perhaps they might, for want of encouragement, become more languid in their opposition. All, all depend on their brawny arms. Better for one man, nay, twenty to suffer innocently than to hold forth such a mercy as might be attended with such dangerous circumstances.

Mrs. Marston: Aye, aye, popularity is the word. 'Tis the God to whom you must sacrifice the dictates of your conscience, the peace of your lives, and your future felicity.

Chairwoman: Come, come, Mrs. Marston, learn to bear and to suffer. Leave off fine reasoning. The more oxen fret in the yoke the more they gall themselves. Tell me, when you are turned out of this house, what hopes have you got? Where will you go?

Mrs. Marston: On what motives have you built your curiosity, pray? I propose to build myself a little log house at the foot of the Great Snake Rock close by Beaver Pond, which, they say, is King's Land.

Eighteenth Century America.

Eltha: King's Land, Mam! Why, you make me laugh in spite of my melancholy. Don't you know, poor soul, that we know of no king in America, and that all King's Lands as you call them, are seized for the benefit of our Congress?

Mrs. Marston: Well, well, Mam, we shall not dispute about the proprietor's name. I meant to erect a little cottage on some such lands as nobody claims, and then to send out two of my daughters a-spinning. As for my son, he vows he will never let his mother want bread. Thus our industry and the kindness of people will, I hope, enable us to go through the rigorous season.

Eltha: Your son, Mam, must go into the militia and perhaps into the Continental service; there you are deceived. 'Tis the least he can do to atone for his father's deficiency. Nor can you depend so much on the assistance of your friends; you mean Tories, I suppose. You may expose them by that, and the committee will have a particular eye to these things.

Mrs. Marston: Would you make it a crime for these people to relieve me in my distresses, me, who have for so many years been so kind and so serviceable to them all? This is the very quintessence of poison. Can this be the genuine spirit of your cause? My son, sir, shall not go into the Continental service. God, I hope, will give me no more to bear than what I can. Help me, help me, Thou protector of widows and orphans! (Somebody knocks.)

Colonel: Walk in, whoever you are. (Enter Major Popino)

Colonel: How does the Major do to-day?

Major: Quite cheerly, and I give you thanks. The Colonel upon private business here?

Landscapes.

Colonel: No, by no means. To-day, you know, is not a day for business except it is that of mercy and consolation, and that is really our errand here.

Major: Why, what is the news here?

Colonel: Nothing worth mentioning, only that Francis Marston is gone to New York. All his effects are to be sold to-morrow, and we came here to prepare his wife lest the shock should be too great.

Major: Ah, oh, Colonel, that is like your work,—always more kind than need be to this sort of cattle. Your neighbours won't thank you for this thrownaway humanity, I am sure, for they are well-known up and down among us. Let them die the death, I say,—and so say many more.

Colonel: (whispers into the major's ears.) I meant principally to see [how] effects stood here. I see everything is well replenished,—'tis a good prize. Won't you be here to-morrow?

Major: By all means. Why, this is a very fine farm: hogs, cattle, and horses in great abundance.

Colonel: Yes, I have just been a-visiting the granaries, chambers, and cellars,—all full. Fine harvest to carry on the war,—my heart merely exults. I want, Major, to purchase to-morrow that large rick of hay, counting maybe forty tons. Won't you bid for me, and I give a hint to you here that I want it for the service, and for the service it will be at last. But they will be sure to triple my advance. These hard times we must turn a penny. The hay will be wanted at the fish kill before the spring.

Major: That's what I will, Colonel. I have been viewing the young fellow leading a fine stallion to the well. I want very much such a war-horse when we train the militia. Could not you help me to the bargain?

323

Colonel: Why, I do not know. The young man claims him as his property. I am at a loss what to do on the occasion.

Major: Why, you must find a couple of the neighbours who will swear that they heard somebody say that they heard F. Marston say that he gave so much for the horse, which in fact I believe is very much so. Then it will be proved to be the father's property and then it will be sold.

Colonel: Well, well, I'll tell you better. First, the horse must be out of the way to-morrow, and we will indulge you with him at private sale in the evening.

Major: Thanks, thanks, noble Colonel. I shall ever acknowledge this as a great and worthy favour indeed. We that bear the brunt of the battle should have some rewards for it. The Congress prodigiously overlooks the merits of the militia; neither tents nor hospitals through the bushes. My lads, that's all we have. We therefore should take care of ourselves at home. And who is better entitled to the spoils of the Tories than we who have the trouble to hunt them, to clap them in gaol, and so forth?

Colonel: You are very right, Major; you speak like unto a man of experience. Did you see anywhere in your travels the great blaze the other night which made us all gaze?

Major: Yes, yes, that's what I did, and with all my heart, too. Why, haven't you heard yet? Why, our folks down below say that New York is all in ashes, and that Howe was like to be Burgoyned.

Colonel: Well, never was a day since the creation crowded with such important events. God is with us; God is with us all; God will abide by us, I believe.

Major: We are in a fair way, that is to be sure. What

Landscapes.

will the dogs do in New York now it is levelled? They say as how our people have caught this lucky moment on a windy night and set it on fire.

Colonel: Hush, hush, Major, there you are wrong. We should never inquire by what means God's divine providence orders things for our good. Suffice it for us that it is done. Let us be thankful. 'Tis the angel, not our own prowess that accomplishes all these great things.

Major: That's well observed, Colonel. As a deacon of a church and a proficient in religion I see that you take things in their proper light; you view every event as good Christians ought to do. I am now of your mind and must haste or else I shall be too late at meeting. I am in hopes to reach there before the sermon begins, and we shall have a fine text, and the minister will handle it well. There is not, you know, such an enemy to Tories, no, not again in fifty miles. How he makes them fly! How he sets them out! And they hate him in abundance for it. Farewell.

Colonel: God with you, Major. Hope yours are all hearty?

Major: Thank you, Colonel; we are all triumphing, happy, and impatient for the last day.

Colonel: Wife, wife (speaking loud); wife, wife, where have you been all this time?

Eltha: Why, Mrs. Marston and I have been visiting up and down and making little bargains which I hope you'll confirm. Upon my word, 'tis a well replenished house and kept perfectly clean.

Colonel: 'Tis high time to go. Who knows but we may reach yet for afternoon sermon? Well, Mrs. Marston, farewell. Take things as patiently as you can. We will try to indulge you all we can to-morrow. Don't distress yourself too much.

Mrs. Marston: Come what will, I shall have on my side God, my innocence, my little children, and, I hope, some bread. Take, take the rest away and then you'll be satisfied. (Exeunt.)

Mrs. Marston: As a county canting, religious hypocrite I had always known thee; now as Congress delegate, and in that service dost thou use thy former qualifications.

Sixth Landscape: On the Road, returning from Francis Marston's house.

> Beatus, *deacon.*
> Eltha, *his wife.*
> Martha, wife to B. Corwin hanged by Lord Sterling; otherwise the woman in despair.

Eltha: Well, Colonel, my dear, did not I tell you that we should sanctify the day, gather a blessing as we went and do good to the cause and to ourselves? What could heaven do more in its most gracious hour? You see that a wife is very often a useful and necessary companion. You see, Colonel, we have relieved Mrs. Marston from that load of anxiety she laid under concerning the pretended death of her husband. We have merely squared her from hiding anything. We have heard the good news of Major Popino, that good man, and here is a bundle containing several very valuable things for which our daughter Dorothy shan't be sorry. The wisest counsellor could not have done more. What say you, my dear?

Colonel: Well, what consideration have you promised this woman?

Eltha: Oh, I have bought nothing, as you may say,

Landscapes.

Eltha: It shows really bad to be received with so much diffidence, and to see suspicions, fears, and terror spread over all those faces.

Mrs. Marston: We are so used to being treated as enemies, to be cut off from every share of compassion and feelings.

Colonel: Enemies, Madam? To be sure the law does not mean that we should show you much mercy; that I will allow.

Mrs. Marston: Poor unhappy man! How many are they who have longed for his blood, that they might glut themselves on his property!

Colonel: Now you are talking of property puts it into my mind to suppose that you know that to-morrow the Board of Commissioners is going to sell all you have, [it] being forfeited to the use of the state by the elopement of your husband.

Mrs. Marston: Sell all I have! How should I fish out of your political abyss such a thought as this? Must I, then, and my children, starve or go a-begging?

Colonel: Aye, aye, and to that and a great many other things the law says it, and the law must be obeyed.

Mrs. Marston: I am not deceived. I expected the very worst that could possibly befall me, and I am ready to submit to my fate. Let us, Mr. Chairman [hear] the whole of it. Would you not please to sit down, you and your wife? Or have I already lost all right and title to what this house contains? (The chairman takes a chair and reads in the Bible.)

Mrs. Chairman: As to that it is but precarious, indeed. However, you hide nothing. You may look at it all until to-morrow, three to six p. m. Upon the whole I am glad to see you so well-prepared. We must try to do something for you and your little ones. I cannot en-

309

Eighteenth Century America.

Colonel: Do, pray, let us hear what this great matter is. Are you insulted, are you abused? There is the precinct; there is the county; there are the united committees of the county. You must apply to them; they replace all other authorities.

Martha: Committee! That name conveys to my brains the most horrid smell; 'tis the most offensive sensation I can receive. 'Tis from them I have received all my distresses and misfortunes, and God in heaven is silent. He lets them hang the innocent, persecute the poor, the widows, the naked orphans.

Eltha: Good woman, you should know before whom you speak: this is the chairman of the committee.

Martha: This the man of the chair! 'Tis you then who have done me all this mischief; 'tis you who have reduced me into despair and reduced me into affliction and poverty lower than ere was a poor living soul reduced. Gracious God, why dost Thou suffer these rulers to plunder the widows and their children, and call their rags their country's inheritance,—a miserable one, which to feed and pamper a few, leaves hundreds desolate, a prey to death and despair? And you are the chairman! Do me justice then,—but, alas, they say you are deaf and blind to remonstrances.

Colonel: What would the woman be at? Why accuse me thus? I know you not, neither the beginning nor the ending of your story. You are mad.

Martha: Does not the sight of me make you recollect some late transactions? Is there nothing in you that vibrates and palpitates as in other men? Is everything tight and rigid? Do you fear neither God nor His judgments? How do you expect mercy at His hands when you show none to no one for His sake?

Colonel: If you won't declare who you are, what it

is that afflicts you so that I may know how to relieve you, I'll get a party to carry you to gaol before night. Depend on it.

Martha: Do so and complete the horrid tragedy. The tears I have shed have dried the milk of my breasts, and my poor baby, by still suckling the dregs, fed a while on the dregs of sorrow. He is now dead, and I was going to look for somebody to bury his emaciated carcass now lying on my straw bed. That is my business, if you must know. The sweet angel will call on you one of these nights and wrench your heart with bitterness and repentance.

Eltha: The woman is surely mad, my dear. Why, she is not worth minding. We shall lose here much more precious time. Do let us haste.

Martha: Aye, Mam, that's spoken like yourself. Mingle religion with obduracy of heart, softness of speech with that unfeeling disposition which fits you so well for a chairman's wife. Despise the poor; reject the complaints of the oppressed; crush those whom your husband oversets; and our gazettes shall resound with your praise. Mad woman! Yes, I am mad to see ingratitude and hypocrisy on horse-back, virtue and honesty low in the dirt.

Eltha: If it was not Sabbath, I'll warrant I'd take you up myself and bring you still lower.

Martha: Well, then I'll defy you, for I am reduced to live alone in a wretched hut with three naked and almost famished children. The fourth lies dead among them. I am past your vengeance, great as you be.

Colonel: Come, wife, let her alone; she is not worth minding.

Martha: That is true, Colonel. I am not worth minding, for what I would ask is mercy and justice, and you have none of that commodity for me.

Colonel: You haven't told me yet who it was that has reduced you so low. I really feel for you, and if I can help it I will relieve you if possible. My head is so perplexed with business that I am apt to overlook.

Martha: Forget me and welcome. I expect nothing at your hands whatever you may say. I'll bury my child and return to feed on despair until death delivers me. Then I'll rejoin my poor unfortunate husband whom your great generals have brutally hanged, and I shall be able to do then without that heifer and three ewes which you have ravished from me.

Colonel: I can't help these things, honest woman. Your random talk does not offend me. You are really so low that your tongue's end does not reach me.

Martha: That is true. What are the shafts of a poor desolate widow? They are blunted by weakness. How can you say that you know nothing of me? Does not the name of that cow and ewe I have mentioned bring to you some distant recollection?

Colonel: I am tired. Good-bye, stubborn woman.

Martha: Do stop. I will tell you all.

Colonel: Well, then, let us hear you out. What have you to say?

Eltha: Ah, no, I am quite weary. The better one is to these people, the worse they are. These Tories are just like the negroes; give them an inch, they will take an ell. I begin to know who she is.

Martha: Do you really? With what emphasis of hatred you pronounce that word "Tory." What [have] they done? Alas, they have neither conspired nor plotted; they have neither banished nor hanged anyone. They are suffering the worst of punishments for the sake of a country which never will thank them, but they act from principles,—hard is their fate.

Colonel: Pooh! pray thee, leave off conscience, principles, etc. These people have none but those of the worst sort, and harder will be still their fate. Come, what have you to say?

Martha: How came you to strip me of all I had after my husband was hanged? How came you to release those effects one day and to have them reseized on the third? On what principles can you take from me and my children our bread and subsistence?

Colonel: Because you are looked on as an enemy.

Martha: Even as an enemy you have no right to starve innocent children. How great a deceiver you have been! Formerly so meek, so religious, so humble; now wild, fiery, and a tyrant.

Colonel: In consideration of your situation, I will have your cattle restored. Go to work, and cease to behave in this frantic manner. I cannot help the sufferings of everyone.

Martha: Great God, give me strength and patience to wait with resignation for that day when the restoration of government shall restore to us some degree of peace and security.

Colonel: That day is far off, good woman. Go home and take care of your children, and leave off your political wishes. (Exeunt)

1. One copper plate representing two men on horseback chained together, a firing gun, and the two men falling.

2. A plate representing Capt. Shoreditch with a bushy head, six militiamen with linsey-woolsey blankets tied from the right shoulder to the left arm, and three Quakers at a tavern door with a post and no sign.

3. The woman in despair leaning on a tree, the Chairman and his wife on horseback talking with her.

4. A stallion rushing from the woods and covering the mare on which Eltha rides, she stoops on the neck, her husband whips the horse but in vain.*

* This last plate may have been designed to accompany another land-scape which Crèvecœur never wrote.

INDEX

333

Index.

Bermuda, 2, 10, 22
Bernier, M., 14, 15
Berry, wild, 231
Bible, 71, 155, 157, 158, 170
Bibliothèque Nationale, 21
Birch, 99
Blackbirds, 86, 114, 116
Black oak, 86
Black worm, 114
Blazed trees, 68
Blue Mountains, 116
Bolting-mills, 147
Bonny, the old faithful mare, 44
Bordeaux, 21
Boston, 5, 6, 9, 12, 174
Bougainville, M. de, 14, 15
Bran, 123
Brandy, 105, 135
Brant, 183, 197, 203
Britain, 218
British, the, 177, 192, 221
British Regulars, 7
Brown (Mr.), 15
Buck-wheat, 117, 120
Budd, Benjamin, 207
Buffon, 59
Bull-frogs, 127
Burgoyne, 221
Butler, Colonel, 197, 198

CABBAGES, 114
Caen, 1, 19
Calf, 134, 142
Canada, 1, 2, 10, 14, 136, 175
Canadian, the, 2, 172, 174
Canker-worm, 90
Canoes, 197
Carlyle (Thomas), 31
Carolina, 135, 137
Carver, Captain, 135

Casgrain D.ès.L., L'Abbé H. R.,
  14
Catalpas, 51
Caterpillars, 86, 117, 168
Cattle, 7, 47, 48, 50, 64, 70, 84,
  103, 109, 111-113, 130, 131,
  137, 142, 145, 150, 201, 203,
  208, 217, 225, 232
Cedar mast, 143
Chadenat, M., 21
Charles the Second, 176
Charleston, 5, 6
Chastellux, Marquis de, 19, 20
Cherry Valley, 221
Chestnuts, 118
Chevrotière, M. la, 14
Chinese, the, 136
Cider, 46, 49, 72, 102, 104, 105,
  134, 145, 149
Cider, gingered, 28, 43, 47
Clams, 109
Clinton, Sir Henry, 8, 15
Cloacina, 111
Cluzant, M. Henri, 21
Columbia University Press, 15
Comb-honey, 123
Commissioners, the, 23
Concord, 7
Congress, 12, 195, 196, 212
Connecticut, 2, 6, 12, 79, 81, 195
Copper kettle, 104
Corn, 51, 86, 114-118, 120, 121,
  123, 142, 143, 150
Corn-cribs, 143
Corn-weevil, 26
"Country Scenes," 32, 34 ff.
Couriers-de-bois, 2
Cows, 43, 44, 70, 71, 110, 112,
  129, 195, 206, 209, 210, 232
Crèvecœur, Hector St. John de,

334

Index.

Index.

Index.

Index.

Index.

339

Index.

Index.

Index.